Modern Logic Design

ELECTRONIC SYSTEMS ENGINEERING SERIES

Consulting Editor **E L Dagless**
University of Bristol

Modern Logic Design

David Green
University of Manchester
Institute of Science and Technology

ADDISON-WESLEY PUBLISHING COMPANY

Wokingham, England · Reading, Massachusetts · Menlo Park, California
Don Mills, Ontario · Amsterdam · Sydney · Singapore · Tokyo · Madrid
Bogota · Santiago · San Juan

Cover design by Sampson/Tyrell Limited.
Typeset by Setrite of Hong Kong.
Printed in Great Britain by Commercial Colour Press.

British Library Cataloguing in Publication Data
Green, David, *1941 May 13—*
   Modern logic design. — (Electronic systems
   engineering series)
   1. Digital electronics   2. Logic design
   I. Title   II. Series
   621.3815'3   TK7868.D5

   ISBN 0−201−14541−3

Library of Congress Cataloging in Publication Data
Green, David, 1941−
   Modern logic design.

   (Electronic systems engineering series)
   Bibliography: p.
   Includes index.
   1. Logic circuits.   2. Logic design.   I. Title.
II. Series.
TK7868.L6G74   1985   621.3815'37   85−20063
ISBN 0−201−14541−3

BCDEF 8987

Preface

Logic design, or, more correctly, switching circuit design, forms a major component of the more general digital systems design process. As such, it deals with the derivation, manipulation and synthesis of switching circuits and processes required to implement the various sections of a digital system. Whereas the digital systems designer may impose a higher-level interpretation on the role and behaviour of the major components of his system, the logic designer may choose to treat each part as essentially the same kind of design problem. In this sense, the logic designer traditionally employs an abstraction wherein the process is converted to some symbolic specification, which in turn leads to the derivation of a set of switching functions. The latter are then manipulated into a suitable form for synthesis in a chosen circuit technology.

The advent of modern highly flexible integrated circuit components coupled with the merging of the hardware and software aspects of a digital system has required new logic design procedures to be formulated which involve the logic designer in a more intimate way with the overall system design. These procedures enable the high-level description of the system to be carried forward through the logic design phase and into the synthesis and implementation of the design. This book presents an introduction to these modern techniques and is aimed at the intermediate level between the introductory text and the research monograph.

It is assumed that readers are familiar with the fundamentals of digital processes. That is, with number representation, Boolean algebra, Karnaugh maps, traditional methods of combinational and sequential switching circuit design, and synthesis by means of basic switching elements and bistable circuits. They should also be acquainted with simple devices such as shift registers and counters, the elements of computer architecture, microprocessor structure and associated components, simple codes and converters, and the elements of programming and software engineering.

Only a few years ago this list of subjects would probably have formed a final year option for an undergraduate course in electrical or electronic engineering. As the importance of digital techniques increased such courses first became compulsory and required for all students and subsequently were transferred to second year and possibly first year syllabuses. The rudiments of these topics are now taught at pre-university level and form part of certain national school examination subjects. This bringing forward of material has allowed more advanced topics, once restricted to specialist M.Sc. courses, to be introduced into the second and third years of under-graduate courses.

Whilst the fundamentals of the subject and the traditional approach are supported by numerous excellent texts and the advanced research area is catered for with a sprinkling of specialist and highly theoretical books, there seems to be a gap in this inter-mediate area. The author has taught courses at all undergraduate and postgraduate levels for many years and has found it increasingly difficult to recommend a single text to cater for this middle ground.

The primary aim of this book is to fill this gap in the literature. There are also a number of other important motivations and objectives. Firstly, the new technology has provided a range of very powerful and flexible devices which the traditional methods are incapable of supporting efficiently. New methods are required to handle these devices and the modern undergraduate course must include these. Secondly, the once well defined boundary between the hardware and software aspects of a digital system has become increasingly blurred by the new technology. The ubiquitous micro-processor is a prime example of this. Whereas the digital hardware designers regard this as just another, albeit more powerful, com-ponent, to be exploited like any other, software engineers view it as an inexpensive way of implementing an order code. Keen arguments and demarcation disputes have raged between departments of electronic engineering and computer science to establish the rightful custody of these devices and their utilization. Of course, the real answer is that they belong in both areas, and to exploit fully these and similar devices it is necessary to be familiar with all aspects. There are signs that this is now being recognized and university courses are beginning to reflect this. There is now a unique oppor-tunity to break down these barriers that have existed since the birth of computers. This move requires support by teaching the methods which can bridge the hardware/software boundary. Although this book is written from the primary viewpoint of producing essentially hardware implementations, due acknowledgement is given to other possible approaches. Thirdly, new emphasis is now being placed on information technology in order to exploit the rapid developments in this field, and those areas of digital circuit design associated with coding and other aspects of digital communications are taking on a new prominence. This book attempts to encompass a background treatment of these systems together with those of 'conventional' digital systems. Thus the study of linear combinational and sequential circuits which provide most of the systems for error control and digital signal processing ought to become an established part of the general course on modern digital processes. They are now and will surely be in the future one of the main areas of application of digital techniques.

In fulfilment of these aims, this book treats the algorithmic state machine as the main vehicle for the design and synthesis of modern integrated digital systems. The methods for synthesizing these designs in a representative set of alternative modern forms are also discussed. The alternative switching function description provided by the Reed–Muller expansion technique is included to enable new forms of implementations to be considered which are amenable to testing and to incorporate the aforementioned linear circuits into the general logic design repertoire.

The modern digital system designer is faced with a formidable task when it comes to verifying his design before attempting to synthesize it, and testing the system when implementation is complete. The introduction of computer-aided design, circuit simulation and fault testing calls for design methods which reflect these developments. Built-in testability and fault tolerance are desirable features of modern designs. An introduction to these problems along with other possible developments are included to enable the student to develop his own opinions as to the future directions of expansion of the subject.

To summarize, therefore, this book is an attempt to provide an intermediate, second-level text to span the range of undergraduate and M.Sc. taught courses, covering aspects of the modern unified approach to digital system design.

Contents

Preface   v

Chapter 1   Review of Traditional Logic Design Methods   1
    1.1   Introduction   1
    1.2   Design of combinational switching circuits   6
    1.3   Design of sequential switching circuits   9
    1.4   Design of asynchronous sequential circuits   15
    1.5   Requirements for modern switching circuit design   20
    1.6   Bibliographical notes   22

Chapter 2   The Algorithmic State Machine Method   23
    2.1   Introduction   23
    2.2   Construction of ASM charts   27
    2.3   ASM state assignments   39
    2.4   Derivation of ASM tables   43
    2.5   Linked state machines   50
    2.6   Bibliographical notes   52
    2.7   Exercises   53

Chapter 3   The Synthesis of ASM-based Designs   55
    3.1   Introduction   55
    3.2   Derivation of next-state excitation functions   56
    3.3   Map-entered variables   59
    3.4   Implementation by discrete gates   72
    3.5   Asynchronous inputs and outputs   77
    3.6   Implementation by multiplexers and ULMs   79
    3.7   Bibliographical notes   90
    3.8   Exercises   91

Chapter 4   Synthesis by Programmable Devices   92
    4.1   Introduction   92
    4.2   Programmable logic arrays   93
    4.3   ROM-based designs   112
    4.4   Application to microprogramming   121
    4.5   Bibliographical notes   128
    4.6   Exercises   128

Chapter 5   Reed−Muller Algebraic Descriptions   131
    5.1   Introduction   131
    5.2   The algebra of GF(2)   133
    5.3   The operational and function domains   136

5.4	Generalized Reed–Muller expansions	142
5.5	Design methods	147
5.6	Applications to coding theory	158
5.7	Bibliographical notes	164
5.8	Exercises	164
Chapter 6	**Linear Sequential Circuits**	**165**
6.1	Introduction	165
6.2	Feedforward filters	165
6.3	Arrangements of filters	172
6.4	Feedback filters	174
6.5	Autonomous feedback sequential circuits	177
6.6	Applications to coding theory	182
6.7	Bibliographical notes	188
6.8	Exercises	188
Chapter 7	**Further Topics**	**191**
7.1	Introduction	191
7.2	Simulation of switching circuits	192
7.3	Automatic testing of switching circuits	197
7.4	Multiple-valued switching circuits	211
7.5	Bibliographical notes	227
7.5	Exercises	228
Solutions to Exercises		230
Bibliography		263
Index		267

Chapter 1
Review of Traditional Logic Design Methods

1.1 INTRODUCTION

Traditionally, switching circuits have been classified into two broad regimes: *combinational* circuits which have outputs that depend only on the present input values; and *sequential* circuits which have outputs that depend on the present input values and on past values of inputs and/or outputs. The latter are inherently more complex since one must take account of the previous 'history' of the circuit and therefore time is an important factor. Whereas the same set of input values applied to a combinational circuit at two different times will yield the same set of output values on each occasion, this may not be the case with sequential circuits. Here, the output will also depend on the behaviour of the circuit during the interval between these two occasions. Sequential circuits can be subdivided further into: *synchronous* types, in which some special input is regarded as supplying the timing input or *clock* which enables all other operations within the circuit to be synchronized and well behaved; and *asynchronous* types which are self-timing and operate in response to changes of input values. Reliable asynchronous circuits are therefore usually more difficult to design than synchronous types.

The main emphasis throughout traditional switching circuit design has been placed on circuit economy. That is, the 'best' design used the fewest, cheapest components. Recently, this simplistic view of circuit economy has been replaced by a much more sophisticated set of criteria. The cost of components has fallen dramatically whereas the cost of design and labour has risen. Mass production of the design obviously involves different economics to the manufacture of a single prototype or a low production run. Also, the emphasis has turned to other considerations such as reliability, testability and wiring costs, and these factors may also enter the economic equation. Furthermore, the advent of LSI and VLSI techniques have yielded very much more powerful and flexible components than were available when the traditional design methods were formulated. Devices such as gate arrays, programmable logic and microprocessors have rendered the traditional methods ineffective. To add to the demise of the traditional methods we have the fact that modern systems themselves are becoming more complex and

Row	x_n	x_{n-1}	x_{n-2}	$\cdots$	x_2	x_1	$f(x_n, x_{n-1}, \ldots, x_1)$	
	n inputs						1 output	
0	0	0	0	$\cdots$	0	0	d_0	
1	0	0	0	$\cdots$	0	1	d_1	
2	0	0	0	$\cdots$	1	0	d_2	
3	0	0	0	$\cdots$	1	1	d_3	
.	.	.	.		.	.	.	
.	.	.	.		.	.	.	2^n rows
i							d_i	
.							.	
.	.	.	.		.	.	.	
2^n-1	1	1	1	$\cdots$	1	1	d_{2^n-1}	

Fig. 1.1 General truth table for n variables.

are now designed by teams, built by teams, and used by teams. The new design procedures are required to facilitate this approach as well as enabling the full exploitation of the new and future components. However it is still useful to study the basic relationships and design tools from the traditional approach since many do carry over into the new regime albeit in modified form.

The most fundamental concept in the description of combinational switching circuits is that of the truth table. This defines the operational behaviour of the circuit by listing the output value for each possible combination of input values. If there are n independent input variables they will exhibit 2^n distinct combinations of values and hence the truth table will have 2^n rows, n input columns and 1 output column. It is convenient to arrange the table so that successive rows follow the normal binary representation of the decimal integers in the progression 0 to $2^n - 1$ as depicted in Fig. 1.1. We can denote the output values as d_i, $0 < i < 2^n - 1$, where d_i is the output value on row i of the table. Since each d_i can be 0 or 1 there must be 2^{2^n} distinct truth tables for n variables. As each of these corresponds to a unique operational behaviour this is also the number of switching functions of n variables. If all the d_i are known, we have a *completely specified* function. However, there may be situations in which certain combinations of input values do not arise during normal operation of a particular circuit. The output value on such occasions is unspecified and these give rise to 'don't care' conditions in which the designer can assume any output value in such a way as to ease

x_3 x_2 x_1	m_0 $\overline{x_3}\overline{x_2}\overline{x_1}$	m_1 $\overline{x_3}\overline{x_2}x_1$	m_2 $\overline{x_3}x_2\overline{x_1}$	m_3 $\overline{x_3}x_2x_1$	m_4 $x_3\overline{x_2}\overline{x_1}$	m_5 $x_3\overline{x_2}x_1$	m_6 $x_3x_2\overline{x_1}$	m_7 $x_3x_2x_1$	$f(x_3, x_2, x_1)$
0 0 0	1	0	0	0	0	0	0	0	d_0
0 0 1	0	1	0	0	0	0	0	0	d_1
0 1 0	0	0	1	0	0	0	0	0	d_2
0 1 1	0	0	0	1	0	0	0	0	d_3
1 0 0	0	0	0	0	1	0	0	0	d_4
1 0 1	0	0	0	0	0	1	0	0	d_5
1 1 0	0	0	0	0	0	0	1	0	d_6
1 1 1	0	0	0	0	0	0	0	1	d_7

Fig. 1.2   Truth tables of the eight minterms of three variables.

the design and implementation of the circuit. Apart from this basic operational definition, the truth table is of little use in the design of switching circuits and traditionally it has been found necessary to convert this either to an algebraic representation or to a more useful form of table or map.

The algebraic equivalent of the truth table is the *canonical* form of expression. Each row of the table can be associated with a unique product term which is true (has value 1) only on that row and is false (has value 0) elsewhere. These fundamental product terms are called *minterms* and symbolized as m_i where i is the corresponding row of the truth table. By summing the minterms corresponding to the rows of the truth table for which the particular function is true we obtain a unique sum-of-products algebraic expression known as the *disjunctive* canonical form (DCF). In the general case we can use the d_i values to select the appropriate minterms and form an equivalent algebraic expression to the truth table. Thus,

$$f(x_n, x_{n-1}, \ldots, x_1) = \sum_{i=0}^{2^n-1} d_i m_i$$

where the summation is the logical OR operation. Each of the 2^n minterms is formed as a different logical product of the n variables x_j and their complements $\overline{x_j}$. Fig. 1.2 shows the truth tables for the eight minterms formed from three variables and this demonstrates that the general function of three variables can be written as:

$$f(x_3, x_2, x_1) = d_0m_0 + d_1m_1 + d_2m_2 + d_3m_3 + d_4m_4 +$$
$$d_5m_5 + d_6m_6 + d_7m_7$$
$$= d_0\overline{x_3}\overline{x_2}\overline{x_1} + d_1\overline{x_3}\overline{x_2}x_1 + d_2\overline{x_3}x_2\overline{x_1} +$$
$$d_3\overline{x_3}x_2x_1 + d_4x_3\overline{x_2}\overline{x_1} + d_5x_3\overline{x_2}x_1 +$$
$$d_6x_3x_2\overline{x_1} + d_7x_3x_2x_1$$

Another useful visual representation of a switching function is provided by the Karnaugh map. This is a cellular structure which contains 2^n cells for n variables which can simultaneously display the operational behaviour and the functional relationship of a switching circuit. Each cell corresponds to one row of the truth table and one minterm of the DCF. Cells are identified by labelling the edges of the map and this is done in such a way as to give a unique combination of variables and their inverses for each cell. Each variable divides the map into two equal halves each containing 2^{n-1} cells. In one half the cells correspond to minterms which include

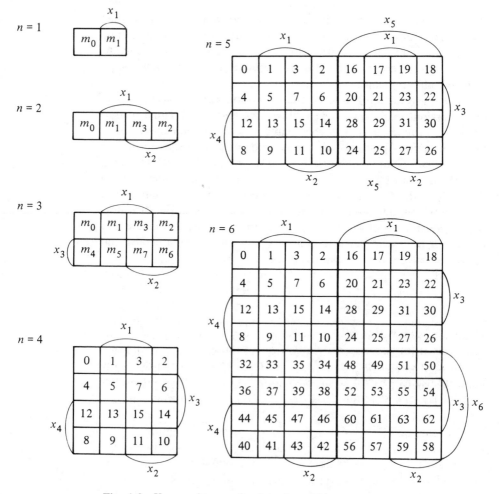

Fig. 1.3   Karnaugh maps for 1 to 6 variables.

the variable in true form; in the other half minterms involve the complement of the variable. This labelling can be achieved in a variety of ways but the method adopted in Fig. 1.3 has the attraction that larger maps can be formed by a doubling operation on a smaller map. The map for $n + 1$ variables can be constructed by adjoining two n-variable maps. Each of these is labelled as for n variables and in addition one is made to correspond to the domain of $\overline{x_{n+1}}$ and the other to the domain of x_{n+1}. Thus, the minterm numbers in the cells of the first half remain as for the original n-variable map, while in the second half each minterm number is increased by 2^n, which is the weighting appropriate to x_{n+1}.

As each cell of the Karnaugh map corresponds to a minterm or one row of the truth table, a function can be plotted if the canonical form or, equivalently, the truth table is known, merely by entering the minterm coefficients or the truth table output values d_i in the appropriate cells. If the expression is not in canonical form it can still be plotted by identifying the area of the map corresponding to each term of the expression. The great power of the Karnaugh map lies in the fact that certain collections of $2, 4, \ldots, 2^j$ cells correspond to single product terms or *implicants*. Implicants which are not completely contained within any other implicant are termed *prime implicants*. The groupings of occupied cells on the Karnaugh map enable the prime implicants of the function to be readily identified. This process is central to the traditional design process for switching circuit synthesis.

The inherently more complex behaviour of sequential switching circuits leads to the introduction of other representations and design aids. It is recognized that the overall behaviour is characterized by two sets of relationships. The first describes the external behaviour as manifested in the output responses to a set of input values applied at a certain time and in relation to previous sets of inputs. The second relates to the internal organization as determined by the transitions between recognized conditions of the memory elements, or internal *states*, in response to sets of inputs and a synchronizing clock. The traditional design process is aimed at reducing some mode of process description to two sets of combinational switching circuits used in conjunction with some type of memory element to synthesize these two forms of behaviour. Thus, the latter stages of sequential circuit design resolve to that of multiple-output combinational circuit design.

This chapter reviews the traditional approach to combinational circuit and sequential circuit design and then leads on to consider the prerequisites for a more flexible approach to employ in conjunction with modern systems and components.

1.2   DESIGN OF COMBINATIONAL SWITCHING CIRCUITS

If we were to implement directly the DCF of a function in terms of basic switching elements such as AND, OR and NOT gates or NOR or NAND elements we would produce a perfectly viable but possibly highly redundant two-level circuit. The first level would implement the product terms and the second would sum these together. Traditional logic circuit simplification aims at deriving the optimum two-level circuit by deducing the optimum sum-of-products expression which has the same canonical form, and therefore truth table, as the original expression to be implemented. The problem lies in the fact that although any expression has a unique canonical form and truth table many expressions share the same canonical form and truth table. They are all different expressions of the same logic function. If we restrict ourselves just to the consideration of sum-of-products forms we can enumerate the possibilities for a given number of variables. In the general product term each variable can be absent, present in true form, or present in complemented form. These three ways of occupying a product term leads us to the conclusion that there are 3^n possible product terms made up from n variables. In a sum-of-products form made up by selecting from these product terms we can arrange 2^{3^n} different expressions. However, we have already observed that there are only 2^{2^n} different functions for n variables. Even for small values of n these two numbers are widely different and the problem of selecting the optimum two-level representation cannot be left to a search through all the possibilities. We require some systematic procedure which provides a good chance of delivering the optimum form with the minimum of effort. Most traditional methods follow the following steps:

1. specification of circuit or statement of switching problem,
2. construction of truth table or algebraic expression,
3. derivation of canonical form of expression,
4. derivation of the implicants and identification of prime implicants,
5. identification of essential prime implicants,
6. selection of non-essential prime implicants to complete the cover of the function,
7. implementation of the circuit.

Steps 1 and 2 are clearly related because any statement or circuit description which employs the connectives of symbolic logic must lead directly to a truth table or algebraic expression. Step 3 follows directly from the table, from the algebraic expansion of the logic expression, or from the Karnaugh map after the expression has been plotted. At this stage all problems have been converted to a standard form of representation and the simplification procedure can now commence. Step 4 is the first difficult step because we have to establish the implicant structure of the function by manipulating the canonical form.

An implicant is either a minterm or some product term made up from a combination of suitable minterms from the original expression by using the reduction formula:

$$(x_n x_{n-1} \ldots x_k \ldots x_1) + (x_n x_{n-1} \ldots \overline{x_k} \ldots x_i) = x_n x_{n-1} \ldots x_1 (x_k + \overline{x_k})$$

$$= x_n x_{n-1} \ldots x_1$$

and the new term no longer contains x_k or $\overline{x_k}$. Similarly, 2^j appropriately related minterms may be replaced or 'implied' by a single implicant which involves only $n-j$ variables. An implicant is called a prime implicant if it is not 'included' in any other implicant of the function, in the sense that all the constituent minterms of the first implicant do not appear in the expansion of the second implicant. The simplification process involves the identification of all the prime implicants of the function and there are two basic types of method for doing this which are well described in numerous introductory texts on switching circuit design. These are the tabular methods such as the Quine-McCluskey method, and map methods based on the Karnaugh map representation of the function. The former methods do not give a design 'feel' for the complexity of the function, nor do they give an immediate indication of the importance of selecting don't care terms or modifications to a function for some other reason, as in CAD situations. However, they are suitable for computerization since an algorithm can be constructed for this purpose, and they are limited only by the number of minterms rather than by the number of variables in the function. On the other hand, map methods have a strong visual effectiveness and are ideally suited to manual interpretation. Unfortunately, the useful size of map is limited to six or seven variables and beyond this they are unwieldy and difficult to interpret. However, there are ways of improving this situation as we shall discover in Chapter 3.

The simplification process continues by selecting from the list of prime implicants a representative set which covers all the minterms of the original function. In attempting to make this selection we may find that some prime implicants must be included because they involve minterms that are not covered by any other prime implicant. Such terms are referred to as *essential* prime implicants and are identified at step 5 of the design process. Up to this point the process is completely deterministic and can always be reached for any function. Step 6 involves the first occasion on which some engineering judgement is called for because an explicit procedure cannot be set up which will be successful for all functions. If the sum of essential prime implicants does not completely cover the function and there remain some uncovered minterms, we require to make a selection from the other prime implicants in order to complete the cover. The search for absolute minimality may involve much effort. Unfortunately, this search is less well rewarded now than in former times. Recent microelectronic developments have reduced component costs which may now be vastly outweighed by computational costs. Thus, a quick sub-optimal solution may be more rewarding. The final step involves the conversion of the minimal or near minimal form into a logic circuit either directly into AND, OR and NOT elements, or, after some slight adjustment, into NAND or NOR components. In this sense, the design has not been completely top-down since the ultimate form of synthesis was known at the beginning and indeed has influenced the complete design process. The newer components and possible means of implementation demand top-down procedures which leave the decisions concerning the synthesis to the last possible moment.

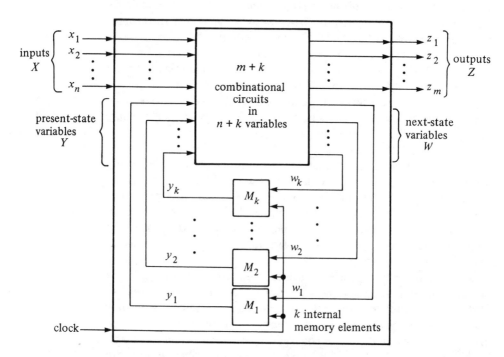

Fig. 1.4   Organization of synchronous sequential machine.

1.3 DESIGN OF SEQUENTIAL SWITCHING CIRCUITS

Sequential circuits differ from combinational circuits in that their outputs are dependent not only on the present values of the inputs but also on past values of the inputs. This more complex type of behaviour requires extra tools and algorithms to describe and synthesize the circuits. Traditionally, the early phases of the design process concerning the description, verification and simplification of the desired sequential behaviour have been performed with an abstract mode of representation using arbitrary symbolic state names. In the final stages a process of assigning binary codes to each identifiable internal state of this abstract *finite-state machine* is performed with a view to representing these by the collective conditions of a number of memory elements. This converts the system into a specific sequential switching circuit. Two sets of combinational functions, one relating to the state transition behaviour and the other providing the desired circuit outputs, are each defined by the state assignment process. This then converts the design problem to that of deducing the optimum synthesis of a collection of combinational switching circuits whose inputs are the system's inputs and the state variables. Fig. 1.4 shows the general arrangement for the traditional design approach. The problem is that of deducing the two sets of Boolean equations representing the finite-state machine equations

$$Z = f(X, Y)$$
$$W = g(X, Y)$$

where Z is the output state, W is the next state, X is the input state and Y is the present state. In terms of the individual system parameters

$$z_i = f_i(x_n, x_{n-1}, \ldots, x_1, y_k, y_{k-1}, \ldots, y_1) \qquad \text{for } i = 1, \ldots, m$$

and

$$w_j = g_j(x_n, x_{n-1}, \ldots, x_1, y_k, y_{k-1}, \ldots, y_1) \qquad \text{for } j = 1, \ldots, k$$

where there are n inputs $x_1, x_2, \ldots, x_n$; k state variables $y_1, y_2, \ldots, y_k$; and m outputs $z_1, z_2, \ldots, z_m$. The number of state variables is usually taken to be the smallest number k such that 2^k is greater than or equal to the number of internal states of the machine.

The complete design process is usually represented by a number of distinct steps and operates from some basic specification of the required sequential behaviour:

1. construction of state diagram,
2. construction of state-transition table,

3. simplification of state-transition table,
4. state assignment,
5. derivation of next-state and output functions,
6. implementation of the circuit.

State diagrams provide a convenient way of depicting the behaviour of a sequential circuit. The states are represented as circles or nodes and the transitions as directed arrows linking the appropriate pair of nodes. There are two accepted models for sequential machines which are manifested by different state-diagram structures. In the first, the Mealy model, the outputs are shown as functions of both the inputs and the internal state variables. On the Mealy state diagram the transition paths are labelled with the combination of input values causing the transition and the combination of output values resulting from the transition. In the second, or Moore model, the outputs are associated with particular states and so appear as labels along with the state name or number at the node. The transitions are labelled only with the input combination giving rise to the transitions. Each mode of representation has its attractions; Moore models tend to require more states to cater for all the output conditions but the corresponding output functions are simpler since they are independent of the input variables. Traditionally, Mealy models are usually adopted for synchronous design, and Moore models are more suited to describing asynchronous systems. As an example, consider a simple synchronous machine with two inputs and one output. The machine is required to detect the occurrence of the sequence of pairs of inputs 00, 00, 11, 10 on the two inputs and to give an output 1 during the final combination of a detected sequence. Fig. 1.5a shows the Mealy state diagram for this machine and four internal states are required. The Moore model, shown in Fig. 1.5b, has one extra state because we need to go to a state where the output is 1 when the sequence is detected.

The state diagram is useful for verifying the sequential behaviour of a machine. Given a starting state and a sequence of input values it is possible to trace the subsequent state-transition behaviour and the sequence of output values. However, it is of little further use in the design process. At step 2 the information contained in the state diagram is transferred to a more useful form of representation provided by the *state-transition table*. On this structure are listed each present state, together with the next states and the outputs for all combinations of input values. Fig. 1.6 shows the state-transition tables corresponding to the Mealy and Moore models of the previous example. For the general machine, represented in Mealy form, there will be k rows, and 2^n columns in both the next-state and output portions of the table. Each entry in

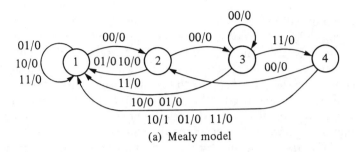

(a) Mealy model

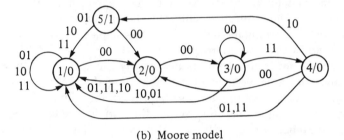

(b) Moore model

Fig. 1.5 Mealy and Moore state diagrams for sequence detector.

Present state	Inputs x_1, x_2							
	Next state				Output z			
	00	01	11	10	00	01	11	10
1	2	1	1	1	0	0	0	0
2	3	1	1	1	0	0	0	0
3	3	1	4	1	0	0	0	0
4	2	1	1	1	0	0	0	1

(a) Mealy model

Present state	x_1x_2	Next state			Output z
	00	01	11	10	
1	2	1	1	1	0
2	3	1	1	1	0
3	3	1	4	1	0
4	2	1	1	5	0
5	2	1	1	1	1

(b) Moore model

Fig. 1.6 Mealy and Moore state-transition tables.

the output half will contain up to m values. Thus, even for a modest machine with relatively few internal states and system inputs and outputs, this table can be very large. The state-transition tables still represent an abstract description of the sequential machine but do enable a systematic search to be performed to identify any redundant states. Procedures can be set up to identify equivalent or *compatible pairs* of states. Also, compatible pairs can sometimes be grouped together to form *maximal compatibles*. In this way the original states of the machine can be partitioned into compatible groups and each group need only be represented by one of its members. The reduced machine needs only to have as many states as there are maximal compatibles. This enables the state table to be reduced in size and complexity.

The motivation behind this state reduction is to attempt to reduce the number of state variables and thereby the number of memory elements required to represent the state. Thus, if the original machine had ten states this would indicate four state variables because $2^3 < 10 < 2^4$. However, if the reduced machine has only eight distinct states only three state variables would be required, thereby eliminating one memory element. More significantly, the number of next-state functions would be decreased by one, and each of the remaining next-state and output functions would involve one fewer variables. If the machine had, say, three inputs and two outputs, the reduced machine could be synthesized with five functions of six variables rather than six functions of seven variables demanded by the original form. This may represent a substantial saving in the synthesis phase and so is in line with the traditional approach of economic implementation viewed from a component cost standpoint.

When the machine is not completely specified because some combinations of inputs, some state transitions or some values of outputs do not arise, the state table will involve don't care conditions in various positions. The problem of deducing the maximal compatibles and their representatives is made more difficult. The new representation represents a covering of the original states rather than a partition because don't care conditions may have been assumed to take on different values on different occasions when implying the equivalence of states. The reduced form has to be checked to ensure that all implied equivalences are in fact still valid. Nevertheless, it is possible to describe algorithms for performing these tasks and they are described adequately elsewhere, in introductory texts.

In practice, providing the original specification of the machine is consistent and covers all contingencies, it is unlikely that redundant states would be introduced during the construction of the state diagram. Realistically, therefore, with well defined problems rather

Present state y_1y_2	Inputs x_1, x_2							
	Next state w_1w_2				Output z			
	00	01	11	10	00	01	11	10
00	01	00	00	00	0	0	0	0
01	11	00	00	00	0	0	0	0
11	11	00	10	00	0	0	0	0
10	01	00	00	00	0	0	0	1

Fig. 1.7 Assigned state table of Fig. 1.6a.

than contrived academic exercises, the chances of performing any significant state reduction is remote. In any event, with the modern emphasis on cost of design rather than cost of implementation, this search for minimality is less well rewarded than in the past. However, simplification performed from the viewpoint of improving reliability is still a worthwhile pursuit.

Up to this point the design process has been completely deterministic and the representation has been an abstract one. In order to synthesize an actual circuit it is necessary to assign codes to the states of the reduced machine. This then enables the truth tables, or Karnaugh maps, of the various combinational functions to be set up. This represents the most difficult step of the traditional design process. Although any assignment which allocates a unique binary code to each state will produce a valid representation, the task of deducing the optimum assignment which will simultaneously yield the most economic forms of all these functions is prodigious. Much effort has gone on over the years to evolve efficient *state-assignment* procedures. Here again, the motivation behind this effort has to a large extent been removed by the introduction of modern forms of circuit synthesis. However, to illustrate the final steps of the design process we show the effects of the arbitrary assignment $1 = 00$, $2 = 01$, $3 = 11$, and $4 = 10$, on the state table of Fig. 1.6a. The fully assigned table is reproduced in Fig. 1.7 and from

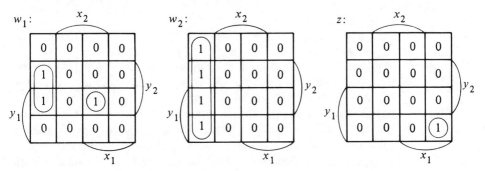

Fig. 1.8 Excitation and output functions from Fig. 1.7.

this we can set up the three four-variable Karnaugh maps of Fig. 1.8. The problem now reduces to that of deriving the economic forms of these three combinational circuits. For this particular assignment we discover that

$$W_1 = g_1(x_1, x_2, y_1, y_2)$$
$$= \bar{x}_1\bar{x}_2 y_2 + x_1 x_2 y_1 y_2$$
$$W_2 = g_2(x_1, x_2, y_1, y_2)$$
$$= \bar{x}_1\bar{x}_2$$
$$Z = f(x_1, x_2, y_1, y_2)$$
$$= x_1\bar{x}_2 y_1\bar{y}_2$$

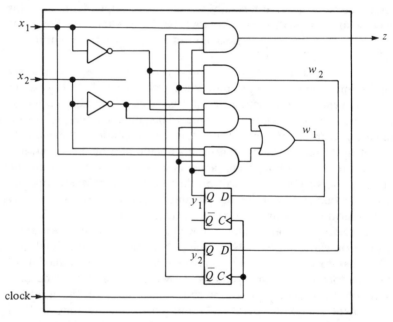

Fig. 1.9 Synthesis of circuit for the sequential machine of Fig. 1.7.

The next-state equations represent the excitation functions of the two bistables representing the two state variables. If D-type bistables were employed in the synthesis, these functions could be used directly to supply the D inputs. Other bistables types would require some adjustment of these equations before implementation. Fig. 1.9 shows one possible form of implementation based on D-type memory elements and AND, OR, NOT switching elements. This represents the final step of the traditional design process.

1.4 DESIGN OF ASYNCHRONOUS SEQUENTIAL CIRCUITS

In asynchronous sequential circuits the internal state transitions and outputs change in response to changes of input values and are not regulated by any form of external timing or clock. If the inputs are allowed to change in any fashion certain malfunctions may arise. The designer has to allow for the possibility that in transitions from one valid or *stable* state to another the system may pass through a number of transient or *unstable* states. These effects arise because all physical devices exhibit a propagation delay and cannot respond instantaneously. For example, if the state is represented by the conditions stored in a collection of SR-bistables which are required to change to a new state this can only be achieved by changing the values on the S and R inputs of each element. Inevitably there will be a short delay, which may differ from element to element, between the change of excitation of each device and also in the response of each device. As a result where one may have anticipated the perfect transition from say 1111 to 0000, in the case of four such units, we may observe a number of intermediate states such as $1111 \rightarrow 1011 \rightarrow 0011 \rightarrow 0010 \rightarrow 0000$. If the outputs of these bistables are used as inputs to other sections of the system they may cause malfunctions. This type of problem is known as a *race*. Certain race conditions can be tolerated if they lead ultimately to the correct next state. However, if an intermediate transient state can be captured by the prevailing input values and converted into an incorrect stable state, this is termed a *critical race*.

Another type of problem which must be considered in the asynchronous domain is that associated with gate configurations such as the circuit given in Fig. 1.10. Simplification of the Karnaugh map in the manner indicated would yield the minimum expression

$$f = x_2 x_1 + x_3 \bar{x}_2$$

and the corresponding circuit would be as shown. This circuit would

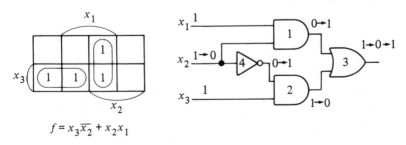

$$f = x_3 \bar{x}_2 + x_2 x_1$$

Fig. 1.10 Simple circuit with hazard.

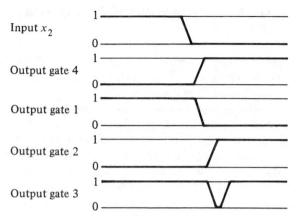

Fig. 1.11   Timing waveforms for the circuit of
Fig. 1.10.

be fine if the gates employed had zero propagation delay. However, problems can arise in certain circumstances when we consider physical devices even if the switching delay is identical for all elements. Suppose $x_3 = x_2 = x_1 = 1$, which would ensure that the output was also 1. If x_2 now changes to 0, the output should theoretically stay at 1, because the output of AND gate 2 changes from 0 to 1 when the output of AND gate 1 changes from 1 to 0. Thus the output of OR gate 3 is maintained at 1. However, if we assume that all gates have a finite propagation delay δt then the two AND gates will not change simultaneously because AND gate 2 will not know about the change of x_2 until δt after gate 1 because of the inverter gate 4. The waveforms of Fig. 1.11 demonstrate that as a result the output of OR gate 3 will switch from 1 to 0 briefly before returning to 1 as AND gate 2 catches up. The spurious pulse produced in this way is due to what is termed a *hazard* and may cause problems elsewhere in the circuit.

Synchronous circuits avoid the problems of races and hazards by taking note of inputs, outputs and states only at certain predefined times dictated by the synchronizing clock. The clock interval

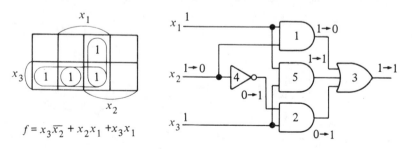

$$f = x_3\overline{x_2} + x_2 x_1 + x_3 x_1$$

Fig. 1.12   Elimination of hazard by an extra gate.

is chosen to be sufficiently long to enable all transients of this nature to die down. Even so, hazards can be important in synchronous systems especially when outputs are used directly, without latching, to instruct some other peripheral device or system which is not therefore completely synchronized to the original system.

Critical races can usually be removed by suitable state assignments. Hazards can sometimes be overcome by using extra gates. Fig. 1.12 demonstrates this technique for the previous problem. The extra AND gate 5, which spans the first two prime implicants, will maintain the output at 1 while x_2 changes. Of course the circuit is no longer the minimum form. Furthermore, if two or more inputs change together it may not be possible to avoid hazards by this method.

The design of asynchronous circuits follows a broadly similar series of steps to the synchronous case but the emphasis is now on producing a reliable race- and hazard-free circuit rather than the most economic form. To improve reliability two stability criteria are usually invoked. First, only one input variable should be allowed to change at any one time, and second, sufficient time should elapse between input changes for the system to reach an equilibrium position.

In asynchronous designs the Moore model for state diagrams is to be preferred since we can relate output states to the internal stable states, thereby achieving some circuit economy. Each stable state on the diagram must be represented with a transition path originating and terminating on itself. This is due to the fact that the particular input change causing the transition to the state will also be responsible for making the system stay in this state. A new transition only becomes possible when the input combination changes. Also, the limitations set on the ways that inputs may change, i.e. one at a time, will reduce the number of legal transition paths appearing on the diagram. As an example, Fig. 1.13 gives the

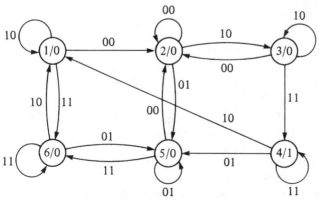

Fig. 1.13 State diagram for an asynchronous sequence detector.

state diagram for a circuit which detects the sequence 00, 10, 11 on two parallel input lines x_1 and x_2 and gives a 1 output during the final combination.

The equivalent of the state-transition table is traditionally referred to as a *primitive flow table*. The stable states are shown circled and are allocated to one particular row of the table. On the same row are given the next states resulting from legal input changes. Input states requiring more than one input change from that of the stable state are illegal and shown as '—' on the table. When a legal input change occurs the machine moves to the state indicated for the new input state and therefore takes up position on the row of the table containing the stable version of the new state. The output column shows the output(s) related to the stable state of each row. Fig. 1.14 gives the primitive flow table for the state diagram of Fig. 1.13.

Flow tables may be simplified in two ways. The first is similar to that for synchronous circuits and involves the recognition of equivalent state pairs. The second is due to *row merging*. Equivalent states give the same outputs and lead to the same next states under all input conditions. They must occupy the same column of the flow table. Equivalent state pairs can be combined to form maximal compatibles which will represent a partition of the states into equivalent groups in the case of a completely specified machine. As before the presence of unspecified and don't care conditions will lead to a covering of the states in terms of the maximal compatibles. In either event, a reduced flow table can be drawn up which now has one row for each of the maximal compatibles used in the representation of the original states. Row merging allows a further compression to take place by permitting two stable states to occupy the same row. This can be done only when there are no conflicting state numbers in any of the positions in the two rows to be merged. Thus, two rows such as:

$$- \quad 4 \quad ③ \quad 5$$
$$1 \quad ④ \quad 3 \quad -$$

can be merged to become the single row:

$$1 \quad ④ \quad ③ \quad 5$$

This is attractive because the state assignment process allocates a code to each row of the reduced flow table and the fewer the rows, the fewer state variables are required to define them uniquely. Thus, two stable states occupying the same row will effectively have the same state assignment but transitions between them can be made by input changes alone.

In the state assignment we must ensure that during a transition only one state variable changes, otherwise a race might occur which

| x_1x_2 | Next state | | | Output |
00	01	11	10	z
2	—	6	①	0
②	5	—	3	0
2	—	4	③	0
—	5	④	1	1
2	⑤	6	—	0
—	5	⑥	1	0

Fig. 1.14 Primitive flow table for Fig. 1.13.

could cause a transition to the wrong stable state. To illustrate this, consider the merged flow table shown in Fig. 1.15 in its symbolic and assigned forms. Now suppose the machine is in state 1 and the input is 00 maintaining this stable condition. If the input changes to 10, a change to state 5 is indicated, i.e. ①→5→⑤. Unfortunately, with this assignment, this transition requires the excitation to change from 00 for state 1 to 11 for state 5. If both y_1 and y_2 change together then we obtain the correct transition 00→11, hence 1→5. However, if y_2 changes first, giving 00→01, this will lead to an incorrect transition to state 4, and the inputs will hold the circuit in this incorrect stable state. This is an example of a critical race. We can also have non-critical races such as occurs if we are in state 2 and the input changes from 01 to 00 indicating a change to state 1. This necessitates the excitation changing from 11 to 00 but it does not matter which variable changes first because we will always arrive at state 1 eventually. In order to avoid critical races we must endeavour to assign in such a way that codes for rows which have transitions possible between them are unit distance. Sometimes the

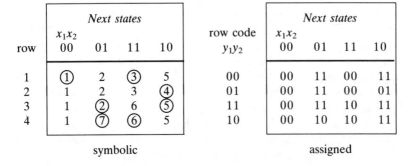

| row | Next states | | | | row code | Next states | | | |
| | x_1x_2 | | | | y_1y_2 | x_1x_2 | | | |
	00	01	11	10		00	01	11	10
1	①	2	③	5	00	00	11	00	11
2	1	2	3	④	01	00	11	00	01
3	1	②	6	⑤	11	00	11	10	11
4	1	⑦	⑥	5	10	00	10	10	11

symbolic   assigned

Fig. 1.15 Symbolic and assigned flow table with critical race.

number of state-code variables has to be increased to achieve this, which can offset the savings brought about by state-table reduction.

Finally, the synthesis of the various excitation and output functions derived from the assigned tables must be performed in a hazard-free manner along the lines indicated earlier.

1.5 REQUIREMENTS FOR MODERN SWITCHING CIRCUIT DESIGN

The traditional techniques of switching circuit design are fragmented and each step of the design process has its own form of representation of the problem. The procedures are top-down only in the sense that they begin with an abstract description which is subsequently converted to a specific circuit. However, even in the early stages, it is always assumed that the synthesis will be in terms of hardware discrete components selected from a limited repertoire of basic circuit elements. These assumptions dictate the design goals at all stages of the process. Modern components, coupled with the new emphasis on the merging of hardware and software aspects of system design, require a more universal top-down approach which can cover the whole spectrum from switching circuits constructed with discrete gates, through the universal and programmable devices, to the complete software implementation of some well defined process. Such an approach must leave the decisions regarding the choice of synthesis technology to the last possible moment and must not be dictated by the available components of the day. Of course, we cannot ignore the fact that ultimately some physical representation has to be produced as an end-product and until the facilities for the design and production of fully customized integrated circuits are readily available to the logic designer, we must take note of the available devices. This new approach must also be suitable for handling small systems with relatively few states as well as large complexes of information processing units.

It is customary for the digital systems designer to partition the system into two sections: first the data-path section comprising the units which perform manipulations on the data; and second the control-path section which dictates and organizes the sequence in which the data-path operations are performed. In a hardware implementation both these sections involve logic circuits, although the control section may contain units which are conveniently implemented as software processes, and thus are designed from the same fundamental principles. This dichotomy is therefore a convenient interpretation of the structural and operational behaviour of the system which helps the systems designer to specify and organize the design of a complex process. The logic designer, however, can choose to disregard this high-level interpretation and treat each unit in a more fundamental abstract sense. The fragmented operations of the traditional approach only tend to reinforce this abstraction. The symbolic representation of the process, whether it be part of the data path or the control path, can be handled in essentially the same way and thereby converted into an optimum arrangement of switching circuits in the chosen circuit technology. Of course, it is desirable that any logic design process can carry forward the system design constructs and be applicable to both data and control parts. It should be related to the higher-level description by more than the mnemonics for inputs, outputs and states.

The most useful approach to adopt in these circumstances is a *modular* one in which large systems can be partitioned into a hierarchy of interconnected and intercommunicating modules. These modules may themselves contain sub-modules and so on until we reach a fundamental level determined by the chosen technology. The common theme in all hardware switching circuits and software processes is that they can be described by an *algorithm*. This defines in an unambiguous way the actions necessary to produce the required results from the given data. Thus a modular algorithmic approach would seem to be one with a wide sphere of application spanning all aspects of modern digital system design. The main vehicle for this design approach is the *algorithmic state machine* or ASM. In the following chapters the ASM technique is used primarily as an aid to the design and synthesis of hardware digital systems but the approach also has wide application in a software engineering environment.

The *documentation* is one of the most vital components of the design process and any design can be considered incomplete if adequate documentation does not accompany the final product. Communication between the customer, designer, constructor and ultimate users of the system is of paramount importance. As these parties may be teams of people rather than individuals, a language common to all levels is imperative. The adoption of a consistent system of terminal mnemonics for identifying the various inputs, outputs, internal states and control lines can greatly ease this communication problem. Each step of the design process generates its own piece of documentation expressed in this common notation so that each stage of the design is meaningful to all others. This set of product documentation could take the form:

1. system specification: some well defined algorithm(s),
2. terminal mnemonics based on commonly agreed principles,
3. a fully assigned ASM chart for each module,

    4. an ASM table for each module,

    5. the excitation and output functions of the ASM(s),

    6. logic diagram in the chosen technology,

    7. wiring diagram with integrated circuit types, placements and connections,

    8. system test procedures.

Most of these steps remain valid for the software-based implementation with perhaps 6, 7 and 8 replaced by a program flowchart, program listing and software verification procedures.

    The following chapters will deal with some of these design phases concentrating on the central activity of converting a well defined sequential behaviour into a physical realization. Perhaps the two most difficult phases to cover are the first and last. Recently, much research effort has been directed towards these aspects, and techniques such as the development of hardware description languages (HDL) on the one hand, and circuit verification and fault trapping on the other, are beginning to emerge.

1.6 BIBLIOGRAPHICAL NOTES

The traditional approach to digital system and logic circuit design has a comprehensive bibliography. Notable amongst the earlier works are Lewin (1972) and (1974), Hill and Peterson (1974) and Mowle (1976). Of the more recent texts Morris (1976), Floyd (1982), Holdsworth (1982) and Bannister and Whitehead (1983) cover the fundamentals of digital systems including the material outlined in Chapter 1, and form an excellent introduction to the subject. Lee (1978) also covers this material in addition to some of the topics discussed in later chapters of this book.

Chapter 2
The Algorithmic State Machine Method

2.1 INTRODUCTION

A fundamental description of the behaviour of any information processing system, whether it be of hardware or software origin, is provided by an *algorithm*. This is a carefully designed sequence of events which are required to produce a set of results or actions from a given set of data. Thus an algorithm inherently links the data flow and the control of the data flow. An algorithm should exhibit *finiteness* and terminate after a finite number of steps, and *definiteness* in that each step must be precisely defined and unambiguous.

The basic abstract definition of a system which performs an algorithm is provided by the *general state machine*. This structure, depicted in Fig. 2.1, comprises three sub-modules:

1. The *next-state* function, as provided by a transform module,
2. The *state*, as provided by a memory module,
3. The *output* function as provided by a transform module,

and operates on a set of inputs X to produce a set of outputs Z. The inputs represent either data-input paths and are used to derive the outputs or control-input paths for the control of the internal behaviour of the machine. In this latter role they can be referred to as *qualifiers*. Similarly, the outputs, in addition to providing the data-exit paths, can also form control-output paths and may be used

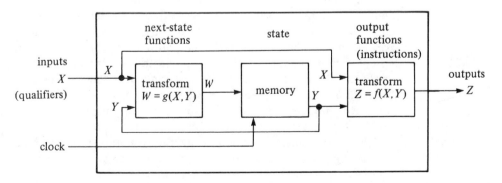

Fig. 2.1 The general state machine.

to initiate actions in other machine modules. In this role they can be referred to as *instructions*. This general structure is sufficiently flexible to cover all classes of combinational and sequential switching circuits as well as some aspects of more complex information processing units or software processes. In each case the sub-modules are interpreted in the appropriate manner. In the general context we will refer to the system as an *algorithmic state machine* or ASM.

As we have seen, the digital systems designer's inclination is to partition the system into the data part and the control part and to design these separately along with their interactions. Fortunately, the ASM method can be employed to describe both these parts because it can specify the data flow and the control of the data flow simultaneously. It is possible to configure the structure of the general state machine to reflect this dichotomy. Essentially, this requires the partitioning of the system inputs into primary (data) inputs and control inputs (qualifiers), and the outputs into data outputs and control or status outputs (instructions). Thus the original system constructs can be passed on to the logic design process. Both parts of the system or the whole can be described by a set of Boolean functions derived from the ASM structure wherein some of the input variables may correspond to data inputs and others to control inputs. The latter may themselves be outputs from other modules. Similarly, the outputs of these functions may be providing the data paths or instructions to other modules. Within the general model of the ASM the memory module stores information from one time interval to another and can be implemented in many forms from single bits stored in bistable elements, registers to hold bytes or words, or blocks of several words. In some cases the memory can be read from or written to simultaneously, others may be read-only memories (ROM) or read-write memories (RWM) where reading and writing cannot be performed simultaneously. Memory modules are obviously time dependent. The transform modules will produce a set of outputs for each set of inputs according to some well defined logical relationship. In hardware terms this may be represented by a combinational switching circuit or some other device to change information from one form of representation to another. In this context they are better known as *interfaces*. Transform modules are not time dependent except for the natural delay of operation present in all physical realizations. Transform modules may also be software components such as a procedure to perform vector or matrix multiplication.

The two transform modules in the general state machine provide the two aspects common to all information processing systems in that the output function transform supplies the data flow paths from input to output, whereas the next-state function transform provides the control of this data flow.

Each state of the machine has a next state determined by the next-state function. The machine resides in each state for a *state time* determined by a periodic input or *clock* to the state register. On entering the new state the next-state function begins to compute a new next state and the output function computes a new set of output values, using the new set of input values provided. In any physical realization of this process there will be a finite delay before these are completed and thus the first part of the state time is taken up by these processes, giving rise to an unstable transition period. The remainder of the state time is a stable period when the outputs are available and the next-state values are ready for the next transition. Fig. 2.2 illustrates this arrangement. Clearly, the state time must be made longer than the unstable period otherwise incorrect system behaviour will result. If $X(j)$ is the set of n inputs $x_1, x_2, \ldots, x_n$, and $Y(j)$ is the set of k state variables $y_1, y_2, \ldots, y_k$, for state time interval j, we can represent this behaviour as

$$Y((i + 1)T) = g[X(iT), Y(iT)]$$

where T is the state time and i is an integer.

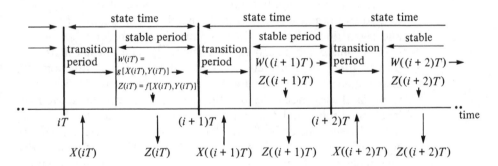

Fig. 2.2 Time relationships for the state machine.

Alternatively, we can define a set W of next-state variables w_1, $w_2, \ldots, w_k$ which are available during the stable period of the current state time. Thus

$$W(iT) = g[X(iT), Y(iT)]$$

or

$$W = g[X, Y]$$

and then the assignment

$$Y: = W$$

signifies the state transition at the end of the state time. Similarly, the set Z of m outputs $z_1, z_2, \ldots, z_m$ is produced by a function of the inputs X and state variables Y, thus

$$Z(iT) = f[X(iT), Y(iT)]$$

or

$$Z = f[X, Y]$$

These two sets of equations characterize the general state machine. So in the initial period of each state time

$$W = g[X, Y]$$

and

$$Z = f[X, Y]$$

are computed and these values become available at the beginning of the stable period. At the end of each state time the assignment

$$Y := W$$

is performed so a new state is entered, and the process is repeated for this new state with the new set of inputs.

The abstract definition provided by the general state machine is related to the particular process by employing a system of terminal and signal identification which is immediately understandable and helps to make the design self-documenting. The normal method is to use three or four letters to identify the signal function; for example, RST for reset, CLR for clear. In addition it is also useful to prefix these mnemonics by other letters to signify the active logic level of outputs and the true logic condition of inputs. Thus, the prefix H. signifies active high (that is, a logic 1 will reset when the signal is called H.RST), whilst the label L.RST signifies an active low signal and a logic 0 will reset. Similarly, it is sometimes useful to annotate inputs or qualifiers with Y. or N. to denote the true logic condition. Thus Y.RED means that the true condition is when the signal RED $= 1$, whereas N.RED indicates that the true condition is when RED $= 0$. We may also wish to distinguish outputs which are to be employed in some explicit function and are therefore immediate, by prefixing with I., from those which result from an assignment statement and therefore involve an inherent delay. Thus, although outputs are always immediate as far as the module under consideration is concerned, they may produce an immediate or delayed response in another module. In the latter case, the outputs are not used until the stable period of the state time, when they are clocked into the next module. Immediate outputs can affect the next module as soon as they become active during the unstable portion of the state time. They are therefore asynchronous in nature and consequently more difficult to handle.

Clearly, it is a matter of choice as to whether this system is adhered to rigorously under all circumstances, or used with discretion and only when confusion may otherwise arise. For example, in the context of this book, where the emphasis is on the explanation of the techniques, rather than the description of actual designs, this notation may prove a hindrance, and so will be used only sparingly for the sake of clarity. However, the intention should be to use this notation at all the design stages and initially in conjunction with a pictorial representation of the state machine behaviour. This is similar in appearance to the well known flowchart technique used in computer program design. There are several significant differences, but the main one is concerned with the representation of time relationships. The flowchart usually represents a continuous time flow from top to bottom to reflect the sequence of operations performed by the program. The ASM chart, on the other hand, has discontinuities in the time frame and time moves on in quantum steps as control passes from one state to the next. Within the portion of the chart devoted to one state there are no assumed time relationships.

2.2 CONSTRUCTION OF ASM CHARTS

The ASM chart provides a diagrammatical representation of the state-transition functions and output functions of a state machine. It is used as an aid to the design of a state machine for the implementation of an algorithm and on completion becomes part of the design documentation. The chart is made up from three basic symbols. These are:

1. the *state box,*
2. the *decision box*, and
3. the *conditional output box.*

The state box represents one state of the ASM. The machine resides in a state box for one state time. The symbol is shown in Fig. 2.3

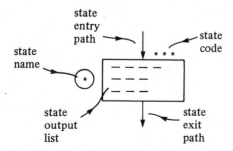

Fig. 2.3 The state box.

and indicates that each state has a *name*, usually a mnemonic or a number, and a *state code*. The latter represents the unique combination of values of the state variables and is defined during the *state assignment* process. Thus, it is probably unknown when the ASM chart is first drawn up and must be added subsequently. The outputs generated during the state, also represented in mnemonic form, are listed in the state box and constitute the *state output list*. A state output is active only when the machine resides in a state which has the output listed in its state output list. State outputs are active for a state time. Each state box has an entry path and an exit path. The exit path may lead to another state box, in which case there is an unconditional or direct state transition, or it may lead to a decision box in the case of a conditional or qualified transition.

The decision box, as shown in Fig. 2.4, involves the inputs to the state machine and gives the conditions that control or qualify the conditional state transitions and conditional outputs. The box contains a Boolean expression, involving the inputs, which defines the condition, and there are two exit paths. If the condition is true, the *true exit path* is followed, if false the *false exit path* is used. These routes are indicated by T and F, but if the Y or N logic condition prefixes are omitted from the logic statement the exit paths can be labelled with 1 and 0, assuming a positive logic convention so that T = 1, F = 0. The exit paths may lead to other decision boxes, state boxes, or to conditional output boxes.

The conditional output box describes those outputs which only become active if certain conditions, defined in terms of the system inputs, are true. Thus a conditional output box contains a *conditional output list* and is always associated with a decision box which describes the condition. The entry path must originate from a decision box but the exit path can lead to another decision box or a state box. The symbol is given in Fig. 2.5.

These primitive elements can be combined together to form the basic unit of an ASM which is the *ASM block*. This is a structure consisting of one state box and a network of decision boxes and

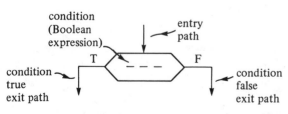

Fig. 2.4   The decision box.

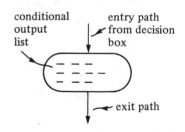

Fig. 2.5   The conditional output box.

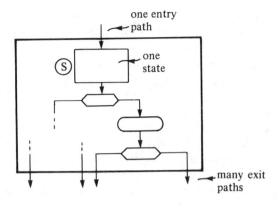

Fig. 2.6   An ASM block.

conditional output boxes as represented in Fig. 2.6. An ASM block
has one entry path and any number of exit paths. Each exit path
must lead to another state and so is an entry path to another ASM
block or to its own block. Each possible path from one state to the
next is termed a *link path*. Each link path corresponds to a single
Boolean expression which contributes to the complete expression
for a conditional output or a next-state function. Within an ASM
block the state box is the only element which indicates a time factor
and all other boxes are assumed to be activated concurrently. Thus
there is a quantum step in time when the block is entered and
the ordering of decision boxes and conditional output boxes is
immaterial from a time point of view as all conditional functions and
outputs are evaluated simultaneously irrespective of their positions
in the block. In this respect the *ASM chart* differs from a program

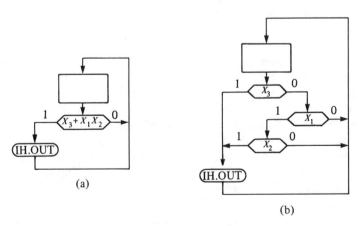

Fig. 2.7   ASM chart for a combinational switching circuit: using (a) a
single decision box, (b) multiple decision boxes.

or signal flowchart. An ASM chart consists of one or more ASM blocks interconnected in a consistent manner and describes the total behaviour of a state machine.

A purely combinational circuit could be described by an ASM chart consisting of one ASM block. Thus, Fig. 2.7 shows the arrangement for the function $I.OUT = X_1.X_2 + X_3$, either as a block containing a single decision box or as several decision boxes each involving only a single primary input. The state box has no physical significance and plays only a formal role in the structure. In the case of an autonomous sequential circuit such as a counter or shift register sequence generator, the corresponding ASM chart will consist of a series of state boxes connected by direct transition link paths. No inputs are involved to qualify the behaviour and the system will endlessly repeat the same sequence of states. Although state outputs are perfectly permissible it is usual in counter circuits to relate these directly to the outputs of the bistables in the state register. Fig. 2.8a gives the ASM chart for an eight-state binary counter which has three state variables, A, B and C. The state assignment is such that the state outputs are redundant because we can easily verify that bit $1 = A$, bit $2 = B$ and bit $3 = C$. Thus the counter outputs are identical to the outputs on the state register. Fig. 2.8b shows a similar arrangement for a counter operating in a unit-distance or Gray code. Here again the state outputs match the state register outputs. However, this need not always be the case, as is shown in Fig. 2.8c. Here the state assignment is such that the state register counts in pure binary but the state outputs deliver the Gray code equivalent. The difference between Figs. 2.8b and 2.8c is clearly that in the former we require that the next-state functions generate the Gray code sequence and then the state outputs are trivial, whereas in the latter the next-state functions ensure a pure binary count and the state output functions perform a transform on this.

Sequential circuits with inputs permit more complex behaviour patterns to be implemented. The inputs are used to modify the state transitions so that conditional or qualified state changes can be allowed. This gives sufficient flexibility to describe any consistent algorithm. The inputs can also be used to qualify outputs and this usually implies some simplification of the system, if not the implementation, since fewer states may be required. Conditional outputs, therefore, support Mealy-type sequential behaviour. If only state outputs are permitted this corresponds to the Moore-type description.

The simplest type of sequential circuit with conditional behaviour is found in the bistable circuits such as clocked SR- or JK-types. Fig. 2.9b gives the ASM chart for a JK-bistable when it is

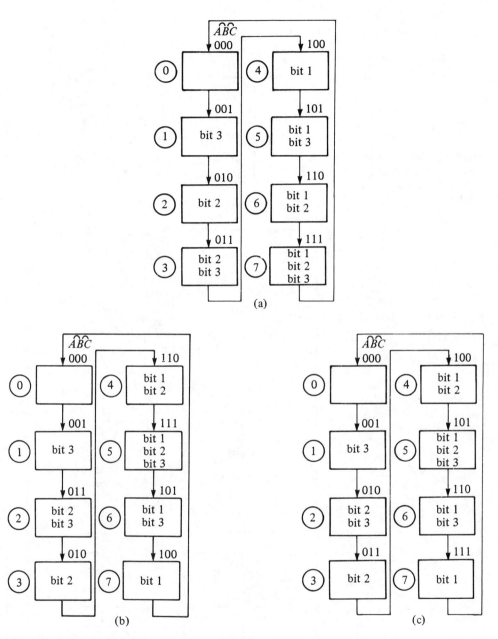

Fig. 2.8   ASM charts for simple autonomous sequential circuits.

regarded as a synchronous sequential machine. The J and K inputs control the state transitions as determined by the dynamic truth table of Fig. 2.9a. Fig. 2.10 shows the ASM chart of a more complex

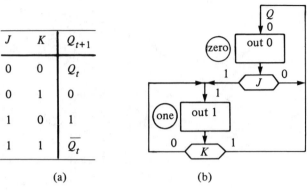

J	K	Q_{t+1}
0	0	Q_t
0	1	0
1	0	1
1	1	$\overline{Q_t}$

Fig. 2.9 ASM chart of a synchronous JK-bistable regarded as a sequential machine.

(a)

(b)

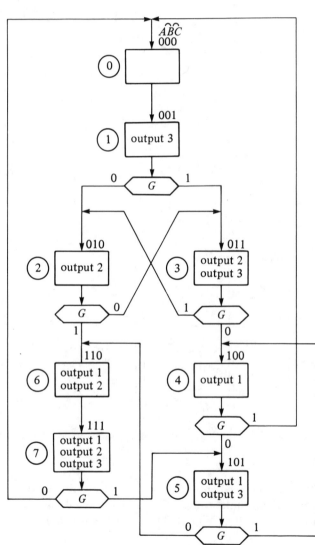

Fig. 2.10 ASM chart for counter controlled by single input G to count either in pure binary ($G = 0$), or in Gray code ($G = 1$).

system which involves a single qualifier G to control the behaviour of an eight-state counter. When G is set to 0 the three outputs deliver the normal binary code; when $G = 1$ the counter progresses through the Gray code sequence. Thus, the next-state transitions depend on the input as well as the present state variables. The outputs, being state outputs, depend only on the state variables.

Another degree of system complexity can be achieved by the inclusion of conditional outputs in some link paths. Thus the most general ASM structure involves next-state and output functions which depend on inputs and state variables. These functions can be built up in a block-by-block manner.

The jth block of an ASM chart describes the jth state Y_j, the state outputs $f_j[Y_j]$, the conditional outputs $f_j^*[X_j, Y_j]$, where X_j are the inputs associated with the jth block, and part of the next-state function $g_i[X_j, Y_j]$. The totality of these components taken over all the blocks on the ASM chart provides the complete next-state and output functions of the ASM with Q states. Thus,

$$g[X, Y] = \sum_{j=1}^{Q} g_j[X_j, Y_j]$$

$$f[X, Y] = \sum_{j=1}^{Q} (f_j[Y_j] + f_j^*[X_j, Y_j])$$

Thus the ASM chart not only depicts the sequential behaviour of a state machine but it also provides the structure of the various functions required for the synthesis of this behaviour. Fig. 2.11

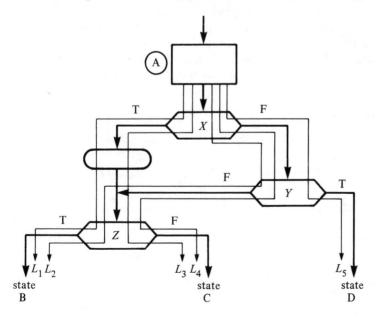

Fig. 2.11 An ASM block and its link paths.

shows an ASM block which is a fragment of some larger ASM chart. We can identify the various link paths through the block and with each one we can associate a Boolean expression. In a well defined ASM at any one instant with a set of stable inputs only one of these link paths should be active and hence only one of these Boolean expressions should be true at any one time. In this example we find:

$$\begin{aligned}
&L_1 \rightarrow XZ &&\text{transition of state A to state B} \\
&L_2 \rightarrow \overline{X}\overline{Y}Z &&\text{transition of state A to state B} \\
&L_3 \rightarrow X\overline{Z} &&\text{transition of state A to state C} \\
&L_4 \rightarrow \overline{X}Y\overline{Z} &&\text{transition of state A to state C} \\
&L_5 \rightarrow \overline{X}Y &&\text{transition of state A to state D}
\end{aligned}$$

These expressions contribute to the complete expression of the next-state functions which will result when all link paths through all ASM blocks have been identified. Any state outputs, as listed in the state box, will become active during the whole of the stable period of the state time for which the machine is in state A, irrespective of which link path is followed. The conditional outputs, as listed in any conditional output boxes, will only become active if the link path containing the conditional output box is followed. Any activated conditional state output will remain active for the whole of the stable period of the state time for which the machine resides in state A. In Fig. 2.11 the conditional output(s) listed in the conditional output box will become active if either link path L_1 or L_3 is followed: that is, if $XZ + X\overline{Z} = X$ is true. This is also obvious from the ASM chart.

In constructing ASM charts care should be taken to ensure that they are meaningful and physically realizable. First, we should always ensure that each state leads to a unique next state for each stable set of input conditions. Fig. 2.12 shows some invalid arrangements. That of Fig. 2.12a is clearly impossible because two next states are indicated simultaneously but the ambiguity of Fig. 2.12b is

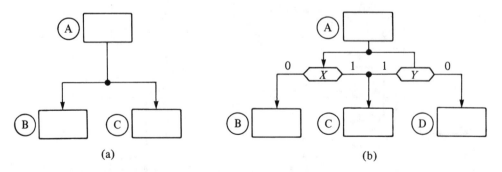

(a)   (b)

Fig. 2.12   Some invalid ASM chart structures.

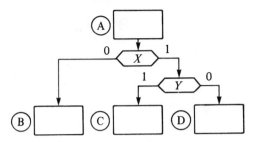

Fig. 2.13 A correct ASM structure for Fig. 2.12b.

less obvious. If both X and Y are true there is a unique state transition. However, if either X or Y is false then two next states are indicated. The probable intended behaviour is that of Fig. 2.13 which has removed the ambiguity by a simple rearrangement of decision boxes. Second, there should be no closed loop which does not contain at least one state box. That is, all loops should leave the ASM block by one of the exit paths and re-enter the block via the normal entry path. Thus, the arrangement of Fig. 2.14a is made clearer by redrafting as in Fig. 2.14b.

Other common errors are due to badly arranged decision boxes which lead to logically impossible conditions, fictitious link paths and ambiguous state transitions. In Figs. 2.15a and b, the apparent link paths between states A and B cannot in fact exist because they would require X to be simultaneously true and false. This would be revealed when the link path expressions were identified and found to be $\bar{X}X = 0$ or $XY\bar{X} = 0$. Similarly, but not so obvious, is the arrangement of Fig. 2.15c where the link path from A to B is impossible because we would require

$$X\bar{Y}(\bar{X} + Y) = XY\bar{X} + X\bar{Y}Y = 0$$

which can never be true. It is perfectly possible for the same qualifier to occur in several decision boxes in an ASM block and still give a valid construction. Fig. 2.16 illustrates two such situations. We are free to use equivalent series or parallel interconnections of

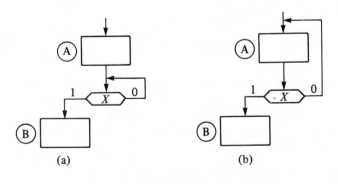

(a)   (b)

Fig. 2.14 Invalid and valid representation of looping.

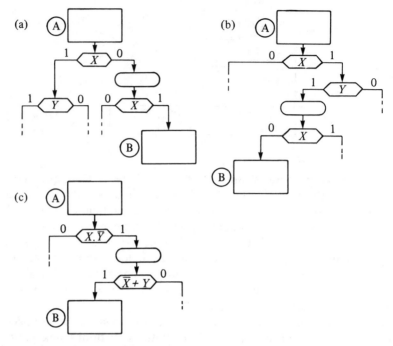

Fig. 2.15 ASM charts with impossible link paths.

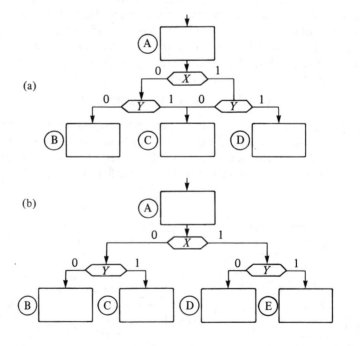

Fig. 2.16 Some valid ASM chart structures.

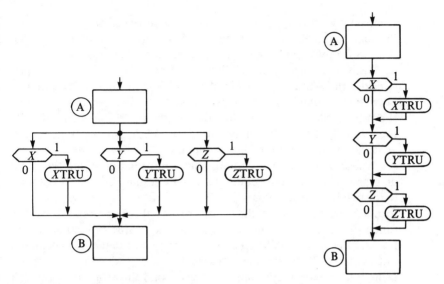

Fig. 2.17 Equivalent series and parallel ASM chart structures.

decision boxes within an ASM block. As no time relation exists in decision or conditional output boxes the two arrangements of Fig. 2.17 are equivalent and all three outputs become available simultaneously, providing the conditions are correct, in both arrangements. Series structures are less likely to lead to ambiguous state transitions but parallel ones may make the chart more compact.

On some occasions it is possible to make the ASM chart more

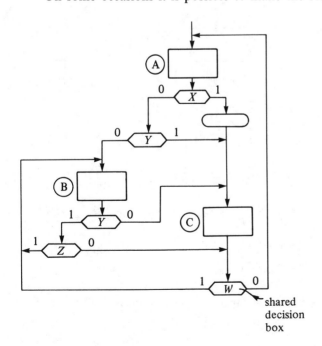

shared decision box

Fig. 2.18 Simple ASM chart.

compact by allowing ASM blocks to share decision boxes or conditional output boxes, thereby avoiding duplication. The fact that the ASM blocks will then overlap is not a problem as they still can be easily identified and the link paths extracted. As an example, consider the ASM chart of Fig. 2.18 which has a shared decision box between the blocks for state B and state C. We can easily extract the three ASM blocks corresponding to the three states and identify their link paths as shown in Fig. 2.19. With practice this can be achieved without redrawing the blocks.

These ASM charts contain more information than the state diagrams of traditional sequential circuit design because in addition to displaying the sequential behaviour of the state machine performing an algorithm, they also reveal the components of the functions required in the synthesis of the ASM. For comparison, Fig. 2.20 gives the ASM chart for the sequence detector considered in Chapter 1. Two forms are shown. In the first, decisions are made using the primary system inputs. The second shows a more compact form with fewer decision boxes but with more complex decision functions. In either case the output, here called I.SEQ, only becomes active on one link path in state 4.

In order to continue the design by extracting the next-state and output functions for synthesis we must first convert the abstract symbolic representation into a specific one by assigning binary codes to the state names.

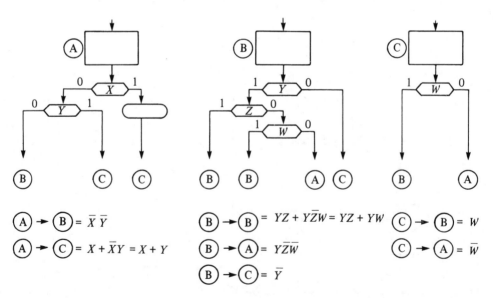

Fig. 2.19   The ASM blocks and their link paths for the ASM of Fig. 2.18.

2.3 ASM STATE ASSIGNMENTS

As in the traditional design methods studied previously, the state assignment problem is the most difficult step to 'solve' in general terms, if one is anxious to derive the optimum assignment. Different assignments will lead to different complexities of solution, but any assignment which provides a unique code to each distinct state will lead to a valid synthesis. The states of the machine will be represented by the condition of a *state register* which, in hardware synthesis, will usually be made up from a collection of individual memory elements, such as SR-, D- or JK-types; one for each state variable. The number k of these variables is chosen so that 2^k is

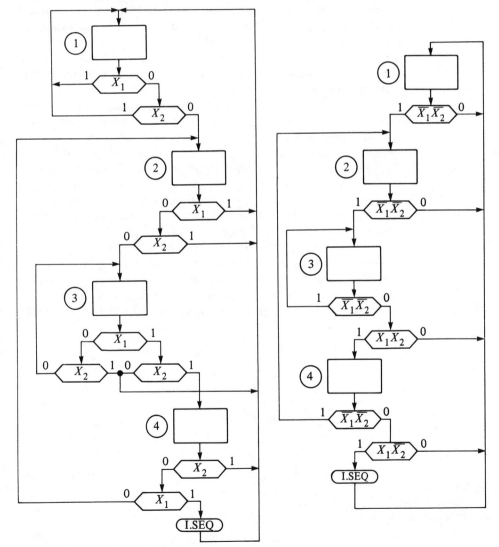

Fig. 2.20 ASM charts for the sequence detector of Fig. 1.5a.

greater than or equal to Q where Q is the number of states. To reduce circuit complexity, k is chosen as the smallest value to satisfy this relationship.

The state assignment is the process of allotting one of the 2^k possible k-bit codes to each of the Q states so that each state is associated with a unique k-bit word. Once selected, this code is entered on the ASM chart as indicated earlier. The state assignment, once completed, by whatever method, converts the abstract symbolic state machine into a definite specific structure in which all the functions f and g are fixed. Only the method of implementation of these functions can influence the overall circuit complexity. A useful way of recording a state assignment is by means of a *state map* which is similar in structure to a Karnaugh map and has one cell for each possible code. The map is labelled with the state variables and the state name corresponding to each assigned code is written in the appropriate cell. Fig. 2.21 shows a state assignment and the corresponding state map for an ASM with five states and therefore three state variables.

A relatively simple method of state assignment which has a high probability of yielding a 'good' solution is based on the concept of the minimum *state locus*. In moving from one state to the next the assigned codes will have to change in $1, 2, \ldots$ or k bit positions. If we list all the possible state transitions in an ASM and sum the number of bit changes required, this gives the state locus. We attempt to assign codes in such a way as to minimize this count on the assumption that this will simplify the excitation functions for the state register. Fewer bit changes are also desirable from a reliability point of view, especially when asynchronous inputs are involved. In effect we can attempt to obtain the minimum locus by assigning a unit-distance code to states which are linked. This is equivalent to placing linked codes in adjacent cells on the state map. This may not be possible for all transitions and some may require two or more bit

State name	State code A B C
a	0 0 0
b	0 1 0
c	0 1 1
d	1 1 1
e	1 0 1

state map:

A \ BC	00	01	11	10
0	a	–	c	b
1	–	e	d	–

– are unassigned codes

Fig. 2.21 A state assignment and the corresponding state map.

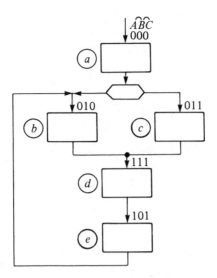

Fig. 2.22 ASM with state assignment of Fig. 2.21.

changes. Consider the ASM chart of Fig. 2.22 which uses the assignment of Fig. 2.21. We observe the following:

transition $a \to b = 000 \to 010$ 1 bit change
transition $a \to c = 000 \to 011$ 2 bit changes
transition $b \to d = 010 \to 111$ 2 bit changes
transition $c \to d = 011 \to 111$ 1 bit change
transition $d \to e = 111 \to 101$ 1 bit change
transition $e \to b = 101 \to 010$ 3 bit changes

Total = 10 bit changes

so the state locus for this assignment is 10. We can reduce this to 7 by using the assignment given in the state map of Fig. 2.23. Here all but the transition e to b are adjacent and have unit distance. If we

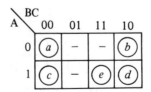

State name	State code A B C
a	0 0 0
b	0 1 0
c	1 0 0
d	1 1 0
e	1 1 1

state map:

A\BC	00	01	11	10
0	a	–	–	b
1	c	–	e	d

Fig. 2.23 Minimum state locus assignment for Fig. 2.22.

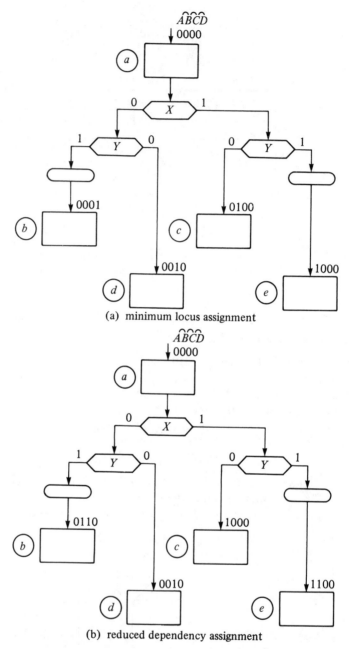

(a) minimum locus assignment

(b) reduced dependency assignment

Fig. 2.24 Comparison of minimum locus and reduced dependency assignments.

assign 011 to *e* this makes *e* to *b* unit distance but also increases *d* to *e* to distance 2. Thus, either of these two assignments represents a minimum state locus, and there are many other possibilities.

The minimum state locus only takes into account the changes of state variables and their effect on the next-state functions. However, the latter are also dependent on the inputs to the ASM as manifested in the decision boxes. Some attempt can be made to assign in such a way as to simplify the functions from an input contributions point of view. Such an assignment is termed a *reduced dependency* assignment. Consider the ASM chart fragment of Fig. 2.24a in which a unit-distance assignment has been made to these interconnecting states. If NA, NB, etc., are the next values of A, B, etc., then for this ASM block of Fig. 2.24 state a, we can derive the following:

$$NA = XY$$
$$NB = X\bar{Y}$$
$$NC = \bar{X}\bar{Y}$$
$$ND = \bar{X}Y$$

and so each function depends on both inputs. With the assignment used in Fig. 2.24b which is not minimum locus, the next-value equations become

$$NA = X$$
$$NB = Y$$
$$NC = \bar{X}$$
$$ND = 0$$

and each function has a reduced dependency on the inputs. This process is attempted on a state-by-state basis for the whole state machine and the overall assignment may show a near-optimum improvement over either an arbitrary or a minimum locus assignment. More formal methods exist, developed for the traditional approach, such as that of stable partitions of states into self-contained subsets, and therefore achieve another form of reduced dependency. However, as with other aspects of system optimization, the rewards for much design effort are less significant in the newer technologies and some forms of implementation discussed later are not influenced by the state assignment.

2.4   DERIVATION OF ASM TABLES

Whilst the assigned ASM chart is a useful tool for the description of a state machine and as such forms an important part of the documentation, in order to proceed to the synthesis phase the information on the chart is best transferred to tabular form. These tables include the state-transition and next-state excitation tables, and the state output and conditional output tables. These can be expressed separately, in both symbolic and assigned forms, or more usefully as a combined ASM table. Consider the ASM chart given in Fig. 2.25. The machine has three inputs Q_1, Q_2, Q_3, and five outputs. Of these CLR and SET are immediate and active high, INC is immediate and active low, and ADD and LAMP are delayed and active high. There are six states and three state variables A, B and C. We can locate six ASM blocks and a total of eleven link paths. These are, where B = block and L = link path:

$$B_1 \; L_1 : 1 \rightarrow 1 \; \overline{Q_1}\,\overline{Q_2} \quad \text{where } B_1 \text{ corresponds to } \overline{A}\,\overline{B}\,\overline{C}$$
$$B_1 \; L_2 : 1 \rightarrow 2 \; Q_1$$
$$B_1 \; L_3 : 1 \rightarrow 3 \; \overline{Q_1}Q_2$$
$$B_2 \; L_4 : 2 \rightarrow 4 \; \overline{Q_3} \quad \text{where } B_2 \text{ corresponds to } \overline{A}\,\overline{B}\,C$$
$$B_2 \; L_5 : 2 \rightarrow 5 \; Q_3$$
$$B_3 \; L_6 : 3 \rightarrow 1 \; \overline{Q_1} \quad \text{where } B_3 \text{ corresponds to } \overline{A}\,B\,\overline{C}$$
$$B_3 \; L_7 : 3 \rightarrow 5 \; Q_1$$
$$B_4 \; L_8 : 4 \rightarrow 5 \; \overline{Q_2} \quad \text{where } B_4 \text{ corresponds to } A\,B\,\overline{C}$$
$$B_4 \; L_9 : 4 \rightarrow 6 \; Q_2$$
$$B_5 \; L_{10}: 5 \rightarrow 1 \; - \quad \text{where } B_5 \text{ corresponds to } \overline{A}\,B\,C$$
$$B_6 \; L_{11}: 6 \rightarrow 1 \; - \quad \text{where } B_6 \text{ corresponds to } A\,\overline{B}\,C$$

The functions required in the synthesis will involve the three inputs and the three state variables. The six-variable map of Fig. 2.26 indicates how the various link paths contribute to these functions.

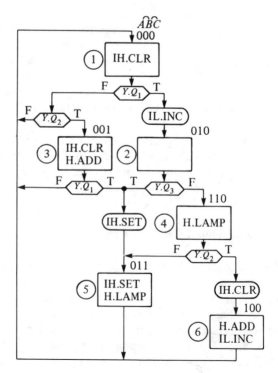

Fig. 2.25 Example ASM with six states.

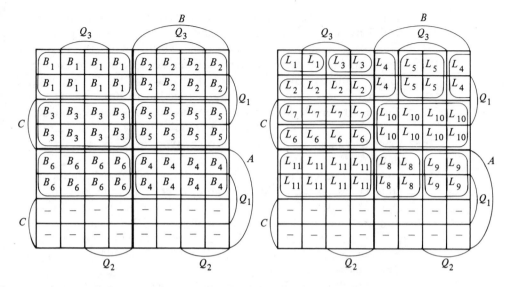

Fig. 2.26 Contributions of ASM blocks and link paths to system functions.

The state-transition table has three sections, the inputs or qualifiers, the present states, and the next states. The number of rows on the table is equal to the number of link paths on the corresponding ASM chart. Fig. 2.27a shows the symbolic form of this table for the state machine of Fig. 2.25. In the assigned form of

Inputs			Present state	Next state	Comments
$Y.Q_1$	$Y.Q_2$	$Y.Q_3$			
F	F	—	1	1	B_1, L_1
T	—	—	1	2	B_1, L_2
F	T	—	1	3	B_1, L_3
—	—	F	2	4	B_2, L_4
—	—	T	2	5	B_2, L_5
F	—	—	3	1	B_3, L_6
T	—	—	3	5	B_3, L_7
—	F	—	4	5	B_4, L_8
—	T	—	4	6	B_4, L_9
—	—	—	5	1	B_5, L_{10}
—	—	—	6	1	B_6, L_{11}

(a) symbolic

Inputs			Present state			Next state		
Q_1	Q_2	Q_3	A	B	C	NA	NB	NC
0	0	—	0	0	0	0	0	0
1	—	—	0	0	0	0	1	0
0	1	—	0	0	0	0	0	1
—	—	0	0	1	0	1	1	0
—	—	1	0	1	0	0	1	1
0	—	—	0	0	1	0	0	0
1	—	—	0	0	1	0	1	1
—	0	—	1	1	0	0	1	1
—	1	—	1	1	0	1	0	0
—	—	—	0	1	1	0	0	0
—	—	—	1	0	0	0	0	0

(b) assigned

Fig. 2.27 Next-state tables for the ASM of Fig. 2.25.

Fig. 2.27b, the state names are replaced by the assigned codes and T and F by the logic values. The state-transition table can be used to set up the next-state excitation table which defines the next-state functions for the particular type of memory element to be employed in the synthesis. The simplest type to consider is the D-type bistable which requires only one excitation function to drive the D input. This can be made identical to the corresponding component of the next-state code; that is, $DA = NA$, $DB = NB$, etc. The derivation of excitation functions for this and other types of memory is discussed more fully in Chapter 3.

The state-output table describes those outputs which appear in state boxes on the ASM chart and therefore has one row for each state of the ASM. These outputs depend only on the state variables and are independent of the input qualifiers. We exclude from this table any state outputs which also occur in conditional output boxes because in this latter role they will also be qualified by the inputs. The tables of Fig. 2.28 list the state outputs for the ASM of Fig. 2.25. On the symbolic table we indicate when the particular output is active and this is interpreted as being active high or low according to the associated prefix and entered on the assigned table.

The conditional output table lists those outputs which appear in conditional output boxes on the ASM charts including those which also appear in state boxes. Since conditional outputs are active only on certain link paths this table has a row for each link path and columns for the inputs and the present states. A conditional output will be shown as active for those link paths containing a conditional output box in which it is listed. If a conditional output also appears in a state box it will be shown as active on all the link paths of the corresponding state. Fig. 2.29 shows the symbolic and assigned

Present state	Outputs H.ADD H.LAMP		Comments	Present state A B C	Outputs H.ADD H.LAMP	
1			B_1	0 0 0	0	0
2			B_2	0 1 0	0	0
3	A		B_3	0 0 1	1	0
4		A	B_4	1 1 0	0	1
5		A	B_5	0 1 1	0	1
6	A		B_6	1 0 0	1	0

A = active
(a) symbolic   (b) assigned

Fig. 2.28   State-output tables for the ASM of Fig. 2.25.

Inputs Y.Q$_1$ Y.Q$_2$ Y.Q$_3$	Present state	Conditional outputs IL.INC IH.SET IH.CLR	Comments	Inputs Q$_1$ Q$_2$ Q$_3$	Present state A B C	Conditional outputs IL.INC IH.SET IH.CLR
F F —	1	A	B_1, L_1	0 0 —	0 0 0	1 0 1
T — —	1	A A	B_1, L_2	1 — —	0 0 0	0 0 1
F T —	1	A	B_1, L_3	0 1 —	0 0 0	1 0 1
— — F	2		B_2, L_4	— — 0	0 1 0	1 0 0
— — T	2	A	B_2, L_5	— — 1	0 1 0	1 1 0
F — —	3	A	B_3, L_6	0 — —	0 0 1	1 0 1
T — —	3	A A	B_3, L_7	1 — —	0 0 1	1 1 1
— F —	4		B_4, L_8	— 0 —	1 1 0	1 0 0
— T —	4	A	B_4, L_9	— 1 —	1 1 0	1 0 1
— — —	5	A	B_5, L_{10}	— — —	0 1 1	1 1 0
— — —	6	A	B_6, L_{11}	— — —	1 0 0	0 0 0

A = active

(a) symbolic   (b) assigned

Fig. 2.29 Conditional-output tables for the ASM of Fig. 2.25.

forms of this table for the ASM of Fig. 2.25, and here again on the assigned form logic conditions are replaced with logic values, state names with state codes, and the active levels with the appropriate binary values.

These tables in their assigned form enable the various functions required to produce the correct next-state transitions and system outputs to be set up. A more compact form of this information is provided by the combined *ASM table*. This includes the inputs, present states and next states, in symbolic and assigned forms, the state outputs and conditional outputs. It is a straightforward com-

Link path	Inputs Q$_1$	Q$_2$	Q$_3$	Present state Sym.	A	B	C	Next state Sym.	NA	NB	NC	Outputs State H.ADD	H.LAMP	Conditional IL.INC	IH.SET	IH.CLR
1	0	0	—	1	0	0	0	1	0	0	0	0	0	1	0	1
2	1	—	—	1	0	0	0	2	0	1	0	0	0	0	0	1
3	0	1	—	1	0	0	0	3	0	0	1	0	0	1	0	1
4	—	—	0	2	0	1	0	4	1	1	0	0	0	1	0	0
5	—	—	1	2	0	1	0	5	0	1	1	0	0	1	1	0
6	0	—	—	3	0	0	1	1	0	0	0	1	0	1	0	1
7	1	—	—	3	0	0	1	5	0	1	1	1	0	1	1	1
8	—	0	—	4	1	1	0	5	0	1	1	0	1	1	0	0
9	—	1	—	4	1	1	0	6	1	0	0	0	1	1	0	1
10	—	—	—	5	0	1	1	1	0	0	0	0	1	1	1	0
11	—	—	—	6	1	0	0	1	0	0	0	1	0	0	0	0

Fig. 2.30 Combined ASM table for the ASM of Fig. 2.25.

bination of the individual tables, except that the state-output table has to be expanded to include all link paths. We then ensure that a state output is shown as active for all link paths through the corresponding ASM block. Fig. 2.30 gives the combined ASM table for the machine of Fig. 2.25.

The combined table represents a complete specification of the state machine and forms part of the system documentation along with the ASM chart. The subsequent synthesis procedures operate on this form of representation. As an initial indication of how this might proceed we can construct the Karnaugh maps of the next-state values and the outputs along the lines indicated in Fig. 2.26. That is, each function will be formed as some combination of the link path expressions as indicated in Fig. 2.31. From the ASM table, or these maps, we find

$$NA = L_4 + L_9 = \overline{Q_3}\overline{A}B\overline{C} + Q_2AB\overline{C}$$
$$= \overline{Q_3}\overline{A}B\overline{C} + Q_2AB$$

using unassigned codes as don't cares, and

$$NB = L_2 + L_4 + L_5 + L_7 + L_8$$
$$= Q_1\overline{A}\overline{B}\overline{C} + \overline{Q_3}\overline{A}B\overline{C} + Q_3\overline{A}B\overline{C} + Q_1\overline{A}BC + \overline{Q_2}AB\overline{C}$$
$$= Q_1\overline{A}\overline{B} + \overline{A}B\overline{C} + \overline{Q_2}AB$$

similarly,

$$NC = L_3 + L_5 + L_7 + L_8$$
$$= \overline{Q_1}Q_2\overline{A}\overline{B}\overline{C} + Q_3\overline{A}B\overline{C} + Q_1\overline{B}C + \overline{Q_2}AB$$
$$\text{IL.1}NC = L_1 + L_3 + L_4 + L_5 + L_6 + L_7 + L_8 + L_9 + L_{10}$$
$$= \overline{Q_1}\overline{A} + B + C$$
$$\text{IH.SET} = L_5 + L_7 + L_{10}$$
$$= Q_1C + \overline{Q_3}B + BC$$
$$\text{IH.CLR} = L_1 + L_2 + L_3 + L_6 + L_7 + L_9$$
$$= \overline{A}\overline{B} + Q_2AB$$
$$\text{H.ADD} = L_6 + L_7 + L_{11}$$
$$= \overline{B}C + A\overline{B}$$
$$\text{H.LAMP} = L_8 + L_9 + L_{10}$$
$$= BC + AB$$

The last two equations representing the state outputs are of course independent of the system inputs and could be derived from much smaller maps labelled only with the state variables as indicated in Fig. 2.31.

The detailed problems involved in the synthesis of these system functions are considered in the following chapters. Up to this point

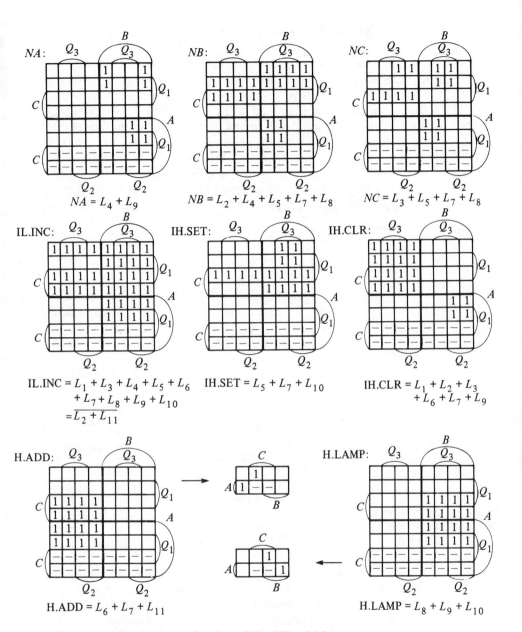

Fig. 2.31 System function maps for the ASM of Fig. 2.25.

no decision has had to be made regarding the form of implementation. We are still free to choose from a wide range of circuit technologies as well as a software implementation.

2.5 LINKED STATE MACHINES

Thus far we have only considered systems which can be described entirely by one ASM chart. It may be convenient to design the data part and the control part of a system by means of separate ASM structures which then have to be linked in some way to realize the complete system. One advantage of the ASM approach is that very large systems can also be separated into a number of ASMs which are linked together in some fashion to provide the overall system. Each individual ASM can be designed separately and then linked according to some strategy. The full exploitation of this technique is beyond the scope of this book but it is of interest to discuss some of the concepts.

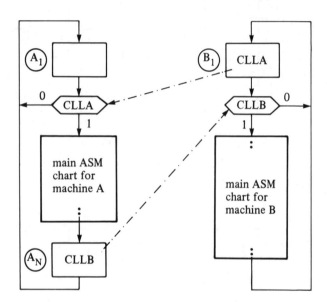

Fig. 2.32 Serial linking of two synchronized ASMs.

The simplest arrangements occur when the various ASM modules share the same clock and therefore have identical state times. Extra precautions have to be taken when the clock of one module is a multiple of, or completely asynchronous to, that of the others. We shall confine our interest to the simple case when all modules operate with the same clock.

The interaction of two machines can involve either a serial or parallel linking. The linking is achieved by making the outputs of one machine form the control inputs to the other, and vice versa. This illustrates the role of ASM outputs as instructions to other machines. Fig. 2.32 demonstrates this principle for two serially linked state machines. Machine A will wait in state A_1 until it receives the call instruction CLLA from machine B. Machine A will then proceed through the other states required to perform its task until it reaches state A_N. This will generate the instruction CLLB which will cause machine B to leave state B_1 and proceed with its task. Meanwhile machine A will return to wait in state A_1. This structure will execute the tasks of machine A and machine B alternately. This arrangement can be elaborated upon by designating one machine as the main control machine which can call several others during the execution of its task. In each case on calling another machine, the main machine must wait until it receives a return call indicating the completion of the other machine's task. This situation includes the case where the same module is called several times during the algorithm of the main machine. Such an arrangement is illustrated in Fig. 2.33. Machine A waits in state A_1 after the first call of the subroutine algorithm, in state A_R after the second call, and in state A_S after the third. We can also imagine structures where one machine calls another, which in turn calls a third, and so on. This arrangement is described in Fig. 2.34. In each case the

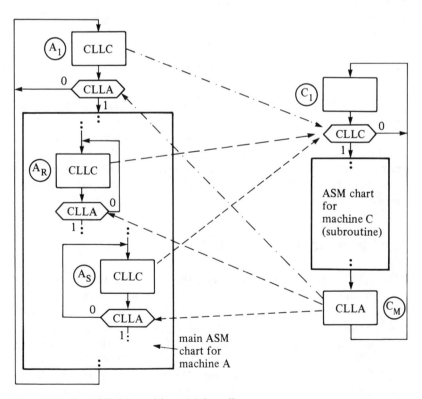

Fig. 2.33 Serial linking with multiple calls.

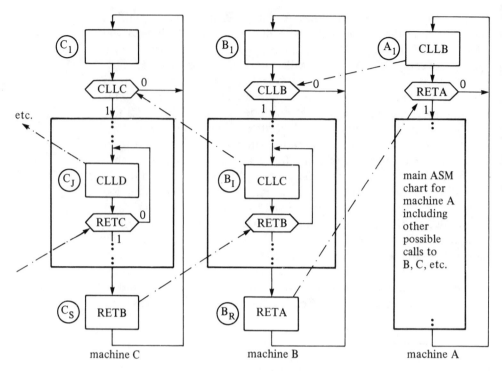

Fig. 2.34 Serial linking with chained calls.

calling machine waits for the return call before proceeding with its own task.

Two machines may also be linked in parallel to enable two processes to be performed concurrently. The simplest parallel mode is when we wish to ensure that two parallel processes are initiated together. In this situation we can make the initial state of each process make a call for the other as indicated in Fig. 2.35.

2.6 BIBLIOGRAPHICAL NOTES

The ASM method was first comprehensively documented by Clare (1972) and only a few other texts have included coverage of this topic. Winkel and Prosser (1980), Davio *et al.* (1983), Comer (1984) and Mano (1984) all include treatments of varying degrees of thoroughness. Relatively few technical papers have been devoted to the ASM method as such; of these, Jablon *et al.* (1977) and Edwards and Aspinall (1983) are prominent. The latter paper shows that the data and the control parts of a system can both be described by an ASM. Dagless (1983) also relates the ASM method and logic design.

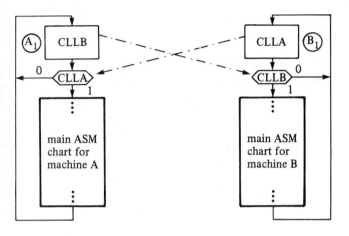

Fig.   2.35 Linking   of parallel processes.

2.7 EXERCISES

2.1 An algorithmic state machine is defined by the ASM chart in Fig. 2.36. Sketch each ASM block and indicate the link paths. Construct the following tables in both symbolic and state-assigned forms:

a) state transition table,
b) state output table,
c) conditional output table.

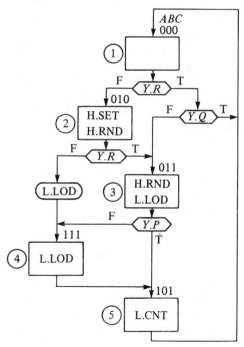

Fig. 2.36 ASM chart for Exercise 2.1.

Inputs			Present state	Next state	Outputs		
X	Y	Z			L.I	L.J	H.K
F	—	T	1	6		A	A
F	—	F	1	1		A	
T	—	—	1	4		A	
—	—	—	2	4			A
—	—	—	3	2		A	
—	—	—	4	1	A	A	
—	T	—	5	2			
—	F	—	5	6			
T	—	F	6	3			
F	—	—	6	4	A		
T	—	T	6	5			

F = false; T = true; A = active.

Fig. 2.37 ASM table for Exercise 2.3.

2.2 Construct the combined ASM table for the machine of Exercise 2.1 and derive the next-state equations.

2.3 Fig. 2.37 shows the symbolic form of ASM table for a certain sequential machine. Draw the corresponding ASM chart and mark clearly each ASM block and link path. Deduce a minimum locus assignment for this machine and construct the fully assigned ASM table. Derive logical expressions for the three outputs.

2.4 A sequential machine has two inputs X and Y, and detects the sequence of input value pairs 00, 11, 00, 10, 00, giving an output $H.SEQ$ on each detection during the final combination of the sequence. Draw an ASM chart for this machine and construct the symbolic form of ASM table.

2.5 Perform a minimum locus state assignment for the machine of Exercise 2.4 and construct the assigned ASM table. Derive the next-state and output functions.

Chapter 3
The Synthesis of ASM-based Designs

3.1 INTRODUCTION

The state assignment process transforms the abstract description of the sequential machine into one in which all the next-state and output functions are specified. The ultimate form of the implementation depends only on the method of synthesis applied to these functions and the manner in which any unspecified or don't care conditions are interpreted.

In order to extract the next-state excitation functions from the assigned ASM table it is first necessary to make some decision regarding the representation of the internal memory of the machine. In hardware implementations this inevitably means some form of register or collection of basic memory elements such as D-type, JK-type or SR-type clocked bistables. The present state of the machine will then be interpreted as the concatenation of output values of this set of bistables. Thus, for k state variables, $Q_1, Q_2, \ldots, Q_k$ the present state Q will be presented as:

$$Q = Q_1 \frown Q_2 \frown Q_3 \frown \ldots \frown Q_k$$

The next states will then be seen to be the set of values applied to the inputs of these bistables. On command of the timing clock these inputs will become the new outputs thereby producing the new present state.

It is necessary to interpret the next values of the state variables in a way suitable to the particular type of bistable to be employed. When this is done it is then possible to derive the next-state excitation and output functions. In general, these functions will be dependent on the present-state variables and the inputs or qualifiers and are thus seen to be functions of up to $k + n$ variables when there are k state variables and n inputs. Thus for even modest ASM structures with, say, less than 16 states and only four inputs, these functions may involve up to eight variables. It is inconvenient to employ Karnaugh maps of this dimension even though the resulting maps may be sparse due to the many unspecified conditions which may be present. However, the Karnaugh map still remains the ideal mode of representation for the visual interpretation and manipulation of functions and it would be useful to retain it in this context.

The technique of employing map-entered variables enables sparse functions of many variables to be compressed onto Karnaugh maps of fewer variables. This form of representation is then suited to the final phase which is that of synthesizing these functions in some preferred form of circuit technology. In addition to synthesis by means of discrete logic gates we can now investigate other forms of implementation via MSI elements such as multiplexers (MUX) and other forms of universal logic modules (ULM). ASM design methods are also highly suited to LSI and VLSI technologies which have produced semi-custom units such as uncommitted gate arrays, and programmable devices such as programmable array logic (PAL), programmable logic arrays (PLA) and programmable logic sequencers (PLS). It is also important to consider implementations based on read-only memories (ROM). This chapter will deal with the extraction of the next-state excitation functions from the assigned ASM table and their representation on compact Karnaugh maps. The synthesis of these functions by means of various circuit technologies will then be investigated.

3.2 DERIVATION OF NEXT-STATE EXCITATION FUNCTIONS

The next-state functions defined on the assigned ASM table need to be interpreted for each type of memory element to be used for the internal representation of the state of the machine. The most straightforward type to use is the simple D-type which has one data input and a clock input. As the clock input is taken high, the value on the data input is transferred to become the new output value of the bistable. Thus, if $D = Q$ before the clock is applied no change of state will be observed and only when $D = \bar{Q}$ initially will the output be seen to switch. In either case we can still say that the new output is the value of D prevailing when the clock goes high. Thus,

$$Q := D$$

If Q represents the present state of the bistable, D represents the next-state value. Thus there is a direct correspondence between the D inputs and the next-state function values when D-type bistables are employed in ASM design synthesis. The next-state variables such as NA, NB, etc., can be expressed directly as DA, DB, etc., where the latter are the inputs to the D-type bistables representing the state variables A, B, etc.

This direct correspondence is not apparent when JK-bistables are employed because these devices have two data inputs, namely J and K, as well as the synchronizing clock input. Furthermore, most JK-bistables are of the master–slave variety in which the values on the data inputs are transferred to the master element as the clock

J	K	Q_{t+1}
0	0	Q_t
0	1	0
1	0	1
1	1	$\bar{Q_t}$

Fig. 3.1 Operation of the JK-bistable.

A	NA	JA	KA
0	0	0	—
0	1	1	—
1	0	—	1
1	1	—	0

Fig. 3.2 Excitation rules for the JK-bistable.

goes high and then from master to slave element when the clock returns low. As the outputs of the device are derived from the slave element the JK-bistable appears to change state on the negative going edge of the clock waveform. Master–slave bistables are to be preferred to the simple devices even though they require more excitation functions because they represent the only sure way of achieving reliable synchronous sequential behaviour. Fig. 3.1 illustrates the more complex behaviour of the JK-bistable. This table can be used to devise rules for generating the values for J and K to enable a given next value of output to be produced from a given present value. It is necessary to apply these rules to each state variable and its next-state value and for each row of the ASM table. Consider the state variable A and its next-state value NA. There are four possibilities. Firstly, Fig. 3.1 indicates that the case $A = 0$ and $NA = 0$ will result if $J = 0$ and $K = 0$ or $J = 0$ and $K = 1$. This implies that it is necessary to ensure only that $J = 0$, and the value of K is not important and is therefore a don't care condition. Similarly, the case $A = 0$ and $NA = 1$ will be achieved for $J = 1$ and $K = 0$ or $J = 1$ and $K = 1$. This is equivalent to making $JA = 1$ and $KA = —$. The complete set of rules is summarized in Fig. 3.2.

We can apply a similar procedure to the case of the clocked SR-bistable. If we assume the S and R inputs are active low then Fig.

S	R	Q_{t+1}
1	1	Q_t
0	1	1
1	0	0
0	0	?

(a) active low inputs

S	R	Q_{t+1}
0	0	Q_t
1	0	1
0	1	0
1	1	?

(b) active high inputs

Fig. 3.3 Operation of SR-bistables.

A	NA	Active low inputs SA	RA	Active high inputs SA	RA
0	0	1	—	0	—
0	1	0	1	1	0
1	0	1	0	0	1
1	1	—	1	—	0

Fig. 3.4 Excitation of clocked SR-bistables.

3.3a applies; for active-high inputs Fig. 3.3b is appropriate. In each case the situation $S = R =$ active must be avoided, unless extra circuitry is incorporated to make the device set-dominant or reset-dominant because this will lead to indeterminate behaviour. The case $A = 0$, $NA = 0$ is achieved by making $S = 1$ and $R = 1$ or $S = 1$ and $R = 0$; i.e. $S = 1$, $R = $ — in the case of active low inputs, or $S = 0$, $R = $ —, for active high inputs. The complete excitation tables are given in Fig. 3.4.

As an example of this technique, consider the assigned ASM table of Fig. 3.5. For the present exercise only the present-state/next-state behaviour is relevant and Fig. 3.6 shows this information translated for D-type, JK-type and SR-type bistable elements. At this stage it can be appreciated that although the two-input devices require twice as many excitation functions as the single-input D-type, the presence of large numbers of don't care terms can result in much simpler functions.

Inputs X Y Z	Present state Sym. A B C	Next state Sym. NA NB NC	Outputs H.J H.K L.L
0 — —	1 0 0 0	2 0 0 1	1 0 1
1 — —	1 0 0 0	3 1 0 0	1 1 1
— 0 —	2 0 0 1	2 0 0 1	0 0 1
— 1 —	2 0 0 1	4 0 1 1	0 0 1
— — 0	3 1 0 0	1 0 0 0	0 0 1
— — 1	3 1 0 0	5 0 1 0	0 0 1
— — —	4 0 1 1	6 1 1 0	0 0 0
1 — —	5 0 1 0	4 0 1 1	1 1 1
0 — —	5 0 1 0	1 0 0 0	1 1 0
— — 1	6 1 1 0	6 1 1 0	1 1 1
— — 0	6 1 1 0	1 0 0 0	1 0 1

Fig. 3.5 Example ASM table.

Inputs	Present state	(a) Next state			(b) Next state						(c) Next state					
X Y Z	Sym. A B C	Sym.	DA	DB DC	JA	KA	JB	KB	JC	KC	SA	RA	SB	RB	SC	RC
0 — —	1 0 0 0	2	0	0 1	0	—	0	—	1	—	1	—	1	—	0	1
1 — —	1 0 0 0	3	1	0 0	1	—	0	—	0	—	0	1	1	—	1	—
— 0 —	2 0 0 1	2	0	0 1	0	—	0	—	—	0	1	—	1	—	—	1
— 1 —	2 0 0 1	4	0	1 1	0	—	1	—	—	0	1	—	0	1	—	1
— — 0	3 1 0 0	1	0	0 0	—	1	0	—	0	—	1	0	1	—	1	—
— — 1	3 1 0 0	5	0	1 0	—	1	1	—	0	—	1	0	0	1	1	—
— — —	4 0 1 1	6	1	1 0	1	—	—	0	—	1	0	1	—	1	0	1
1 — —	5 0 1 0	4	0	1 1	0	—	—	0	1	—	1	—	—	1	0	1
0 — —	5 0 1 0	1	0	0 0	0	—	—	1	0	—	1	—	1	0	1	—
— — 1	6 1 1 0	6	1	1 0	—	0	—	0	0	—	—	1	—	1	1	—
— — 0	6 1 1 0	1	0	0 0	—	1	—	1	0	—	1	0	1	0	1	—

Fig. 3.6 ASM table of Fig. 3.5 assigned for the excitation of (a) D-type, (b) JK-type and (c) SR-type bistables.

3.3 MAP-ENTERED VARIABLES

It is possible to display and manipulate sparse functions of many variables on Karnaugh maps of smaller dimension by entering the excess variables on the map along with the 0s and 1s where appropriate. This is especially effective if there are numerous don't care terms. As we have observed, ASM designs usually produce sparse functions of many variables with numerous don't care terms and so this technique is particularly appropriate here. Consider the three-variable Karnaugh map in Fig. 3.7a. The corresponding general function is:

$$f(X_3, X_2, X_1) = d_0\overline{X}_3\overline{X}_2\overline{X}_1 + d_1\overline{X}_3\overline{X}_2X_1 + d_2\overline{X}_3X_2\overline{X}_1 +$$
$$d_3\overline{X}_3X_2X_1 + d_4X_3\overline{X}_2\overline{X}_1 + d_5X_3\overline{X}_2X_1 +$$
$$d_6X_3X_2\overline{X}_1 + d_7X_3X_2X_1$$

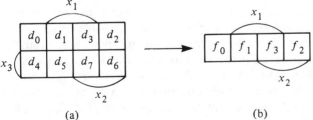

(a)   (b)

Fig. 3.7 Three-variable Karnaugh map and its compression to two-variable form.

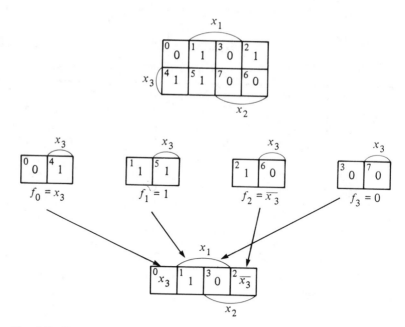

Fig. 3.8   Example function and its residues.

This may be rearranged to give

$$f(X_3, X_2, X_1) = (d_0\overline{X_3} + d_4 X_3)\overline{X_2}\overline{X_1} + (d_1\overline{X_3} + d_5 X_3)\overline{X_2}X_1 +$$
$$(d_2\overline{X_3} + d_6 X_3)X_2\overline{X_1} + (d_3\overline{X_3} + d_7 X_3)X_2 X_1$$
$$= f_0\overline{X_2}\overline{X_1} + f_1\overline{X_2}X_1 + f_2 X_2\overline{X_1} + f_3 X_2 X_1$$

This appears to be a two-variable function with coefficients f_i and as such could be plotted on a two-variable Karnaugh map as depicted in Fig. 3.7b. The f_i are in fact all functions of one variable, in this case X_3, or less. Thus

$$f_i = d_j\overline{X_3} + d_k X_3$$

and as d_j and d_k go through their four possible combinations of values, each f_i resolves to 0, 1, $\overline{X_3}$ or X_3.

For a given function we can resolve each of these sub-functions and enter the results on the lower-order map. This process is illustrated in Fig. 3.8. In practice, it is possible to identify each of these residues of the third variable by inspection of the original map. Also, it is equally valid to select one of the other variables as the residue variable. In each case we can identify a pair of map entries for each residue function and we can resolve these to determine the entries on the reduced map. Fig. 3.9 demonstrates this process for the previous function using each of the variables in the map-entered role.

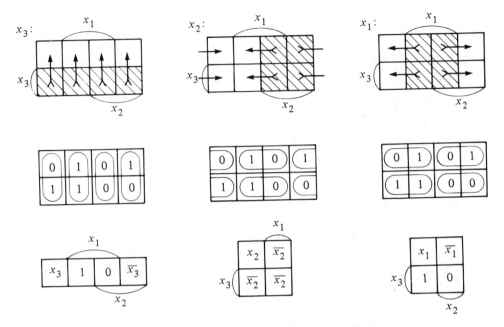

Fig. 3.9 Three possible ways of compressing a three-variable function.

The process is readily extended to larger functions. For four variables we can select the residue variable in four ways. In each case we require to resolve eight residue functions and enter these in the appropriate cells on the three-variable map. Fig. 3.10 shows this technique for an arbitrary function. In addition, we can extend the compression process so that we may enter two or more variables. The canonical form of a four-variable function can be rearranged as

$$
\begin{aligned}
f(X_4, X_3, X_2, X_1) = &(d_0\overline{X}_4\overline{X}_3 + d_4\overline{X}_4X_3 + d_8X_4\overline{X}_3 + d_{12}X_4X_3)\overline{X}_2\overline{X}_1 + \\
&(d_1\overline{X}_4\overline{X}_3 + d_5\overline{X}_4X_3 + d_9X_4\overline{X}_3 + d_{13}X_4X_3)\overline{X}_2X_1 + \\
&(d_2\overline{X}_4\overline{X}_3 + d_6\overline{X}_4X_3 + d_{10}X_4\overline{X}_3 + d_{14}X_4X_3)X_2\overline{X}_1 + \\
&(d_3\overline{X}_4\overline{X}_3 + d_7\overline{X}_4X_3 + d_{11}X_4\overline{X}_3 + d_{15}X_4X_3)X_2X_1 \\
= &f_0\overline{X}_2\overline{X}_1 + f_1\overline{X}_2X_1 + f_2X_2\overline{X}_1 + f_3X_2X_1
\end{aligned}
$$

which has similar structure to a two-variable function but now the coefficients f_i are functions of *two* variables X_4 and X_3. There are now 16 possible forms that these residue functions may take and only six of these are trivial in that they resolve to 0, 1, $\overline{X}_4$, X_4, $\overline{X}_3$ or X_3; the remaining ten involve non-trivial Boolean expressions such as $X_4\overline{X}_3$ or $X_4 \oplus X_3$. If a large number of the latter arise amongst the f_i the resulting map can appear confusing and difficult to manipulate. This process of compression by two variables is demonstrated in Fig. 3.11a where X_4 and X_3 are used in the formation of

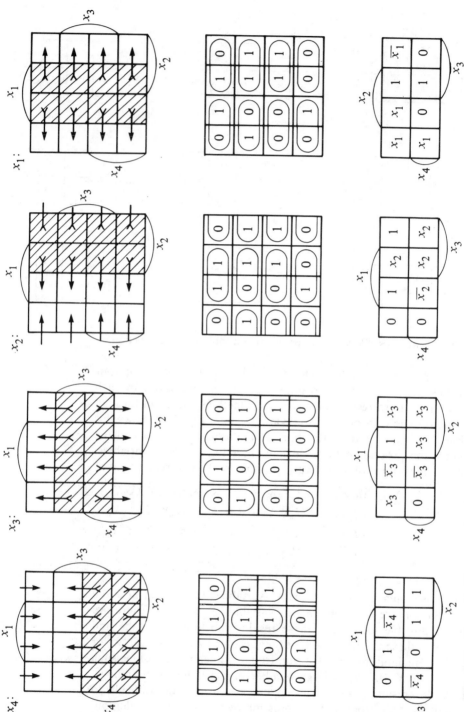

Fig. 3.10 Four possible ways of compressing a four-variable function.

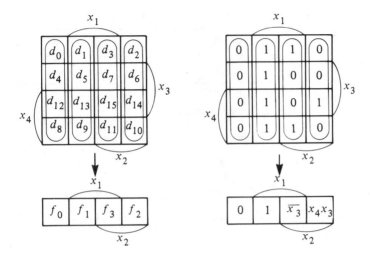

Fig. 3.11 Map entering two variables.

the residue functions. Fig. 3.11b shows this reduction applied to an actual function. As before, we could equally well have selected any two of the variables to form the residue functions. In this case there will be six possible choices and each one will correspond to a different grouping of the coefficients on the original map as depicted in Fig. 3.12. The process of identifying the residue functions is eased somewhat in the presence of any don't care terms in the original function. These can be employed to advantage to simplify the residues and thereby clarify the compressed map.

In order to employ this technique in the synthesis of ASM-based designs we need to consider three questions. First, how do we decide which variables are to be used as map-entered variables and which are to be designated as mapping variables and used to label the function maps? Second, how do we construct the function maps directly from the assigned ASM table? Third, how do we simplify or extract functions from maps containing map-entered terms?

In ASM designs we have already identified two sets of system variables; the state variables and the inputs or qualifiers. The nature of ASM structure is such that state transitions are unlikely to depend on all the qualifiers and the outputs depend on either the state variables alone or on certain link paths which in turn depend only on certain of the qualifiers. Thus, a reasonable tactic in ASM designs is to employ the state variables as mapping variables and the inputs as map-entered variables. This choice is attractive for several reasons. First, the function maps which result will have dimension equal to the number of state variables which in turn is dictated by the number of states. As the Karnaugh map is only usable with ease

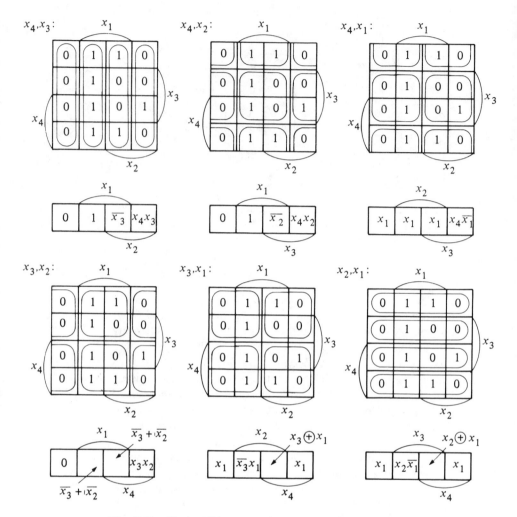

Fig. 3.12 Six possible ways of reducing by two variables.

up to five or six variables we should still be able to accommodate systems with up to six state variables or 64 states. This is probably a realistic limit on the size of the ASM design, at least when the design is to be performed or interpreted manually. In any case, larger systems can usually be broken down into separate modules each containing less than this number of states. Second, the format of each function map will be identical to that of the state map resulting from the state assignment process and each cell on the function map will correspond to the behaviour during one state on the ASM chart or table. Thus each ASM block will correspond to one cell on the function map. Third, the residue functions will involve only the inputs or qualifiers and will be independent of the state variables.

Inputs		State		
X	Y	A	B	DA
1	–	0	0	1
0	–	0	0	0
–	1	1	1	0
1	0	1	1	1
0	1	0	1	1
1	0	0	1	1

(a)

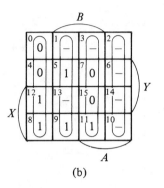

(b)

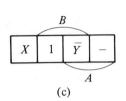

(c)

Fig. 3.13 Derivation of map-entered function map from complete map.

One method of constructing the function maps would be to begin by setting up Karnaugh maps with dimension equal to the total number of system variables. Subsequently, these maps could be compressed using the procedures described previously after selecting the qualifiers as map-entered variables. Consider the fragment of a simple ASM table given in Fig. 3.13a. The function for DA depends on the two state variables A and B, and on the two qualifiers X and Y. We can therefore depict this function on a four-variable Karnaugh map as indicated in Fig. 3.13b. The first three rows of the ASM table each define *two* cells on the map because each has an unspecified value for one of the inputs. Thus

$$d_8 = d_{12} = 1,$$
$$d_0 = d_4 = 0,$$
and
$$d_7 = d_{15} = 0.$$

The other three rows are all completely specified and therefore correspond to only *one* cell in each case. It follows that

$$d_{12} = d_5 = d_9 = 1.$$

All remaining cells on the Karnaugh map are unspecified and therefore correspond to don't care terms. The selection of X and Y as map-entered variables results in a two-variable Karnaugh map labelled with the state variables A and B. The residue functions can be identified on the complete map and entered into the corresponding compressed map as shown in Fig. 3.13c.

This method is not very attractive since we wish to avoid using the full-size maps at any stage in the process. This can be achieved by reading off the residue functions directly from the ASM table. The fact that each cell on the function map corresponds to one ASM block of the table considerably eases this problem. For each cell on the compressed map the state variable values are fixed and to

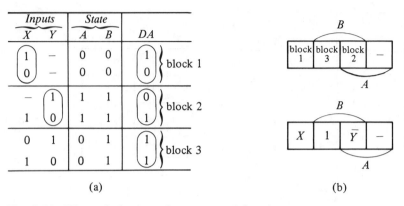

(a)   (b)

Fig. 3.14   Direct derivation of map-entered function map.

deduce the entry we need only express DA as a function of the input variables. Thus we partition the ASM table into the various ASM blocks as indicated in Fig. 3.14a. We can then deduce the function for DA for each block of the partition ignoring the values under A and B. For the first block $DA = X$, $DA = \bar{Y}$ for the second block, and $DA = 1$ for the third block. The location of these components of the complete function is determined by the state assignment and indicated by the corresponding state map. The fourth state code is unused and therefore appears as a don't care term on the function map of Fig. 3.14b. We have achieved the same result as the previous method without setting up the larger function map.

As a more complete example, let us return to the ASM table of Fig. 3.6. The corresponding state map and the various excitation functions for each type of memory element are each depicted in compressed form in Fig. 3.15. Here we have managed to express all these functions, which involve up to six system variables, including three state variables and three qualifiers, on three-variable Karnaugh maps. This demonstrates the high degree of compactness which the map-entered variable technique can provide.

The process of setting up these compact function maps is greatly eased by the fact that in both the previous examples there is at most one qualifier per ASM block. This in turn dictates that there are at most two link paths per ASM block and therefore the corresponding residue functions are either don't care terms, in the case of direct state transitions and one link path, or a function of one qualifier in the case of two link paths. Although functions such as that for DB involve all six system variables, during any one ASM block they are dependent on at most four of these variables; that is, the three state variables and one of the qualifiers. In situations where there are more qualifiers per ASM block the residue functions may involve

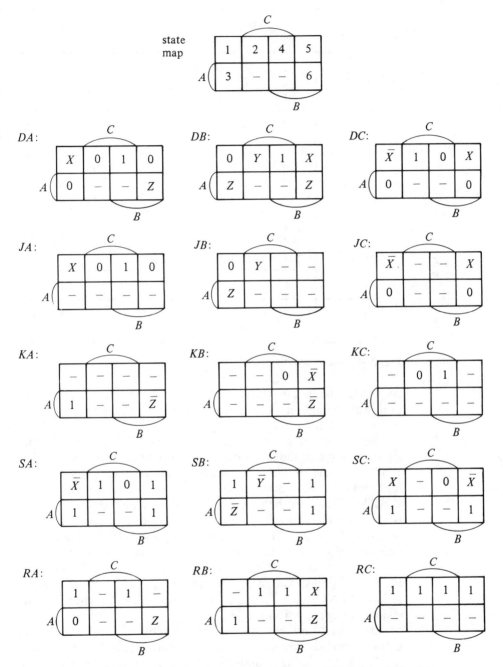

Fig. 3.15 State map and excitation functions maps for the ASM table of Fig. 3.6.

more than one qualifier and therefore may not resolve to a single variable but rather will take the form of a Boolean expression. Even

Inputs			Present state				Next state			
X	Y	Z	Sym.	A	B	C	Sym.	NA	NB	NC
1	—	—	1	0	0	0	2	0	0	1
0	0	—	1	0	0	0	3	1	0	1
0	1	—	1	0	0	0	4	1	0	0
—	—	1	2	0	0	1	3	1	0	1
—	—	0	2	0	0	1	5	0	1	1
0	—	—	3	1	0	1	5	0	1	1
1	1	—	3	1	0	1	3	1	0	1
1	0	—	3	1	0	1	2	0	0	1
—	1	0	4	1	0	0	3	1	0	1
—	0	0	4	1	0	0	2	0	0	1
—	—	1	4	1	0	0	6	0	1	0
—	—	—	5	0	1	1	2	0	0	1
—	0	—	6	0	1	0	6	0	1	0
—	1	—	6	0	1	0	1	0	0	0

Fig. 3.16 More complex ASM table.

so, this technique can still be used because it is unlikely that any link path will depend on all the system qualifiers and the resulting maps will not be too confusing.

For example, consider the ASM table of Fig. 3.16. In this structure some of the ASM blocks contain more than one qualifier. When we come to derive the maps for the next state functions we find that on some occasions the residue functions will involve two variables. Thus, for the function NA during state 3 the contribution is given by the expression $NA = XY$, and during state 4 the component is $NA = Y\overline{Z}$. These are readily obtained since NA is true on only one of the three link paths. Other situations are slightly more complex. For example NC during state 1 is true on the first two rows (link paths) and thus NC is given by $NC = X + \overline{X}\overline{Y}$ which reduces to $NC = X + \overline{Y}$. The complete functions, together with the state map, are given in Fig. 3.17.

In order to establish the means whereby we may simplify and extract functions expressed using map-entered variables let us return to the ASM fragment and the full function map of Fig. 3.13. Simplification of this complete map using the don't care terms to advantage reveals that one possible minimum form of DA is

$$DA = \overline{A}B + \overline{A}X + A\overline{Y}$$

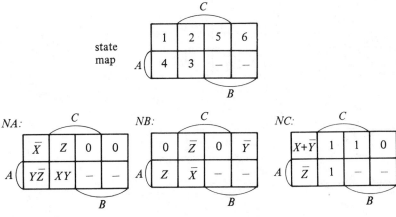

Fig. 3.17   Next-state functions for the ASM of Fig. 3.16.

as demonstrated in Fig. 3.18a. We require to obtain the same expression directly from the compact map. This can be achieved by the following process:

1. Set all variables to 0 and simplify on the 1s remaining on map.
2. Restore variables, set 1s to don't care and minimize for each variable or residue function in turn.
3. Combine the expressions generated in 1 and 2 to form the complete expression.

Applying this technique to the compact map yields:

Step 1 $DA = \bar{A}B$
Step 2 $DA = X\bar{A} + \bar{Y}A$
Step 3 $DA = \bar{A}B + X\bar{A} + \bar{Y}A$

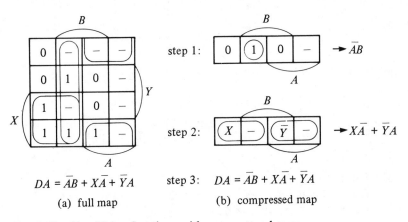

Fig. 3.18   Simplifying functions with map-entered terms.

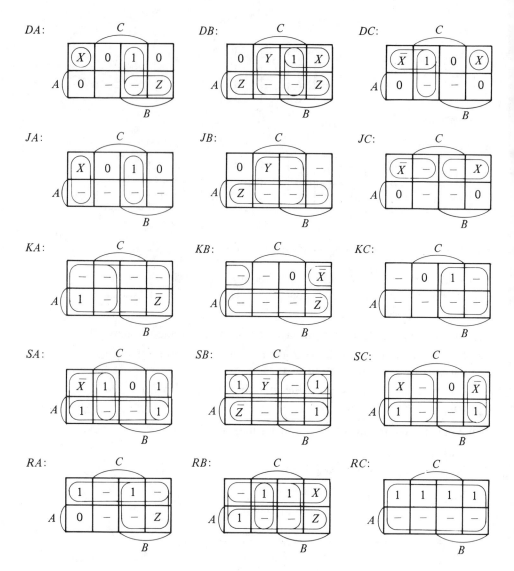

Fig. 3.19 Simplification of the system functions of Fig. 3.15.

as indicated in Fig. 3.18b. If we use this technique on the maps of Fig. 3.15 the following set of expressions are obtained as indicated in Fig. 3.19:

$$DA = BC + X\overline{A}\overline{B}\overline{C} + ZAB$$
$$DB = BC + YC + X\overline{A}B + ZA \left.\begin{array}{c}\end{array}\right\} \text{D-type bistables}$$
$$DC = \overline{B}C + \overline{X}\overline{A}\overline{B} + X\overline{A}B\overline{C}$$

$$JA = BC + X\overline{B}\overline{C}$$
$$KA = \overline{B} + \overline{Z}$$
$$JB = YC + ZA$$
$$KB = \overline{X}\overline{A}C + \overline{Z}A$$
$$JC = \overline{X}\overline{A}\overline{B} + X\overline{A}B$$
$$KC = B$$

JK-type bistables

$$SA = \overline{B}C + B\overline{C} + \overline{X}B + A$$
$$RA = \overline{A} + ZB$$
$$SB = \overline{A}\overline{C} + B + \overline{Y}\overline{A} + \overline{Z}A$$
$$RB = \overline{B} + C + X\overline{A} + ZA$$
$$SC = A + X\overline{B} + \overline{X}B\overline{C}$$
$$RC = 1$$

SR-type bistables

Thus far we have considered the derivation of only excitation functions from ASM tables. An exactly similar technique can be employed to determine the output functions. Here again the technique of map-entered variables can be used with the state variables acting as mapping variables and the qualifiers as map-entered terms. However, in the case of unconditional state outputs which are active, either high or low, during the state time, irrespective of which link path is followed, the resulting maps will not contain any map-entered variables. Rather, they will contain 1s in cells corresponding to states in which they are active, in the case of active high outputs, and 0s in cells corresponding to inactive states. This situation is reversed for active low outputs. Conditional outputs will have functions which contain map-entered variables corresponding to the link paths for which they are active. Fig. 3.20a

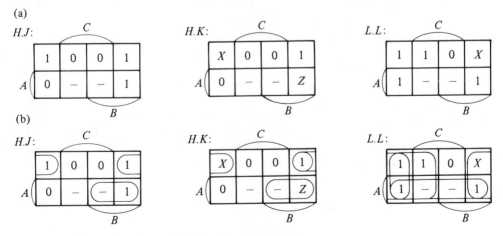

Fig. 3.20 Output functions of ASM table of Fig. 3.5.

shows the maps obtained for the three outputs of the ASM table defined in Fig. 3.5. Output J is an active high state output and is active during states 1, 5 and 6, and its map contains no map-entered variables. Output K, also active high, is a conditional output during states 1 and 6, and is unconditional during state 5. We therefore encounter map-entered variables in the cells for states 1 and 6. Similarly, output L, which is active low, is conditional during state 5 and unconditional during state 4. The corresponding expressions derived as indicated in Fig. 3.20b are:

$$HJ = \overline{A}\overline{C} + AB$$

i.e. function of state variables only, and

$$HK = \overline{A}B\overline{C} + X\overline{A}\overline{C} + ZAB$$
$$LL = A + \overline{B} + X\overline{C}$$

i.e. functions of state variables and modifiers.

3.4 IMPLEMENTATION BY DISCRETE GATES

The derivation of the excitation functions, corresponding to a chosen bistable element, and the output functions enables an implementation to be performed in the desired form of circuit technology. Traditionally, in prototype development, a direct implementation in terms of discrete devices such as NAND or NOR elements would be appropriate at this stage so that the design could be evaluated and verified. Recently, the availability of computer-aided design facilities incorporating logic simulation packages has permitted the verification of designs without the need for expensive and time-consuming prototyping. However, it still remains valid in some circumstances, such as uncommitted gate-array synthesis, to consider implementations in terms of discrete switching elements.

The Boolean expressions derived from the ASM designs by the straightforward simplification of the function maps will represent two-level sum-of-products circuit forms. This AND–OR arrangement is ideally suited to direct translation to NAND. Each gate can be replaced by a NAND element with the same number of inputs. The inversion produced at the output of the first level of NANDs provides the necessary inversion for the inputs to the second level of NANDs in order to ensure the latter behave as OR elements. This type of direct implementation is easy to perform and the circuit of Fig. 3.21 represents the ASM defined in Fig. 3.5 when D-type bistables and NAND elements are employed.

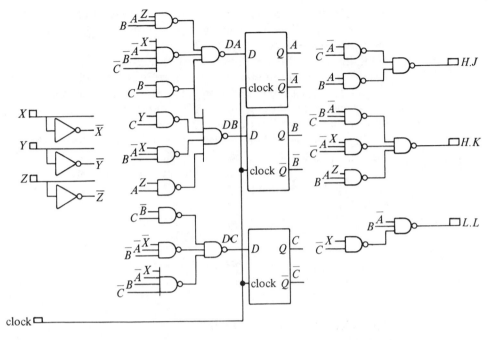

Fig. 3.21 Direct implementation of the ASM of Fig. 3.5 in terms of D-type bistables and discrete NAND elements.

Unfortunately, the direct implementation of the two-level functions derived by the independent simplification of each function map does not necessarily yield the optimum synthesis in terms of circuit complexity. Very often further simplification of each individual function may prove possible by employing some form of factorization technique. This will enable common terms to be factored out, thereby reducing the fan-in requirement of some product terms at the expense of increasing the number of gate levels. However, this factorization is not necessarily best suited to the minimum form of the function and better factorizations may emerge from expressions with some redundant content. In addition, further savings can usually be found by sharing terms amongst the various functions to be synthesized. Here again, there is no standard explicit technique for ensuring that optimum term-sharing is achieved. In short, these procedures form part of the art of logic design which can only be mastered with design experience. In the past much research effort was devoted to the development of systematic procedures for the efficient design of multiple-level and multiple-output functions. Changing circumstances, made manifest by the rapid shift of balance from cost of implementation towards cost of design have rendered these second-order improvements ineffective from a cost-saving viewpoint. Simplification with a view to improving reliability or testability is probably still a worthwhile pursuit in some circumstances. Otherwise, there is little to recommend the search for absolute minimality beyond the straightforward simplification and the more obvious factorizations and term-sharing revealed by these manipulations. However, the incorporation of these traditional methods into CAD systems will no doubt assist the designer who has access to such packages.

A useful method for obtaining a multilevel solution directly from the truth table values rather than by manipulation of the reduced forms is based on a general circuit tree which can be constructed from a simple basic module. Let F_i be a function of i variables expressed in disjunctive canonical form. Thus we can write:

$$F_0 = d_0$$
$$F_1 = d_0\bar{x}_1 + d_1x_1$$
$$F_2 = d_0\bar{x}_2\bar{x}_1 + d_1\bar{x}_2x_1 + d_2x_2\bar{x}_1 + d_3x_2x_1$$
$$= (d_0\bar{x}_1 + d_1x_1)\bar{x}_2 + (d_2\bar{x}_1 + d_3x_1)x_2$$
$$= F_1\bar{x}_2 + F_1^*x_2$$

and, in general,

$$F_n = F_{n-1}\bar{x}_n + F_{n-1}^*x_n$$

where F_i^* has a similar structure to F_i but has a different set of coefficients. We could represent this function with a circuit module of the form given in Fig. 3.22. In this arrangement we may replace both F_{n-1} and F_{n-1}^* by similar modules and by repetition build up a general multilevel circuit tree which has only the variables and truth table values as inputs.

In this complete form this circuit tree is an example of a *universal* circuit in that it can realize any Boolean function of n variables by applying the appropriate truth table values to the corresponding inputs. Fig. 3.23 shows the circuit tree corresponding to three-variable functions. This arrangement automatically yields a multilevel representation which employs only two-input gates.

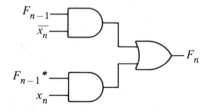

Fig. 3.22 Basic circuit module.

For any particular function, many of the gates in the tree will prove to be redundant and could therefore be removed from the structure. The process of locating and eliminating these redundant gates can form a method of simplification which yields a multilevel synthesis of two-input gates. The original universal tree forms a template on which all such possible functions will fit. The elimination process commences at the input side where the truth table values are applied to the first level of AND gates. Thus, if $d_i = 0$ the output of this AND gate will be zero independently of the value of x_1. On the other hand, when $d_i = 1$, the output of the AND gate will be equal to the value of x_1 or $\bar{x}_1$. In both cases the AND gates can be removed and the appropriate values applied to the OR gates in the next level. The inputs to these OR gates will therefore be 0, x_1 or $\bar{x}_1$. The OR function applied to any pair of these inputs will produce 0, 1, x_1 or $\bar{x}_1$, so the OR gates are not required. This means that the first level of modules can be removed for every function but

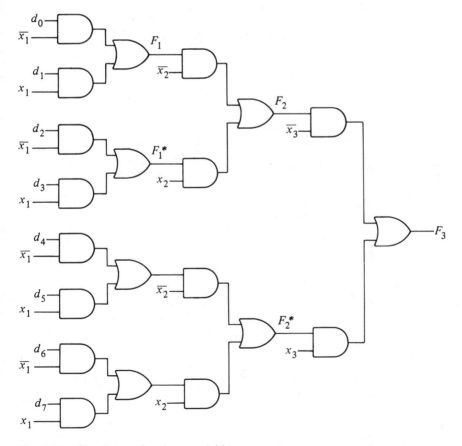

Fig. 3.23 Circuit tree for three variables.

the inputs are no longer truth table values but rather the residue functions of the variable x_1. Thus, the function

$$F_1 = d_0\bar{x}_1 + d_1x_1$$

can only take the values 0, 1, $\bar{x}_1$ or x_1, for all possible combinations of d_i values.

The process of gate elimination can continue into further levels of the tree and possibly more gates can be removed by using simple rules devised from the terminal characteristics of the AND or OR gates. As an example, consider the three-variable function defined by the truth table of Fig. 3.24a. Applying these values to the inputs of the three-variable circuit tree enables us to eliminate all the gates in the first level of modules, as indicated in Fig. 3.24b. Three of the AND gates in the next level can be eliminated directly and the fourth is also redundant because otherwise the next OR gate is performing

$$\bar{x}_1 + x_2x_1 = \bar{x}_1 + x_2.$$

The resulting multilevel circuit is given in Fig. 3.24c.

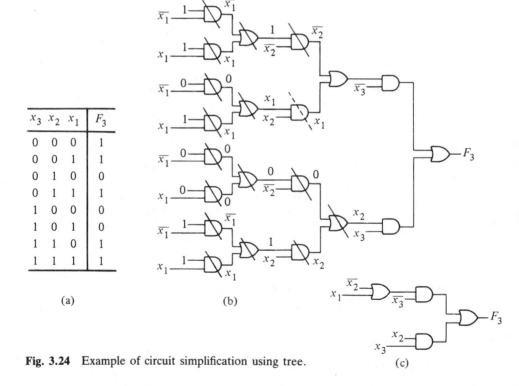

x_3	x_2	x_1	F_3
0	0	0	1
0	0	1	1
0	1	0	0
0	1	1	1
1	0	0	0
1	0	1	0
1	1	0	1
1	1	1	1

(a)

(b)

(c)

Fig. 3.24 Example of circuit simplification using tree.

The particular configuration of the circuit tree (that is, an AND-OR-AND-OR cascade) is suitable for direct conversion to NAND elements, or, if all inputs and the output are inverted, to NOR elements. The fact that only two-input elements are required may also make this technique attractive in uncommitted gate-array synthesis.

3.5 ASYNCHRONOUS INPUTS AND OUTPUTS

When the synthesis of an ASM is performed with clocked memory elements, and when all inputs are synchronous, problems due to races leading to incorrect state transitions are avoided. However, if unclocked bistables are employed or if some inputs are asynchronous, this may not be the case and care must be taken in the state assignment to eliminate critical races. Whereas the uncertainties regarding synchronous inputs and state variables are restricted to the unstable transition period of the state time, asynchronous inputs can change at any time and so carry an uncertainty 'window' into the stable period as well. Thus, if an asynchronous input changes towards the end of a state time, we are uncertain about its value and those of functions derived from it at the critical time of state transition. Fig. 3.25 shows one block of an ASM chart and table, which contains an asynchronous qualifier, denoted $^*X$. A minimum locus state assignment has been made and the partial next-state functions of this block are found to be:

$$NA = {}^*X.\overline{Y}$$
$$NB = {}^*\overline{X}.\overline{Y}$$
$$NC = Y$$

and so two state variables depend on the asynchronous input. If $Y = 1$ these equations will produce the next-state code 001 without ambiguity because this link path is independent of the asynchronous input. However, when $Y = 0$ there will be uncertainty in two of the state variables. If $^*X$ is changing in the region of a state transition there will be uncertainty about the value of $^*X$ and $^*\overline{X}$ and thus the next-state code could take on values other than those corresponding to correct transitions from this block. Thus we may get an incorrect transition along an erroneous link path.

Although this uncertainty can never be removed, its effect can be limited by judicious state assignment. In the reduced dependency

Inputs		Present state				Next state			
*X	Y	Sym.	A	B	C	Sym.	NA	NB	NC
—	1	a	0	0	0	b	0	0	1
1	0	a	0	0	0	c	1	0	0
0	0	a	0	0	0	d	0	1	0

$$NA = {^*X}.\overline{Y} \quad NB = {^*\overline{X}}.\overline{Y} \quad NC = Y$$

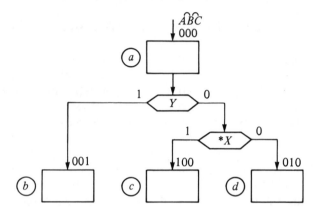

Fig. 3.25 Minimum locus assignment with possible race.

assignment of Fig. 3.26, which is not minimum locus, the partial next-state equations are:

$$NA = {^*X}.\overline{Y}$$
$$NB = \overline{Y}$$
$$NC = 1$$

and now only one state variable is uncertain when $Y = 0$. Thus, the next-state code could be interpreted as 011 or 111 and both of these correspond to valid transitions from this block. We have therefore reduced the uncertainty by assigning adjacent codes to states which are reached from the two link paths separated by one asynchronous qualifier. This is a good general principle for these situations.

Another source of incorrect behaviour in ASM-based designs is concerned with immediate outputs. Whereas delay functions respond only to the stable period of the state time, an immediate function begins to respond as soon as any of its input variables change and so can be regarded as an asynchronous output. Thus, if races occur due to more than one synchronous variable changing during the unstable period of the state time, spurious pulses may occur on these immediate outputs. Also, these output errors can be caused by asynchronous inputs changing during any part of the state

Inputs		Present state				Next state			
*X	Y	Sym.	A	B	C	Sym.	NA	NB	NC
–	1	a	0	0	0	b	0	0	1
1	0	a	0	0	0	c	1	1	1
0	0	a	0	0	0	d	0	1	1

$$NA = *X.\overline{Y} \qquad NB = \overline{Y} \qquad NC = 1$$

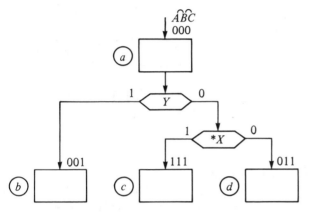

Fig. 3.26 Race-free reduced dependency assignment.

time. Output races can only be removed by careful state assignments tailored to the particular ASM structure.

The asynchronous nature of immediate outputs also makes them prone to hazards when they are implemented with discrete gates. Thus the synthesis of these functions should be checked and suitably modified, if necessary, using the technique described in Chapter 1.

3.6 IMPLEMENTATION BY MULTIPLEXERS AND ULMS

One type of MSI component which has been widely available for many years is the data selector or multiplexer (MUX). In addition to their obvious roles they can also be exploited as a form of universal logic module (ULM) for the implementation of combinational switching circuits such as those associated with ASM-based designs. This universal property can be an attractive feature in hardware prototyping or design development because modifications may be more readily accommodated than in equivalent discrete gate implementations. In addition to the exploitation of these devices in their discrete forms there is also the possibility of employing similar structures in semi-custom integrated form. For

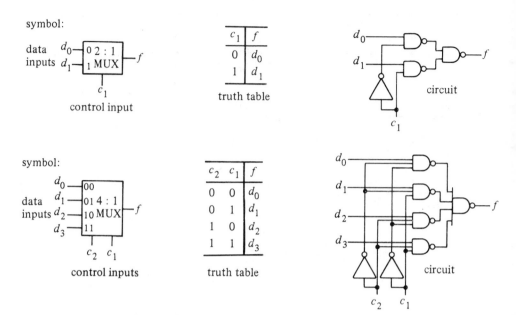

Fig. 3.27 The 2:1 and 4:1 multiplexers.

example, the multiplexer configuration is particularly amenable to implementation in nMOS pass transistor structures. These MUX devices consist of 2, 4, 8,..., 2^k data inputs, 1, 2, 3,..., k control inputs and one output. They are referred to as 2:1, 4:1, 8:1,..., 2^k:1 multiplexers. The combination of values placed on the k control inputs selects one of the 2^k inputs and switches it to the output. The symbol, truth table and possible internal circuitry for the 2:1 and 4:1 MUXs are given in Fig. 3.27.

It is readily appreciated that these devices can directly synthesize functions of one and two variables respectively, if the variables are connected to the control inputs and the truth table output values of the function are applied to the data inputs. Thus the 2:1 MUX can mechanize any function of one variable and the 4:1 MUX can support two variables. In this role these devices are referred to as universal logic modules (ULM), and it becomes of interest to investigate the means whereby general functions in many variables can be implemented by ULMs either of a single type or from a repertoire of basic modules.

An important point to appreciate is that these devices can support functions of larger numbers of variables than there are control inputs by applying the residue functions of these extra variables, rather than the raw truth table values, to the data inputs. If these residue functions involve at most one variable, not necessarily the same variable in all cases, then they will invoke no extra

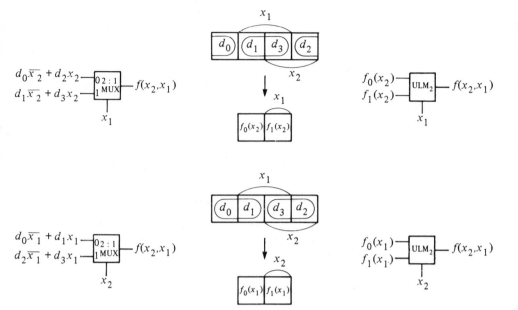

Fig. 3.28 Implementing functions of two variables on a 2:1 MUX.

cost to implement when we assume that inverses of variables are available. Thus, a 2:1 MUX can always synthesize any function of two variables and we can refer to this device as a ULM_2. The 4:1 MUX can always support functions of three variables and is therefore a ULM_3. The general $2^k:1$ MUX is therefore a ULM_{k+1}. The data inputs to these devices will be the residue functions of one of the system variables, the remaining variables being applied to the control inputs. These devices will also be capable of supporting some functions of more than one extra variable without additional cost providing the residue functions of these extra variables all resolve to zero cost terms. Alternatively, we could employ additional circuits to implement any non-trivial residues before input to the ULM.

For the moment let us consider only the simple case of one extra variable. The first task is to select a variable to act as a residue variable. This task and its implementation is directly analogous to selecting map-entered variables for Karnaugh map compression. For each choice of residue variable X_i we can isolate a set of pairs of map entries on the complete function map, each of which resolves to 0, 1, $\overline{X}_i$ or X_i. These residues can then be used as inputs to the ULM. Fig. 3.28 shows the possibilities for the ULM_2 device. The equivalent arrangements for the 4:1 MUX in the role of a ULM_3 are given in Fig. 3.29. There are now three possible choices for the

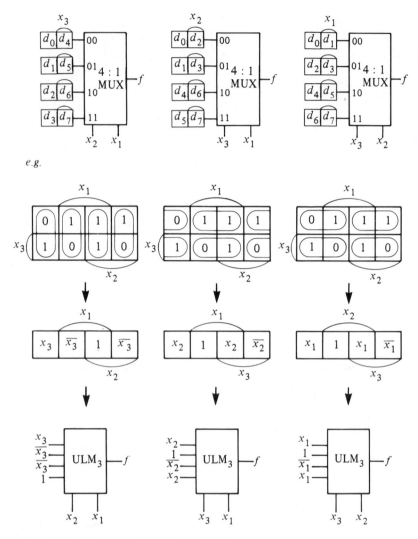

Fig. 3.29   Using a 4:1 MUX as a ULM_3.

residue variable each of which results in a different set of residues. Care must be taken to ensure that each residue function is applied to the appropriate data input. This is determined by the order in which the control variables are applied to the control inputs. Thus if the order is X_2X_1, as shown in the first case, the sequence of residue functions, reading from the top input down, is f_0, f_1, f_2, f_3. However, if we interchange the control variables to give X_1X_2, then this will permute the sequence of the residues to become f_0, f_2, f_1, f_3. Similar relationships can be determined for the other arrangements of Fig. 3.29.

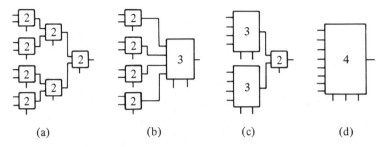

Fig. 3.30 Possible ULM$_4$ structures.

These concepts clearly apply to single multiplexers of any dimension. Thus the larger types of 8:1 MUX (ULM$_4$) and 16:1 MUX (ULM$_5$), etc., can be employed in a similar way to the smaller versions. Alternatively, we can consider the implementation of larger functions in terms of combinations of smaller ULMs. For example, we could devise a ULM$_4$ either from a single 8:1 MUX or from combinations of ULM$_3$ and ULM$_2$ elements. Fig. 3.30 shows the four symmetrical arrangements which can be achieved without redundancy of inputs. In each case there are three control inputs for three of the variables, and eight data inputs for the residue functions of a fourth variable. From a hardware point of view there is clearly a dramatic difference between these functionally equivalent structures, both in terms of the number of devices and the number of connections required to input and output terminals. Both of these factors provide some measure of the cost and complexity of an implementation. The general ULM$_k$, as we have seen, has $k-1$ control inputs, 2^{k-1} data inputs, and one output, giving a total of $2^{k-1}+k$ pins, each of which will represent a soldered or wrapped connection. Thus the ULM$_2$ has four pins, the ULM$_3$ has seven pins, and the ULM$_4$ has 12 pins. The first ULM$_4$ structure requires seven ULM$_2$ devices and therefore involves 28 connections, the second has four ULM$_2$ and one ULM$_3$ giving 23 connections, and the third needs 18 connections to the two ULM$_3$ and one ULM$_2$ elements. All of these structures have more connections than the single ULM$_4$ device.

In the case of the ULM$_5$ there are eight possible symmetrical arrangements as shown in Fig. 3.31, ranging from a network of 15 ULM$_2$ elements requiring 60 connections, to the single 16:1 MUX with 21 pins. In between are various arrangements of ULM$_2$, ULM$_3$ and ULM$_4$ elements each involving an intermediate number of connections.

The single device would seem to offer the most compact form of module. However, for a particular function some of the smaller devices in the other arrangements may be redundant and could be

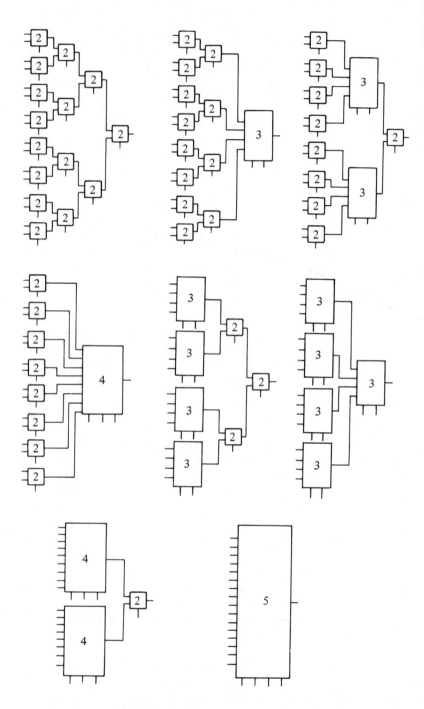

Fig. 3.31 Possible ULM$_5$ structures.

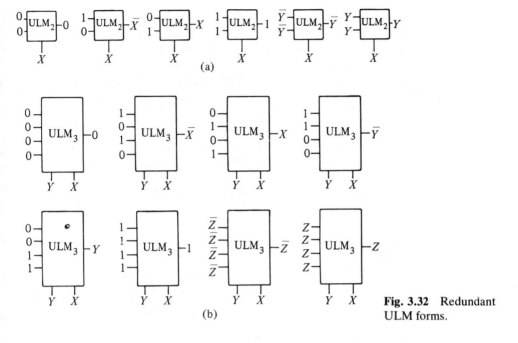

(a)

(b)

Fig. 3.32 Redundant ULM forms.

removed from the structure without altering the overall behaviour of the circuit. For example, consider the six ULM_2 circuits of Fig. 3.32a. Each of these is redundant because the outputs are 0, 1 or a single variable. Similar rules exist for the ULM_3 element as indicated in Fig. 3.32b where there are now eight redundant forms, and for larger ULMs. If any of these redundant forms appear in the process of implementing a particular function with a network of ULMs, the structure may be simplified. Consider the function of Fig. 3.33a. Here W has been selected as the map-entered variable to

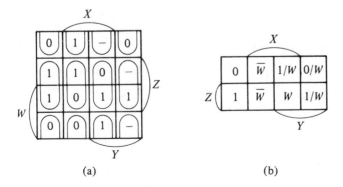

(a)   (b)

Fig. 3.33 Example four-variable function for ULM implementation.

give the compact map of Fig. 3.33b. The presence of don't care terms in the original map means that we have alternative forms of residue function in some cases. If we now implement this function of four variables using the various forms of ULM_4 structures and remove any redundant sub-modules, we arrive at the reduced forms given in Fig. 3.34. The first form reduces to just two ULM_2 elements, the second to one ULM_3, and the third to one ULM_3 and one ULM_2. The single ULM_4 element cannot of course be simplified and thus represents the most expensive form of this function in terms of pin connections required. Note that the sequence of residue functions changes each time, even though the order of connecting the control variables remains the same. We can use this

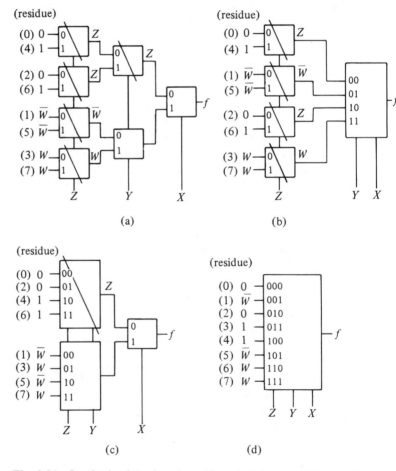

Fig. 3.34 Synthesis of the function of Fig. 3.33 on the ULM_4 structures of Fig. 3.30.

fact to advantage sometimes by changing the order of the control variables, thereby permuting the residue functions and possibly creating more redundant sub-modules than in the original ordering. We observe that the chances of locating redundant sub-modules are higher when the smaller elements are involved, especially on the input side of the network.

We now turn our interest towards the implementation of the functions derived from ASM-based designs with multiplexers in the ULM role. The most direct procedure would be to select a ULM of appropriate dimension to implement each function with one device. This can be achieved for an ASM with k state variables by employing a ULM_{k+1} for each function. If the k state variables are used as control variables each cell on the function map will correspond to one data input on the ULM. A direct translation from function map with map-entered terms to ULM inputs is possible if all the residues are functions of at most one qualifier. As we have seen, this only

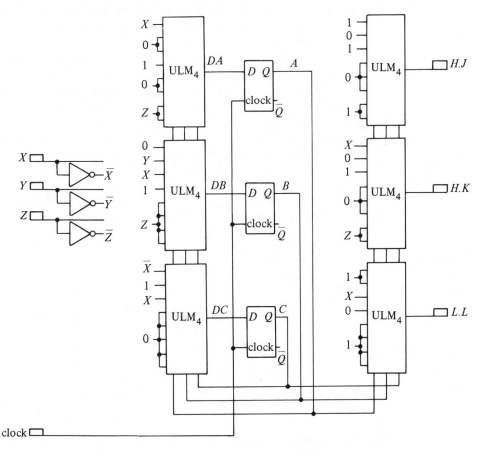

Fig. 3.35 Synthesis of the ASM of Fig. 3.5 in terms of ULM_4 elements.

arises if there is at most one qualifier in any ASM block of the system. This direct method of synthesis has the attraction that it retains a certain degree of universality. The same circuit configuration will support any ASM design with the same values of k, n and m, which involves at most one qualifier per block. A modification such as a new state assignment will require only a re-ordering of the new residue functions onto the ULM data inputs. For our previous example of Fig. 3.5, we could synthesize each function with a single ULM_4 element as depicted in Fig. 3.35. Here, each set of inputs to the multiplexers has been taken directly from the corresponding function maps of Figs. 3.15 and 3.20, thereby avoiding the need to simplify or even extract the functions from the latter. Alternatively we could attempt some simplifications by adopting one of the alternative ULM_4 structures and proceeding as outlined earlier.

When large numbers of don't care terms are present a more immediate form of simplification may be apparent. Consider the implementation of the ASM of Fig. 3.5 by means of JK-bistables. The functions for the J and K inputs of each bistable as listed in Fig. 3.15 all exhibit a large number of don't care terms. In fact it is possible to ignore one of the state variables in each function, thereby effectively reducing the maps to two-variable structures. These latter can then be implemented with ULM_3 elements. For example, the function JA has don't care terms in the whole domain of A and thus the function can be made independent of A by making the lower half of the map identical to the top half. Thus JA can be implemented with a ULM_3 using B and C as control inputs and the four map entries in the top half of the map as data inputs. This process can be repeated again on the function KA which, as a result, can be implemented using only a single ULM_2. Also, $KC = B$ and requires no ULM element. The complete excitation circuits are shown in Fig. 3.36. Of course, this new arrangement no longer retains the universal property mentioned earlier.

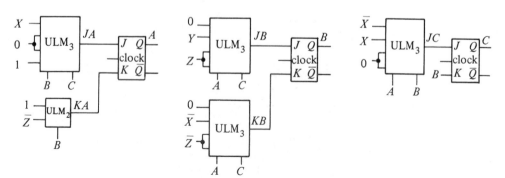

Fig. 3.36 Synthesis of JK-bistable excitation functions.

$$\bar{Y} \text{—}\boxed{\text{ULM}_2}\text{—} \begin{matrix} \overline{XY} \\ \overline{X+Y} \\ \text{(NOR)} \end{matrix} \quad \begin{matrix} 0 \\ \bar{Y} \end{matrix}\text{—}\boxed{\text{ULM}_2}\text{—} X.\bar{Y} \quad \begin{matrix} Y \\ 0 \end{matrix}\text{—}\boxed{\text{ULM}_2}\text{—} \bar{X}Y \quad \begin{matrix} 0 \\ Y \end{matrix}\text{—}\boxed{\text{ULM}_2}\text{—} \begin{matrix} X.Y \\ \text{(AND)} \end{matrix} \quad \begin{matrix} Y \\ \bar{Y} \end{matrix}\text{—}\boxed{\text{ULM}_2}\text{—} \begin{matrix} \overline{X}Y + X\overline{Y} \\ X \oplus Y \\ \text{(EOR)} \end{matrix}$$

$$X \qquad X \qquad X \qquad X \qquad X$$

$$\begin{matrix} Y \\ 1 \end{matrix}\text{—}\boxed{\text{ULM}_2}\text{—} \begin{matrix} X + Y \\ \text{(OR)} \end{matrix} \quad \begin{matrix} 1 \\ Y \end{matrix}\text{—}\boxed{\text{ULM}_2}\text{—} \bar{X} + Y \quad \begin{matrix} \bar{Y} \\ 1 \end{matrix}\text{—}\boxed{\text{ULM}_2}\text{—} X + \bar{Y} \quad \begin{matrix} 1 \\ \bar{Y} \end{matrix}\text{—}\boxed{\text{ULM}_2}\text{—} \begin{matrix} \bar{X} + \bar{Y} \\ \overline{X.Y} \\ \text{(NAND)} \end{matrix} \quad \begin{matrix} Y \\ \bar{Y} \end{matrix}\text{—}\boxed{\text{ULM}_2}\text{—} \begin{matrix} \overline{X}\overline{Y} + XY \\ X \equiv Y \\ \text{(ENOR)} \end{matrix}$$

$$X \qquad X \qquad X \qquad X \qquad X$$

Fig. 3.37 The ten non-trivial functions of two variables and their ULM$_2$ forms.

A problem arises when the residue functions involve more than one variable. As we have observed, this can occur when there is more than one qualifier in any of the blocks of the ASM chart. When such terms arise we cannot use them directly as inputs to ULMs and some additional circuits are required. If these residue functions involve only two qualifiers, as in the earlier example of Fig. 3.16, we can synthesize these extra terms with ULM$_2$ elements and thereby achieve a two-level structure. Fig. 3.37 shows the ten possible functions of exactly two variables and their implementation via ULM$_2$ elements. We can now select the appropriate form for the non-trivial residues that occur on our function maps of Fig. 3.17 and use these along with simple residues as inputs to the main ULM$_4$ devices representing the next-state functions. The final arrangement is shown in Fig. 3.38. Alternatively, we could arrange that each data input to the main ULM is fed from a ULM$_2$ element and this would retain the universal property. The inputs to these auxiliary ULMs could be derived directly from the ASM table. This technique can be extended to deal with larger residue functions by employing

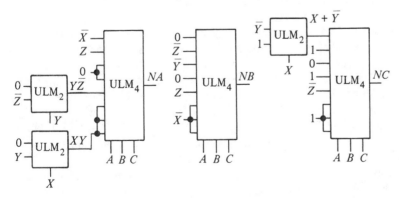

Fig. 3.38 Synthesis of next-state functions of Fig. 3.17 using ULM$_4$s and ULM$_2$s for the non-trivial residues.

larger sub-modules to preform the residue functions before input to the main multiplexer unit as indicated in Fig. 3.39.

The whole procedure can obviously be extended to handle much larger ASM structures. However, it may be inconvenient to use large dimension multiplexers for the direct implementation of functions and it may prove necessary to adopt some form of network structure involving combinations of smaller devices and employing the consequent possibilities for simplification along the lines indicated previously.

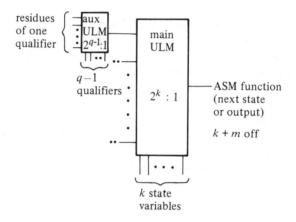

Fig. 3.39   General form of direct ULM synthesis of an ASM function. Complete system will require $k + m$ such modules.

3.7   BIBLIOGRAPHICAL NOTES

Clare (1972) contains extensive coverage of the synthesis of ASM designs. The use of map-entered variables is also included in many of the recent texts referred to previously. In addition, Blakeslee (1975) and Hurst (1978) are useful sources. The use of multiplexers as ULMs has received widespread attention. Notable here are the papers by Yau and Tang (1970a, b) and Edwards and Hurst (1976). Tabloski and Mowle (1976) and Almaini and Woodward (1977) discuss the problem of synthesizing general switching functions with optimum arrangements of ULMs. Bennett (1978) studies the application of map-entered variables in multiplexer synthesis and also relates this to ASM-based designs.

3.8 EXERCISES

3.1 Using the ASM defined in Fig. 2.32, derive the next-state excitation tables for the synthesis by means of:

a) JK-bistable memory elements,
b) SR-bistable memory elements with active low inputs.

3.2 Express the next-state excitation functions of Exercise 3.1 as maps with map-entered variables. Derive the minimum forms in each case.

3.3 Derive a simplified circuit tree for the function:

$$f(X_3, X_2, X_1) = \overline{X}_2 X_1 + \overline{X}_3 X_2 + X_3 \overline{X}_2$$

3.4 Synthesize the four-variable switching function

$$f(X_4, X_3, X_2, X_1) = X_3 \overline{X}_1 + \overline{X}_4 \overline{X}_3 X_2 + \overline{X}_4 X_3 \overline{X}_2 + X_4 \overline{X}_2 \overline{X}_1$$

using:

a) only ULM_2 elements,
b) only ULM_3 elements,
c) both ULM_2 and ULM_3 elements,
d) a ULM_4 element.

3.5 Synthesize the ASM of Exercise 3.1 using JK-bistables and multiplexer elements.

Chapter 4
Synthesis by Programmable Devices

4.1 INTRODUCTION

Recent developments in integrated circuit technology have made possible the production of highly flexible switching circuit components. It has long been recognized that most realistic switching problems involve relatively few terms covering large numbers of variables; that is, sparse functions in many variables. As we have observed, the traditional theoretically based design procedures are best suited to problems involving larger numbers of terms in only a few variables.

Of the newer components, programmable array logic (PAL), programmable-gate arrays (PGAs), the more complex programmable logic arrays (PLAs) and programmable logic sequencers (PLSs), which are now widely available, enable simple functions in many variables to be customized from a standard package. This family of devices is 'programmed' by blowing fusible links at appropriate points in the array of gates within the package. In the case of volume production this programming can be performed by the manufacturer on instruction from the customer but there are versions which are field programmable and the customer can perform this programming of individual devices with the aid of a special piece of equipment. These field-programmable versions are referred to as FPGAs, FPLAs and FPLSs, and they are especially useful for prototype development. They are also highly suited to the synthesis of ASM-based designs.

Another familiar device which has been available for many years and whose rapid development has accompanied that of the microprocessor is the read-only memory (ROM) and its related form the programmable read-only memory (PROM). These devices are also highly flexible and provide an opportunity for the synthesis of combinational switching circuits in the most direct possible way; that is, by storing the truth table of the required function. In this context the input variables are used to define an address in the memory array and the contents of this address is arranged to be the appropriate output values of the required functions. Thus, the ROM has to be programmed in a similar way to the PLAs. However, in practice, unless functions are known to be correct or a large production run is required, it is more useful to employ a reprogrammable version; that is, an 'erasable' PROM, or EPROM. These devices can be erased electrically or by ultraviolet radiation and reprogrammed. This enables errors to be corrected, modifications to be incorporated, or the device to be re-used for completely new functions. From this point on we shall use, for simplicity, the mnemonic 'PLA' to mean either PLA or FPLA unless otherwise stated. Similarly, 'ROM' will stand for ROM, PROM or EPROM, to be interpreted in the context of its use.

Another type of semi-custom component which can be considered to fall into this 'programmable' category is the uncommitted gate array. This is usually a large array of basic components which can be configured into simple logic cells such as two-input NOR elements. These cells can be interconnected to form larger logic elements, including memory elements, which in turn may be joined to form complete systems. The interconnections are performed during the final phase of integration by depositing a metal layer on the predefined matrix which provides the tracks between components within the cells to form gates, between gates to form the switching circuit, and between the circuits and the input and output pins of the device. This process is performed by the manufacturer using a mask prepared from information supplied by the designer. As this is obviously a one-time process, there is a vital need for error-free designs and very accurate circuit masks. This is usually provided by a computer-aided environment where designs can be built up using libraries of macros for common modules, and simulated and verified before 'committing' the array to the particular functions.

Ultimately, we can also include here devices which might be regarded as providing a 'software' implementation of a digital system. Thus, through the implementation of an algorithm by programming a microprocessor with its associated memories and interfaces we can obtain an entirely different kind of synthesis. The borderline between hardware and software, once fairly well defined, is now becoming increasingly blurred. The ASM technique is capable of exploitation right across this region and into the software realm itself.

4.2 PROGRAMMABLE LOGIC ARRAYS

The gate arrays, logic arrays and logic sequencers represent a progression of increasing complexity of structure of these programmable devices. The gate arrays consist of the functional equivalent of one level of switching elements, such as multi-input NAND devices. The logic arrays consist of two levels, an AND array connected to an OR array, which enables switching functions

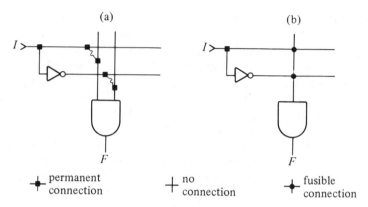

Fig. 4.1 Arrangement of fusible links in programmable arrays.

in sum-of-products form to be implemented. The logic sequencers have two levels of logic, together with a number of memory elements, some of which have outputs which are fed back to the AND array. These components allow certain types of sequential circuit to be synthesized on a single integrated circuit.

In all these devices the programming involves the blowing of fusible links to break connections at certain strategic points in the array. The basic arrangement is shown in Fig. 4.1a. An input and its internally generated inverse are each connected to the inputs of the gate by a pair of fusible links. Initially, in the unprogrammed state, all links are intact. We usually depict the arrangement in the more

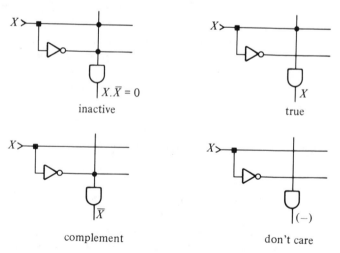

Fig. 4.2 The four possible situations after programming a single node.

compact form of Fig. 4.1b. The act of programming, which involves applying a special programming voltage to the input pins by means of a special piece of equipment, can selectively blow none, one or other, or both of these fuses thereby resulting in the four possible outcomes of Fig. 4.2. If both fuses are left intact then we have effectively X and $\bar{X}$ connected to the two inputs of the gate. Since $X.\bar{X} = 0$, the output of the gate will be zero irrespective of the conditions of fuses on any other input pairs. If one or other of the fuses is blown then either X or $\bar{X}$ remains connected to the gate and this will form part of the product along with the contributions from other inputs. Finally, if both fuses on a particular input are blown this isolates the particular input X from the gate and its output will be independent of the value of X. This represents treating X as a don't care input.

A typical FPGA is depicted in Fig. 4.3. Here the basic elements are NAND gates but the programming rules are the same in principle as above. In this particular device there are nine NAND gates

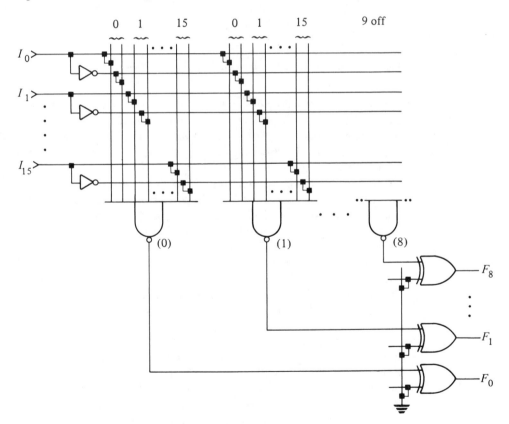

Fig. 4.3 Layout of a typical FPGA.

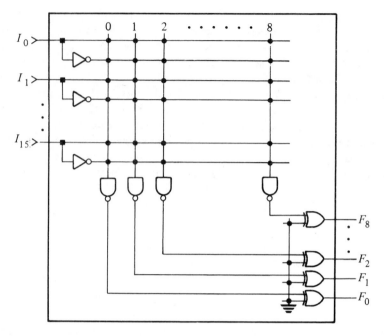

Fig. 4.4 More compact representation of the FPGA of Fig. 4.3.

whose inputs are fusibly linked to any of 16 inputs and their inverses. These NAND gates have the equivalent of 32 inputs, but in order to use a gate we must blow at least one fuse for each input pair and so they are effectively 16-way gates. In addition, the output of each gate is connected to an exclusive-OR gate. The other input of the EOR is fusibly linked to logic value 0. If this fuse is blown the input will rise to logic level 1 via a pull-up resistor. Since $f \oplus 1 = \overline{f}$ this enables the inverse of the gate output to be delivered to the device output. Equivalently, this also permits the definition of active high or active low outputs. The complete device has $9 \times 32 + 9 = 297$ fuses and Fig. 4.4 shows a more compact symbolic representation of the structure. All inputs to a gate are shown on a single line. A dot on the intersection with an input or its inverse indicates that the corresponding fuse is still intact and connection remains. The absence of a dot means the link is broken and no contact exists at this point. Fig. 4.5 illustrates how simple functions can be implemented on these gate arrays. Here we consider a simple model with only three inputs, but this could in fact be a fragment of a much larger array. On the first gate all fuses to the input inverses have been blown and so its output will correspond to $\overline{A}.\overline{B}.\overline{C}$. However, the fuse on the EOR gate associated with the first NAND element has also been blown so the output F_0 will be

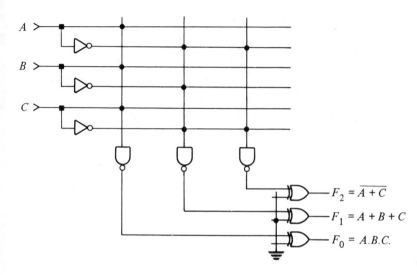

Fig. 4.5 Example of a programmed FPGA.

$$F_0 = \overline{A.B.C} \oplus 1 = A.B.C$$

and we have a straightforward AND function. The second NAND element has been programmed to give $\overline{\overline{A}.\overline{B}.\overline{C}}$ and the EOR allows this to pass unmodified. Since

$$F_1 = \overline{\overline{A}.\overline{B}.\overline{C}} = A + B + C$$

we have implemented an OR function. On the third NAND gate both connections concerned with the B input have been removed so the output is $\overline{\overline{A}.\overline{C}}$. The EOR gate inverts this to give

$$F_2 = \overline{\overline{A}.\overline{C}} \oplus 1 = \overline{A}.\overline{C} = \overline{A + C}$$

and we obtain a NOR function. Thus by judicious application of de Morgan's theorem and suitable inversion of inputs and/or outputs we can generate a wide variety of one-level functions with these devices. However, they are fairly limited in application. We could cascade these devices by using the outputs of one set of PGAs as inputs to other devices. This would enable more complex two-level functions to be realized. However, the PLAs provide this degree of complexity on a single device.

Logic arrays consist of two arrays of logic elements. Fig. 4.6 shows the layout for a typical FPLA which has 48 AND gates each fusibly linked to 16 inputs and their inverses. The second level consists of an array of eight 48-way OR gates which are fusibly linked to the 48 AND gates of the first array. The arrangement of this OR array is depicted in Fig. 4.7. This also incorporates EOR gates on each output in a similar role to that on the gate arrays. The

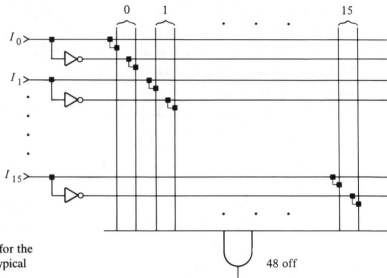

Fig. 4.6 Layout for the AND array of a typical FPLA.

48 off

complete layout is given in Fig. 4.8 in its more compact symbolic form. We observe that there are

$$(32 \times 48) + (8 \times 48) + 8 = 1928$$

fuses in this device and so it is a much larger system than the gate

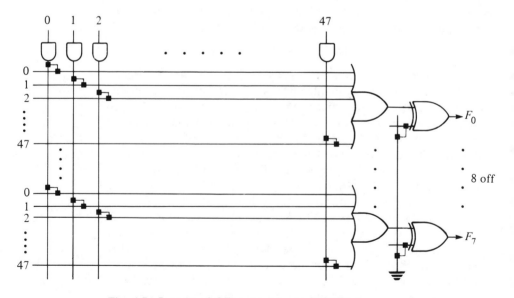

Fig. 4.7 Layout of OR array of a typical FPLA.

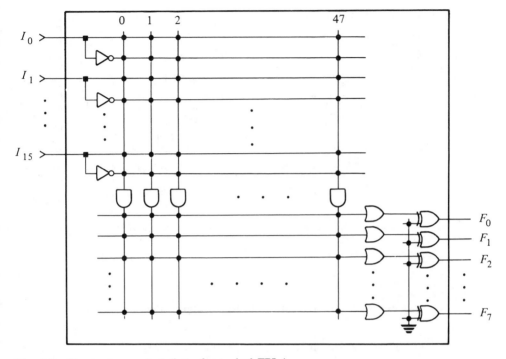

Fig. 4.8 Compact representation of a typical FPLA.

array. The OR array enables the product terms generated by the AND array to be shared between the eight outputs. Alternatively, we can arrange to accommodate completely separate functions of different variables by a simple partition of the arrays. However, this represents an inefficient application of these components. Fig. 4.9

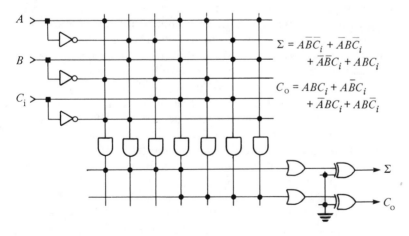

$$\Sigma = A\bar{B}\bar{C_i} + \bar{A}B\bar{C_i}$$
$$+ \bar{A}\bar{B}C_i + ABC_i$$

$$C_o = ABC_i + A\bar{B}C_i$$
$$+ \bar{A}BC_i + AB\bar{C_i}$$

Fig. 4.9 Example of a programmed FPLA.

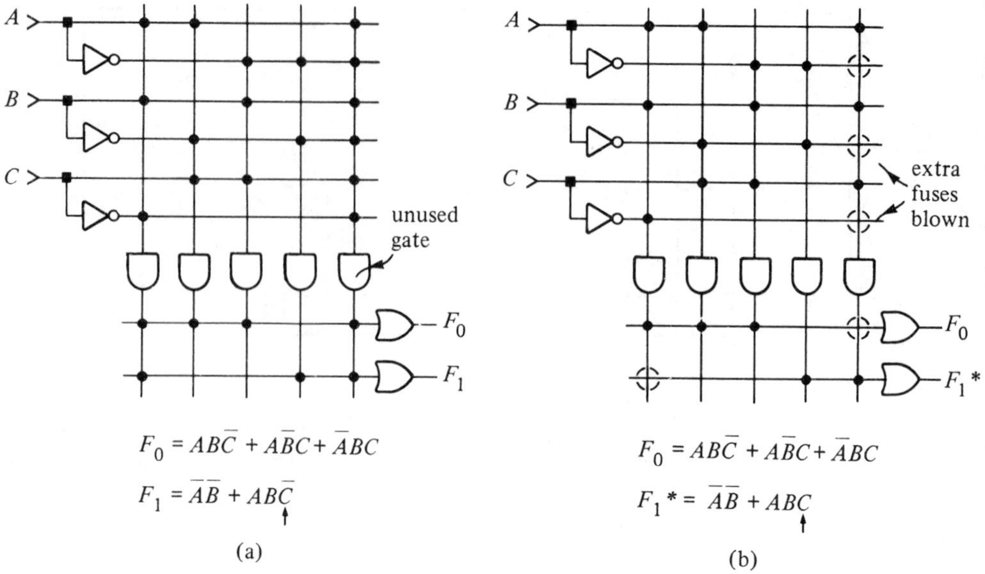
A
B
C
unused gate
F_0
F_1
$F_0 = AB\overline{C} + A\overline{B}C + \overline{A}BC$
$F_1 = \overline{A}\overline{B} + AB\overline{C}$
(a)
A
B
C
extra fuses blown
F_0
F_1*
$F_0 = AB\overline{C} + A\overline{B}C + \overline{A}BC$
$F_1* = \overline{A}\overline{B} + ABC$
(b)

Fig. 4.10 Use of spare gates to perform limited modifications.

shows a simple example for the implementation of a full-adder which requires two functions of the same three variables to compute the sum Σ, and carry-out C_o, from two inputs A, B and a carry-in digit C_i. These two equations each involve four product terms but one of these, ABC_i, occurs in both expansions and needs to be generated only once on the AND array. It can then be used by both outputs.

The obvious drawback of these devices is that once programming has been performed and a fuse has been blown it cannot be reconnected so errors and modifications cannot be tolerated. However, it is possible on certain occasions to accommodate a limited amount of editing. The golden rule is to leave all fuses intact unless they are definitely required to be blown. Certainly, it is wise to leave any unused product terms intact for possible future exploitation. Consider the simple example of Fig. 4.10a where we have two functions of three variables programmed on a portion of a PLA and there is one unused gate. Note that this gate does not affect the output of either function even though it is still connected to the OR array and its inputs remain connected to the device inputs. This is due to the fact that its output is 0 because we have $A.\overline{A}.B.\overline{B}.C.\overline{C} = 0$, irrespective of the values applied to A, B or C. Suppose, for some reason, we require to modify the second function to become that indicated in Fig. 4.10b. That is, we wish to substitute the term ABC for $AB\overline{C}$ in this function. We can do this by blowing the extra fuses

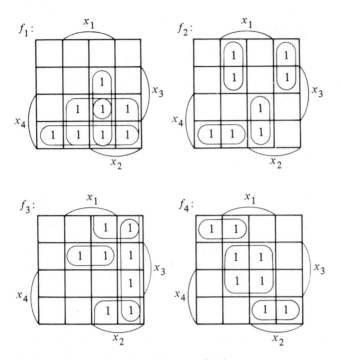

Fig. 4.11   Example functions for FPLA synthesis.

as indicated. This will remove the original term from F_1 and will replace it with the new version programmed onto the spare gate.

Thus, the PLA structure is ideally suited to implementation of sum-of-products forms of switching functions. However, we now have the situation that the cost of all product terms is the same since each will occupy one column of the AND array irrespective of the number of inputs involved in the product. Thus the amount of PLA area occupied by a set of functions will depend on the number of different product terms involved in the whole set. Consider the four functions of four variables depicted in Fig. 4.11. Inspection of these functions reveals that 14 different minterms are involved in the various functions so one direct way to perform PLA synthesis would be to program these 14 minterms on the AND array and to select the appropriate ones for each function with the OR array. This gives the situation of Fig. 4.12a. On the other hand we could attempt to derive the minimum two-level forms of each function and to implement these on the PLA as indicated in Fig. 4.12b. We discover that there are also 14 different prime implicants shared between the functions. Thus our efforts have been wasted. Although these terms are significantly 'simpler' than the original minterms and would represent a considerable saving in conventional synthesis techniques

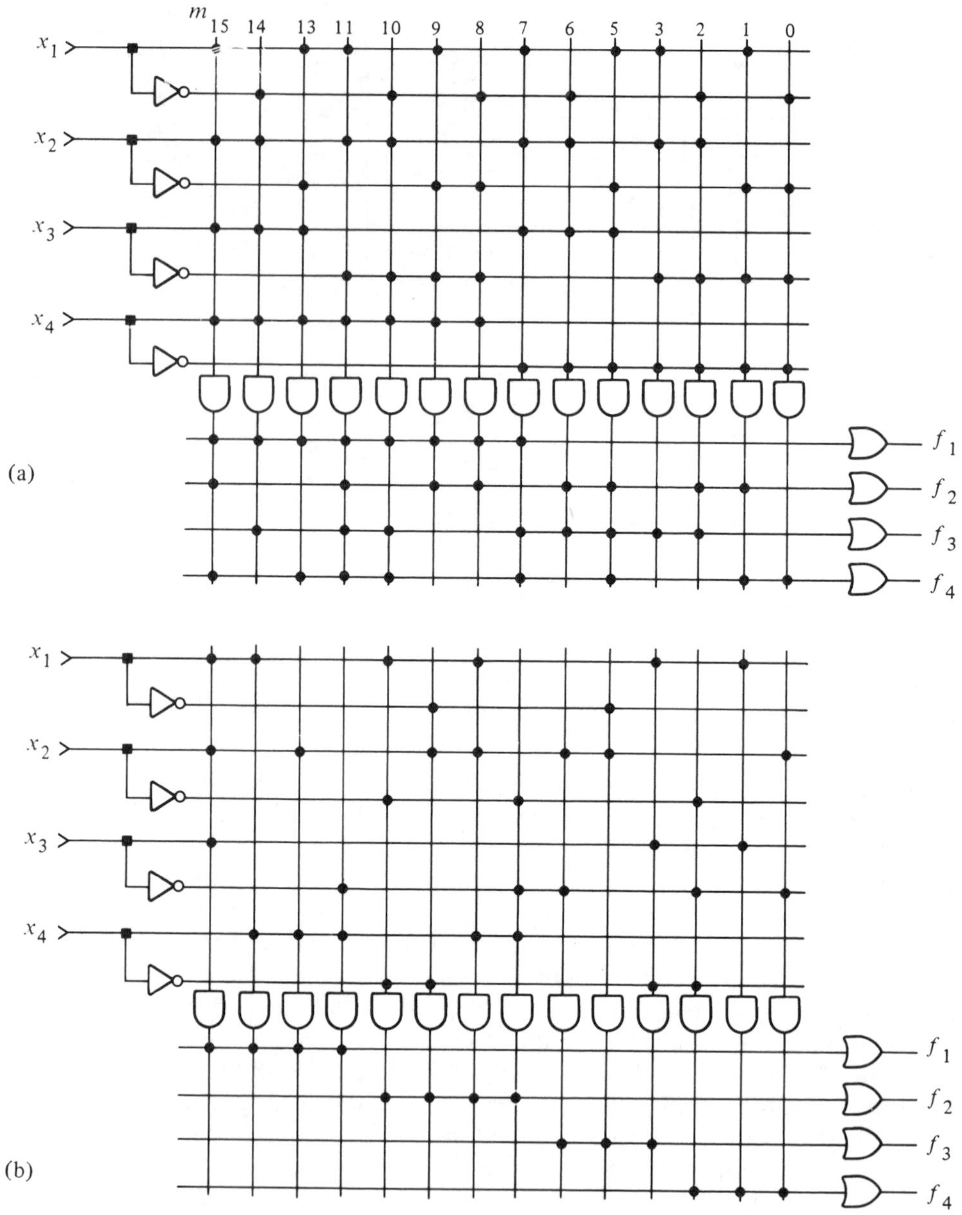

Fig. 4.12 Programming of (a) minterms, and (b) prime implicants.

we do not gain any PLA space over that of the direct method. Of course this is not always the case but this does illustrate that the traditional approach may not always be appropriate for these newer components. If we are interested in optimizing the compactness of a

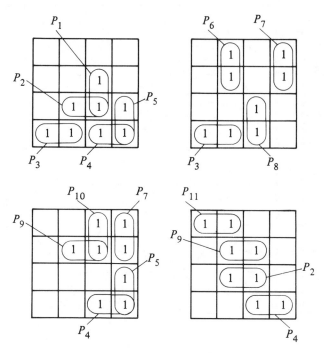

Fig. 4.13 Covering the four functions with 11 product terms.

PLA synthesis we require to search through the complete implicant structures of all the functions involved. Between the two extremes of selecting the minterms of the functions or their prime implicants the optimum form may involve implicants which are not prime. For instance, the four functions of Fig. 4.11 can be covered by just 11 product terms as indicated by the loopings on Fig. 4.13 and of these P_2 and P_5 are not prime implicants of any of the functions.

The essential features of a programmable logic sequencer are given in Fig. 4.14. In addition to extended AND and OR arrays, a number of on-board memory elements are included. These are clocked SR-bistables with active high inputs, and the outputs of some of these are fed back to act as auxiliary inputs on the AND array. Their inputs S and R are derived from extra outputs on the OR array. The remaining bistables act as latches for the system outputs. The inputs to these are also derived from the OR array. Facilities are also provided for presetting the conditions of the bistables. This structure enables certain types of sequential circuit to be modelled on a single device. The bistables with feedback can represent the internal state variables and their inputs can be programmed to be sums-of-products functions of their outputs and the system inputs. The system outputs, as held in the other bistables,

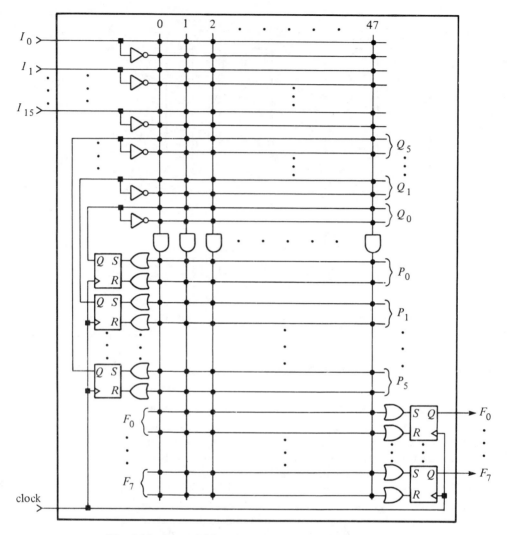

Fig. 4.14   Essential features of a programmable logic sequencer.

can also be programmed to be functions of the state variables and
system inputs. The device as shown will support machines with up to
16 inputs, up to 64 internal states, and up to eight outputs, providing
the required functions involve no more than 48 product terms of the
inputs and state variables. The number of internal states can be
extended by using one or more of the bistables associated with
device outputs as extra state variables and providing the feedback
loops externally through the normal device inputs.

These programmable devices are very flexible in that they are
capable of holding several independent systems simultaneously as

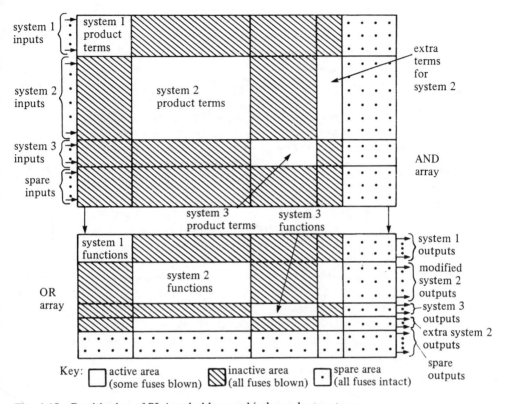

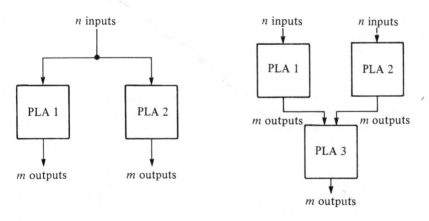

Fig. 4.15 Partitioning of PLA to hold several independent systems.

(a) $2 \times m$ functions of n variables

(b) m functions of $2 \times n$ variables

Fig. 4.16 Combinations of PLAs to expand outputs or inputs.

depicted in Fig. 4.15. Alternatively, they can also be employed in combinations to expand the numbers of outputs or inputs as illustrated by the arrangements of Fig. 4.16. This enables us to build up very large systems.

They are also ideally suited to the implementation of ASM-based designs although the number of outputs available can prove to be a limitation. With a PLA, some inputs are designated as state variables and some outputs as next-state variables. We then require some external memory elements. As before, the simplest to use are the D-types since only one excitation function is required for each bistable. The ASM defined in Chapter 3 by Fig. 3.5 is shown as a PLA and D-type implementation in Fig. 4.17. Here no attempt has been made to optimize the PLA area occupied and this represents a straightforward translation of the reduced expressions derived earlier from the function maps with map-entered variables. If this structure were mapped on to the $(16 \times 48 \times 8)$ PLA described above it would occupy six inputs, 17 product terms and six outputs and the remaining area would be effectively a $(10 \times 31 \times 2)$ PLA. It is unlikely that this would be usable for another system since only two outputs remain. Thus much of the PLA area is unused and so there is no real incentive to reduce the AND array occupancy. If a JK- or SR-based synthesis were required, we would need to use up all the available outputs because we would require two excitation functions for each bistable element. In this situation the unused areas of the AND array are wasted. Thus, D-type bistables are best suited to PLA synthesis because they reduce the number of outputs required from the PLA. The complexity of the single excitation functions is easily handled on the PLA.

This limitation is eased slightly with the FPLS structure because the state variables and their feedback to the AND array are contained internally and do not have to take up valuable outputs and inputs. At the time of writing, the available FPLSs have the outputs of the OR array latched into SR-bistables and, furthermore, these have a common clock line with the state-variable bistables. This arrangement denies us the possibility of obtaining immediate outputs because the output latches have to be clocked to obtain the output values on the device outputs. This same clock command will initiate another change of state and so the outputs will only be available during the next state time. In order to implement ASM designs with FPLSs we have to take this into account and, if possible, modify the ASM chart accordingly. Fig. 4.18 depicts a direct implementation of the ASM of Fig. 3.5 interpreted for SR-bistables with active high inputs on an FPLS. In order to ensure correct latching of the outputs in their respective SR-bistables we require to establish the S and R functions, in each case avoiding the condition

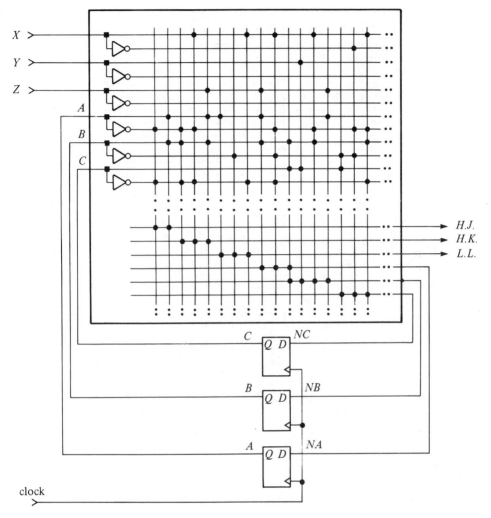

Fig. 4.17 FPLA synthesis of the ASM of Fig. 3.5 employing simplified expressions.

$S = R = 1$. The most straightforward way of achieving this is to make S equal to the output function and then $R = \overline{S}$. Clearly, these outputs are delivered during the next state time to that of the equivalent FPLA synthesis. This situation would be avoided if outputs were not latched or if the output bistables and state-variable bistables made independent clock lines. Then a biphase clock could be employed; one phase to cause state transitions, the second to latch the outputs.

A modified view of these PLA and PLS structures provides us with a more direct means of implementing ASM designs. The AND array and its associated inputs can be regarded as an addressing

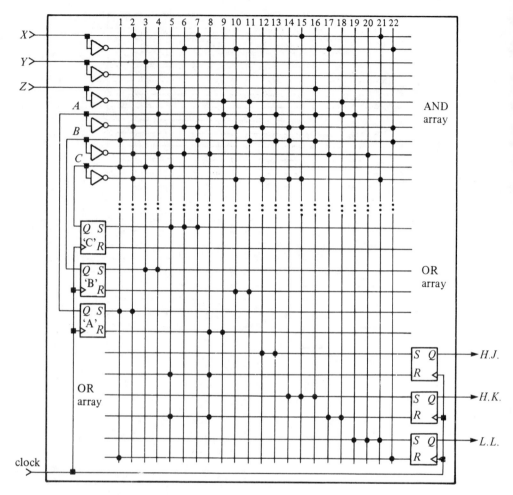

Fig. 4.18   FPLS synthesis of the ASM of Fig. 3.5 using simplified expressions.

mechanism which can select one or more columns on the OR array. We could arrange to give a complete decode of all the inputs as would be the case if the AND array were programmed to hold all the possible minterms. Then any combination of input values, acting as an address, would activate only one AND gate and therefore one column of the OR array. Those outputs connected to this column would then become active. Thus the conditions programmed on each column of the OR array can represent the 'contents' of the 'address' selected by the inputs on the AND array. To implement an ASM chart or table we require a pattern of output values, including next-state values, to be delivered for certain combinations of input values, including present-state values. As not all combinations

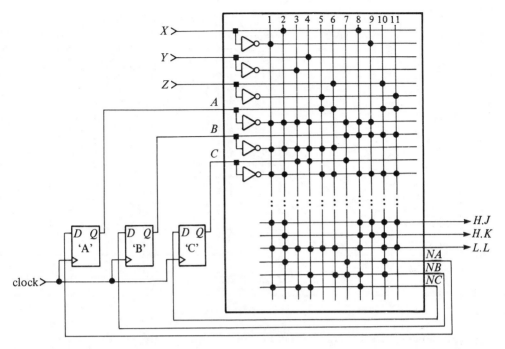

Fig. 4.19 FPLA synthesis of the ASM of Fig. 3.5 using direct mapping of link paths.

are represented we require only a partial decode of the input and state variables. We can exploit the programmable nature of the 'addressing' AND array to decode only those combinations corresponding to the link paths on the ASM chart or table. We therefore program each link path as one column on the PLA. The inputs and present-state variables appear on the AND array and act as an address to select the required pattern of next-state and output values which appear on the same column in the OR array. This technique will employ as many columns on the PLA as there are link paths on the ASM table. This is an attractive proposition since it avoids the use of intermediate maps and function simplification. Also, it is unlikely that, for small systems, the derivation and simplification of the functions yield fewer product terms than there are link paths and so PLA occupancy will usually be less in this direct mapping method. In any case, as we have observed, the number of outputs required is usually the limiting factor and this number remains the same in both methods.

Fig. 4.19 shows the PLA resulting from a direct mapping of the link paths of the ASM of Fig. 3.5 and we observe this uses only 11 product terms rather than the 17 required by the previous method. This technique remains valid for the more complex ASM structure with several qualifiers in each block, which caused problems in

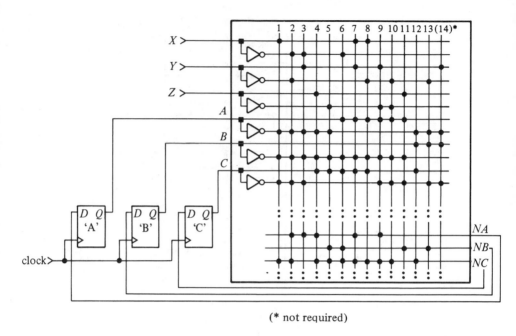

(* not required)

Fig. 4.20   FPLA synthesis of the ASM of Fig. 3.16 using direct mapping of link paths.

discrete gate and multiplexer synthesis. Fig. 4.20 shows the direct link path mapping of the ASM for Fig. 3.16 onto a PLA and here again we require only one column for each link path. A similar compression occurs in the case of PLS synthesis. In addition, if a link path corresponds to a loop back to the same state and there are no outputs associated with this then it may be omitted from the AND array as the truth table for the SR-bistable will ensure the correct behaviour in this case. Whereas our earlier attempt to synthesize the ASM of Fig. 3.5 required 22 product terms on the PLS, Fig. 4.21 reveals that only 11 columns are required on the AND array.

Once the PLA or PLS configuration has been derived for a given system, it is necessary to draw up some kind of programming chart for use by either the manufacturer or, in the case of field-programmable versions, by the designer in conjunction with some form of programming equipment. The pattern of fuses to be blown on the various arrays and the designation active-high or active-low outputs is put into a suitable format for input to the programming device. These patterns can be expressed simply as hexadecimal codes or possibly as actual Boolean expressions which the system converts automatically to fuse patterns. Most systems have 'personality' cards or modules to enable a whole range of

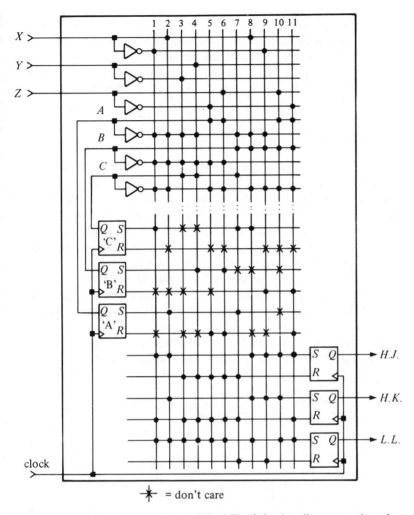

Fig. 4.21 FPLS synthesis of the ASM of Fig. 3.5 using direct mapping of link paths.

devices to be handled on one piece of equipment. Usually, some form of display is incorporated to observe the current state of the device and to enable corrections or modifications to be made before finally programming the device.

Programmable array logic provides another type of programmable fuse logic which in a sense represents an optimization of the PLA structure, especially for the implementation of general switching circuits. These devices also contain a programmable AND array but the OR array is fixed and combines terms from the AND array in a predetermined way. A wide variety of device types are available which provide a range of OR combinations. A function inverse technique is also available in the devices so de Morgan's theorem can be exploited to improve the packing density of functions. Thus, PAL devices represent an attractive alternative to random logic for circuit prototyping but their structure is not as amenable as that of the PLA for the direct synthesis of ASM-based designs.

4.3   ROM-BASED DESIGNS

We have observed that the PLA can be regarded as a storage or memory system with only a partially decoded addressing mechanism. Only a small fraction of the possible combinations of input values can correspond to actual memory locations. In the read-only memory we have a similar arrangement but the address part is fully decoded and there is a memory location for each possible input combination. Furthermore, the addressing part is not programmable and only the contents of the address can be selected by the programmer. This information has to be placed in the memory either during the manufacture or subsequently by a special process distinct from the normal operation. In this normal mode it is not possible to change the contents of the address locations and so the device is 'read-only'. Potentially more attractive for switching circuit synthesis are the field-programmable versions, in a form which is also

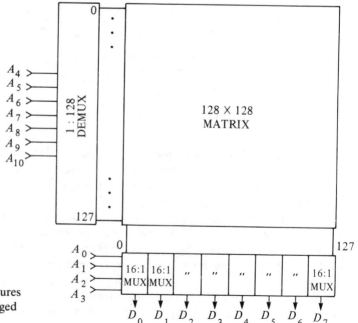

Fig. 4.22   Essential features of a 16K-bit ROM arranged to deliver 2K bytes.

erasable so that they can be reprogrammed to accommodate modifications or completely new designs.

The ROM (PROM or EPROM) provides an opportunity for the most direct form of switching circuit synthesis; that is, by storing the truth table of the required function. In this arrangement the input variables are employed to define an address in the memory and the contents of the address forms the appropriate output values.

In the ROM, the programmable AND array of the PLA is replaced by a fixed addressing mechanism such as a $1:2^n$ demultiplexer. This device supplied with n address bits will select one of 2^n output lines. These lines are then ORed together to form the outputs. It is this OR array which forms the programmable memory part of the system. Usually, the outputs of this OR array are subjected to further selection by multiplexers whose control inputs form another component of the overall address in order to optimize the dimensions of the memory array. Fig. 4.22 shows the component parts of a typical large ROM which incorporates this two-dimensional addressing scheme. Seven address bits A_4 to A_{10} select one row of the 128×128 OR array. These 128 lines form the data inputs to eight 16:1 MUXs which are controlled by four more address bits A_0 to A_3. Thus each combination of 11 address bits gives an 8-bit output and the 16K bits are therefore configured into 2K bytes. This arrangement is clearly highly suitable for use in conjunction with microprocessor systems, but it may not be the best form for switching circuit synthesis. Consider the switching function defined on the six-variable map of Fig. 4.23. The 64 values of this

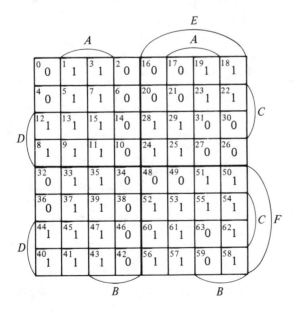

Fig. 4.23 Example function(s) for ROM synthesis.

function could be stored in a 64-bit ROM addressed by the six variables as indicated in Fig. 4.24. As the variables go through all possible combinations of values, the output Z will take on the values of the map or truth table. This may be a convenient realization of this completely specified function or any other combination of functions which completely fills the array. For example, we could interpret the map of Fig. 4.23 as two functions of five variables, or four functions of four variables, etc., or as combinations such as one function of five variables, one of four and two of three. All these cases can be accommodated on the ROM by using the inputs either as function variables or to select a particular function. Thus if the map were interpreted as containing the four functions indicated in Fig. 4.25 then $f_1(E, D, C, B, A)$ can be obtained by setting $F = 0$ and using the other variables to drive the function. The function $f_2(C, B, A)$ is obtained when $F = 1$, $E = 0$ and $D = 0$, whereas $f_3(C, B, A)$ results when $F = 1$, $E = 0$ and $D = 1$. Finally, making $F = E = 1$ will select function $f_4(D, C, B, A)$. Note that, in this arrangement, the four functions are not available simultaneously.

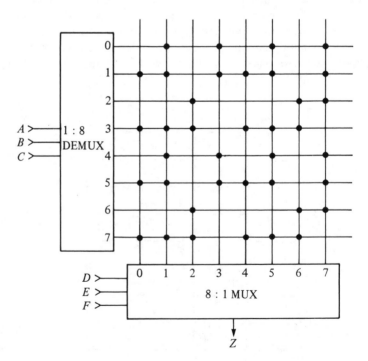

Fig. 4.24   Synthesis of function(s) of Fig. 4.23 on a small ROM.

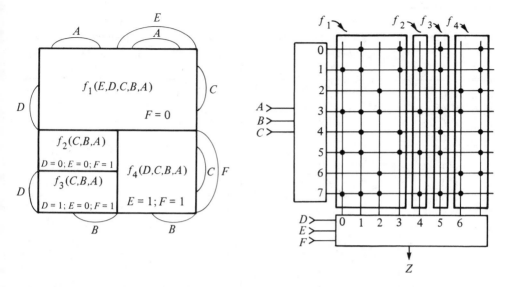

Fig. 4.25   Packing several functions into a single ROM.

Thus the ROM is ideally suited to functions which are fully specified and involve relatively few variables, such as simple code conversions where one binary pattern acting as the address is converted into another pattern found at the address location. As we have seen, most realistic switching functions, and especially those arising from ASM designs, are not of this type and so the ROM-based approach may not be an attractive alternative form of synthesis in these cases.

The problem lies in the fact that not every combination of input and present-state variables is meaningful and certainly they are not all shown explicitly on the ASM table. In order to perform a direct mapping into ROM of the various functions associated with an ASM design we need to expand the ASM table to cover all possible combinations of input values. The ASM defined in Fig. 3.5 has three inputs and three state variables and so there are 64 possible combinations of values. Fig. 4.26 lists this fully decoded table along with the corresponding ASM location, expressed as the ASM block and link path, and the appropriate next-state and output values represented for convenience as a hexadecimal number. In this latter portion we have assumed that each ROM location, addressed by the concatenation $XYZABC$, will be an 8-bit word formatted as $NA\,NB\,NC\,HI\,HJ\,LL$, with the last two least significant bits not used. We can store this information in a 64-byte ROM as indicated in Fig. 4.27. It can be seen that there is a great deal of duplication in the stored array and some locations, corresponding to unassigned

Address X Y Z A B C	ASM location Block	Link path	Contents (hex)		Address X Y Z A B C	ASM location Block	Link path	Contents (hex)	
0 0 0 0 0 0	1	1	3	4	1 0 0 0 0 0	1	2	9	C
0 0 0 0 0 1	2	3	2	4	1 0 0 0 0 1	2	3	2	4
0 0 0 0 1 0	5	9	1	8	1 0 0 0 1 0	5	8	7	C
0 0 0 0 1 1	4	7	C	0	1 0 0 0 1 1	4	7	C	0
0 0 0 1 0 0	3	5	0	4	1 0 0 1 0 0	3	5	0	4
0 0 0 1 0 1	—	—	—	—	1 0 0 1 0 1	—	—	—	—
0 0 0 1 1 0	6	11	1	4	1 0 0 1 1 0	6	11	1	4
0 0 0 1 1 1	—	—	—	—	1 0 0 1 1 1	—	—	—	—
0 0 1 0 0 0	1	1	3	4	1 0 1 0 0 0	1	2	9	C
0 0 1 0 0 1	2	3	2	4	1 0 1 0 0 1	2	3	2	4
0 0 1 0 1 0	5	9	1	8	1 0 1 0 1 0	5	8	7	C
0 0 1 0 1 1	4	7	C	0	1 0 1 0 1 1	4	7	C	0
0 0 1 1 0 0	3	6	4	4	1 0 1 1 0 0	3	6	4	4
0 0 1 1 0 1	—	—	—	—	1 0 1 1 0 1	—	—	—	—
0 0 1 1 1 0	6	10	D	C	1 0 1 1 1 0	6	10	D	C
0 0 1 1 1 1	—	—	—	—	1 0 1 1 1 1	—	—	—	—
0 1 0 0 0 0	1	1	3	4	1 1 0 0 0 0	1	2	9	C
0 1 0 0 0 1	2	4	6	4	1 1 0 0 0 1	2	4	6	4
0 1 0 0 1 0	5	9	1	8	1 1 0 0 1 0	5	8	7	C
0 1 0 0 1 1	4	7	C	0	1 1 0 0 1 1	4	7	C	0
0 1 0 1 0 0	3	5	0	4	1 1 0 1 0 0	3	5	0	4
0 1 0 1 0 1	—	—	—	—	1 1 0 1 0 1	—	—	—	—
0 1 0 1 1 0	6	11	1	4	1 1 0 1 1 0	6	11	1	4
0 1 0 1 1 1	—	—	—	—	1 1 0 1 1 1	—	—	—	—
0 1 1 0 0 0	1	1	3	4	1 1 1 0 0 0	1	2	9	C
0 1 1 0 0 1	2	4	6	4	1 1 1 0 0 1	2	4	6	4
0 1 1 0 1 0	5	9	1	8	1 1 1 0 1 0	5	8	7	C
0 1 1 0 1 1	4	7	C	0	1 1 1 0 1 1	4	7	C	0
0 1 1 1 0 0	3	6	4	4	1 1 1 1 0 0	3	6	4	4
0 1 1 1 0 1	—	—	—	—	1 1 1 1 0 1	—	—	—	—
0 1 1 1 1 0	6	10	D	C	1 1 1 1 1 0	6	10	D	C
0 1 1 1 1 1	—	—	—	—	1 1 1 1 1 1	—	—	—	—

Fig. 4.26 Expanded truth tables for the functions of the ASM of Fig. 3.5 for direct mapping into ROM.

state codes, are not used. This is because the ASM has only six states, 11 link paths and at most one qualifier per ASM block. The full decode covers all contingencies and permits us to have all eight states assigned and up to 64 link paths, as would result if all three qualifiers were used in each block. For an ASM with k state variables, n inputs and m outputs, the fully decoded table would require a ROM with up to $2^{k+n}(k + m)$ bits.

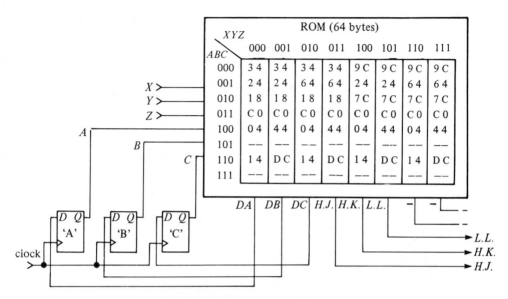

Fig. 4.27 ROM-based implementation of the ASM of Fig. 3.5 using full decode of inputs and state variables.

We can dramatically reduce the ROM space occupied by ASMs which involve at most one qualifier per block because we need only cater for a maximum of 2^{k+1} link paths for k state variables. In the general case the maximum ROM size would be $2^{k+1}(k + m)$ bits and

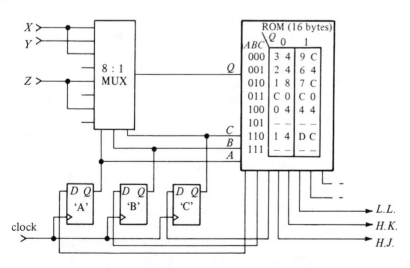

Fig. 4.28 ROM-based implementation of the ASM of Fig. 3.5 using qualifier selection.

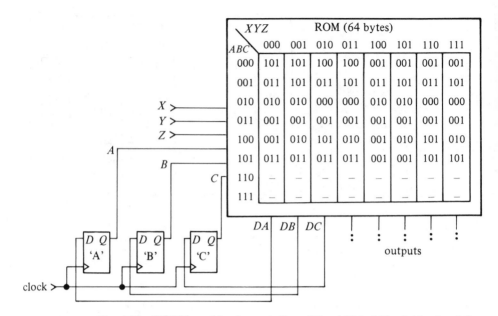

Fig. 4.29   ROM-based implementation of the ASM of Fig. 3.16 using full decode of inputs and state variables.

in our example we require only 16 bytes. We can address these with the three state variables and one qualifier.

As the qualifier may be different for each ASM block we need to select the appropriate input, if any, for each combination of state variables. This can conveniently be done using a multiplexer controlled by the state variables as indicated in Fig. 4.28. Here, Q becomes X, Y or Z where appropriate and the value of this input selects one of two alternative bytes each of which gives the next state and output values corresponding to the associated link path. For the more complex ASM structure, such as that defined in Fig. 3.16 which has two qualifiers in some ASM blocks, we must allow for up to four possible link paths per block. The fully decoded implementation given in Fig. 4.29 still requires 64 locations because we have three state variables and three inputs. In this diagram only the three next-state values are given because no outputs were defined for this ASM. We can extend the modifier selection procedure by using two multiplexers again controlled by the state variables and which select two, one or no qualifiers for each state as in Fig. 4.30. The ROM now requires 32 locations and these can be addressed with the three state variables and the two qualifiers. Note that the same configuration could support an ASM with eight states and four link paths in each block. The general ASM with up to two qualifiers per block would require a ROM with $2^{k+2}(k + m)$ bits.

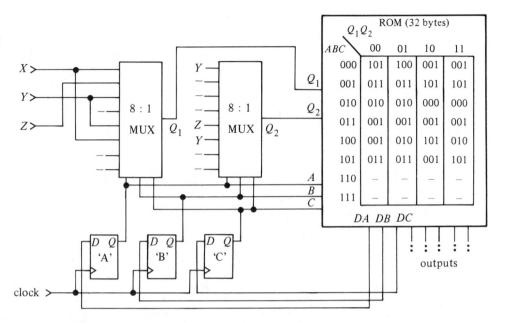

Fig. 4.30 ROM-based implementation of the ASM of Fig. 3.16 using qualifier selection.

An alternative method to that of preselecting the qualifiers for the addressing of the ROM is to make selections on the outputs from the ROM. This also reduces the ROM size since we need use only the state variables as address bits. However, in each location we need to store all the alternative link paths and outputs associated with each state. This is fairly straightforward for simple ASM structures with at most one qualifier per block as there will be a maximum of two alternatives in each case. Fig. 4.31 illustrates this technique using the simple ASM of Fig. 3.5. Each ROM word is addressed by a state code and is formatted to indicate which input, if any, is used as the qualifier for the state, and also to include the two alternative next states and output combinations. As each ROM word is produced the qualifier section is used to select and test the appropriate input. The value of this input controls a set of 2:1 MUXs which extract the appropriate next-state code and the output values for the cases $Q = 0$ or $Q = 1$. For an ASM with k state variables, n inputs, m outputs and at most one qualifier per block, the maximum ROM size is $2^k(n + 2k + 2m)$ bits using this method.

We can also extend this idea to the more complex ASMs with up to two qualifiers per block. We now need to store on the ROM the two qualifiers for each state, and the four possible link path next states and output combinations. One possible ROM word format is

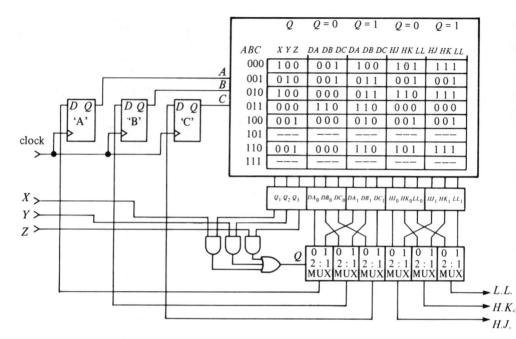

Fig. 4.31   ROM-based implementation of the ASM of Fig. 3.5 using stored link paths and output alternatives.

given in Fig. 4.32 for a machine with three inputs and three state variables. Fig. 4.33 gives the ROM contents corresponding to the ASM defined in Fig. 3.16 using this word format. For the general case the ROM size for the two-qualifier per block ASM would be $2^k(2n + 4k + 4m)$. For the situation where there are up to q qualifiers per block this would indicate a ROM with $2^k(qn + k2^q + m2^q)$ bits. This compares with the smaller number $2^{k+q}(k + m)$ bits required by the preselection technique and larger $2^{k+n}(k + m)$ for the fully decoded system. In the first two cases a significant amount of external circuitry would be required as q approaches n and this would probably far outweigh the savings in ROM space, and so the

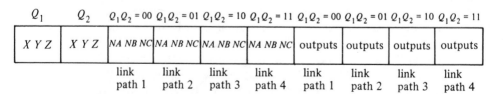

Fig. 4.32   Possible ROM word format for ASM with at most two qualifiers per ASM block.

| | Q_1 | Q_2 | | | | | outputs |
ABC	X Y Z	X Y Z	NA NB NC	NA NB NC	NA NB NC	NA NB NC	
000	1 0 0	0 1 0	1 0 1	1 0 0	0 0 1	0 0 1	· · · · · · · ·
001	0 0 1	0 0 0	0 1 1	0 1 1	1 0 1	1 0 1	· · · · · · · ·
010	0 1 0	0 0 0	0 1 0	0 1 0	0 0 0	0 0 0	· · · · · · · ·
011	0 0 0	0 0 0	0 0 1	0 0 1	0 0 1	0 0 1	· · · · · · · ·
100	0 1 0	0 0 1	0 0 1	0 1 0	1 0 1	0 1 0	· · · · · · · ·
101	1 0 0	0 1 0	0 1 1	0 1 1	0 0 1	1 0 1	· · · · · · · ·
110	— — —	— — —	— — —	— — —	— — —	— — —	— · · · · · · —
111	— — —	— — —	— — —	— — —	— — —	— — —	— · · · · · · —

A >— B >— C >—

Fig. 4.33 ROM composition for the ASM of Fig. 3.16.

full decode which requires no extra external circuitry would become attractive in this situation.

The choice between employing PLA- or ROM-based synthesis depends heavily on the functions involved. In addition there are several other considerations which may affect the decision. PLAs, having only two levels of logic gates, are inherently faster than ROMs, for a given circuit technology, and all their outputs are available simultaneously. This may not always be the case with ROM synthesis when several functions are packed in and can be accessed only by address selection. On the other hand, the programming of FPLAs is a once-and-for-all process with very little room for subsequent error correction or function modification whereas PROMs can be erased and reprogrammed. However, to confuse the issue, fast ROMs and reprogrammable PLAs are now available. As we have seen, for ASM-based systems with the types of functions they include, the PLA approach to hardware synthesis seems to be superior to the ROM-based implementation.

4.4 APPLICATION TO MICROPROGRAMMING

The implementations of ASMs by means of PLAs, and especially ROM-based synthesis, begin to take on the appearance of primitive computer architectures. The system functions stored in the arrays can be regarded as the 'program' which the primitive computer uses to execute the algorithm specified by the ASM. This represents a very simple example of a more general method of machine organization and control. In fact, the concept of microprogramming introduced by Wilkes in 1951 anticipated the ASM method of design and the modern synthesis techniques in quite a remarkable way. In

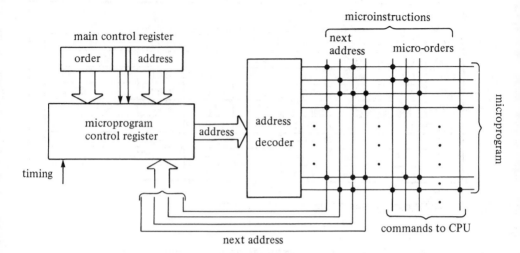

Fig. 4.34 General architecture for a microprogrammed machine.

this approach the orders in the basic order code of the computer are themselves described in terms of a set of more fundamental 'micro-orders' which are arranged in sequences or 'microprograms' which are executed when the machine order is decoded from a machine instruction. The general organization is as depicted in Fig. 4.34. As each order is decoded from the instruction held in the main control register it is used to invoke a sequence of micro-orders stored in the microprogram control store. The contemporary technology limited Wilkes to the description of a microprogrammed machine in terms of hardwired diode-matrix units to form the microcode table. Each row of this matrix consisted of an address part to find the next instruction and a micro-order part which contained the command instruction. This took the form of the bit pattern which was necessary to open the required gates in the central processing unit in order to execute the appropriate component of the microprogram sequence. Thus, each row formed a microinstruction and the set of rows a microprogram. The advent of cheap memory arrays has now enabled the microprogramming concept to develop its full potential. Microprogrammable machines exhibit several desirable features. As only the micro-orders need to be implemented in hardware, the processor design and implementation becomes simpler. The microprogram store can also include diagnostic tests to improve reliability and maintenance. The set of microprograms can easily be enhanced to provide extra features in the machine order code or to emulate another machine, thereby enabling the transportation of programs from one machine to another.

Microprogramming and its associated techniques have recently been given a renewed impetus with the introduction of bit-slice microprocessor devices. This family of components enables special purpose or customized processors to be designed and synthesized by combining basic units which are then operated under microprogram control.

The concept of table-driven control units used in the later generations of computers as foreseen by Wilkes represented the first example of the merging of hardware and software aspects of a digital system. Dedicated hardware units of the machine were replaced with more flexible 'programmable' units which had aspects of both regimes. Eventually, the term 'firmware' was coined to describe this new mode of implementation.

Microprogramming represents another level of programming activity inserted between that of machine language and the genuine hardware of the machine. The normal user is unaware of this primitive structure when operating at the higher levels of compiled, interpreted, assembled or even machine code language. Thus in this multilevel software environment the microprogram's function is to execute interpreters for other virtual machines, and it represents the boundary between the genuine hardware and software components. It is not surprising therefore that the ASM techniques find application in microprogram design and implementation. In this application we must interpret the charts and tables in a slightly different way. Usually, each state represents a single microinstruction and the command part will be represented as the state outputs. The state assignment will now correspond to the address of the microinstruction in the microprogram store. The link paths will correspond to the possible branch or jump addresses in the sequence of microinstruction execution. These link paths will be controlled by qualifiers which will represent control signals originating in the microprogram control unit or CPU.

The micro-orders are usually limited in number and complexity and are confined to such things as register transfer, bit testing and branching. As Wilkes foresaw, the resulting microprograms correspond to state machines with at most one qualifier per state block. We have observed that this type of ASM is a fairly straightforward structure to implement via random logic, multiplexers, PLA or ROM-based synthesis. In this particular application we are normally interested in implementation using ROMs. The techniques of preselecting the qualifier of each state or of postselecting the appropriate link path address from a list of alternatives were both aimed at reducing the required ROM space at the expense of providing extra external components. Under normal circumstances this may not always be a rewarding exercise since ROM is relatively cheap and more flexible than dedicated hardwired circuitry. However, in the microprogramming activity, where speed and code optimization are important, the compression of ROM occupancy will pay high dividends. Thus the full decode is not an attractive possibility in these circumstances.

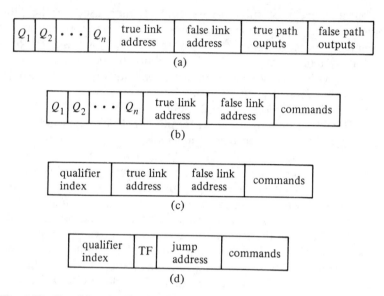

Fig. 4.35   Possible microinstruction formats.

There are several ways to improve the situation by compressing the microinstruction format. If we avoid conditional outputs there will be no need to provide alternative sets of outputs for the qualifier-true link path and the qualifier-false link path. Thus, the only outputs will be state outputs which are therefore independent of the condition of any qualifier. As mentioned above, these outputs will now represent the microinstruction command which will be a bit pattern required to control the hardware enabling the instruction to be executed.

Thus, the original general ROM-word format suggested previously for this situation and reproduced in Fig. 4.35a can be simplified to that of Fig. 4.35b. We can also compress the amount of information required to select the appropriate qualifier by using a qualifier index which will be some agreed code. In this way, for example, up to seven qualifiers could be coded with only three bits instead of seven used in the previous method. Thus the micro-instruction format becomes that of Fig. 4.35c. The need to carry both the condition-true link address and the condition-false link address within the microinstruction format can also be overcome by ensuring that one of these is always the next in sequence to the present address. Whereas the conventional structure is related to the ASM chart of Fig. 4.36a, this new format results from the arrangement of Fig. 4.36b. Here the condition-false link address is the next address in sequence whereas the condition-true link address represents a branch or jump to another location in the micro-program store. This enables us to derive the next address either by incrementing the present address or by loading the jump address. Thus we need only carry the jump address in the microinstruction word. To enable the jump address to be associated with either the true or the false link path we can carry an extra bit, TF, which will indicate whether to increment or load the next address. This new word format is given in Fig. 4.35d and represents a significant compression on the original description.

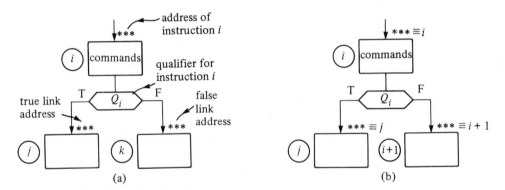

Fig. 4.36   ASM representations for single microinstructions.

This compression is also reflected in a reduction in the associated hardware of the microprogram controller. Fig. 4.37a shows the main requirements for the microinstruction format of Fig. 4.35b. The qualifier MUX selects the appropriate qualifier and its value controls a second MUX which selects either the true or the false link address as the next address which is then fed to the microprogram address register. With the microinstruction format of Fig. 4.35d the qualifier index is decoded into the appropriate qualifier. If its value matches the TF bit, the jump address is loaded in the microprogram counter which replaces the address register. If a match does not occur, the counter is incremented to the next address in succession.

In order to implement the counter-driven microprogram controller it may be necessary to reassign the addresses of the micro-instructions so that when a decision box is involved one link path

(a)

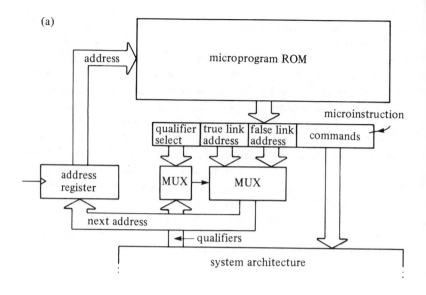

(b)

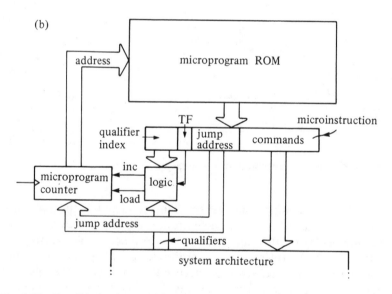

Fig. 4.37 Possible implementations of microprogram controller.

can lead to the successive storage location. Fig. 4.38a shows a sample ASM chart for a fragment of microprogram. The command outputs represent the controls to five logic gates $G_1, G_2, \ldots, G_5$ which are opened to execute the corresponding instruction. With the assignment shown it is not possible to arrange a sequential address for one link path on all occasions. However, the assignment

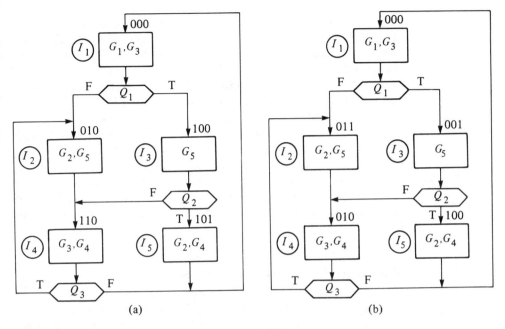

Fig. 4.38 Example fragment of microprogram ASM.

of Fig. 4.38b does permit this provided we associate direct state transitions with the jump addresses. Thus when the qualifier index is 00 a direct transition to the jump address is performed. For qualified state transitions the jump address is used when the TF bit matches the condition of the qualifier denoted by the qualifier index; otherwise a sequential transition results. The corresponding microcode is shown in Fig. 4.39.

The ASM technique can also be employed in conjunction with designs using higher levels of programming activity such as machine

Inst.	Address	Qualifier index	TF	Jump address	Commands G_1 G_2 G_3 G_4 G_5				
I_1	0 0 0	0 1	0	0 1 1	1	0	1	0	0
I_3	0 0 1	1 0	1	1 0 0	0	0	0	0	1
I_4	0 1 0	1 1	0	0 0 0	0	0	1	1	0
I_2	0 1 1	0 0	1	0 1 0	0	1	0	0	1
I_5	1 0 0	0 0	1	0 0 0	0	1	0	1	0

microinstruction

Fig. 4.39 Microcode resulting from Fig. 4.38b. $Q_1 = 01$; $Q_2 = 10$; $Q_3 = 11$, direct $= 00$; T $= 1$; F $= 0$.

or assembly language where there is still a close association with the hardware structure of the machine. When higher-level languages are involved it becomes little more than an alternative form of program flowchart technique unless each high-level instruction is interpreted with some other ASM structure described in terms of machine or microprogram instructions. This gives rise to a hierarchy of interpretively linked state machines.

This viewpoint leads us on across the hardware–software boundary to the implementation of algorithms by means of fully programmable devices such as microcomputers incorporating the normal components of microprocessor, control and memory. As we have seen, in this environment the basic design philosophies still hold, but the design goals and evaluations take on new parameters.

4.5   BIBLIOGRAPHICAL NOTES

The technical literature relating to PLA- and ROM-based synthesis of switching circuits is rapidly expanding. Data sheets and applications notes such as Mullard (1981) and Memory Devices (1980) give useful information on the basic properties and exploitation of the programmable devices. Texts such as Blakeslee (1975), Winkel and Prosser (1980), Davio *et al.* (1983) and Mano (1984) also discuss the general principles of their use. Clare (1972) explores the use of ROM structures in the synthesis of ASM-based designs. Forrest and Edwards (1983) relate PLAs to ASM descriptions. Kinnemint (1983) and Dagless (1983) also consider the exploitation of programmable logic in digital system designs.

4.6   EXERCISES

4.1 A certain FPLA can support up to three functions of four variables which together involve eight or less product terms. Draw the connection diagram for this device when it is programmed to synthesize the following function:

$$f_1 = \sum(1, 4, 6, 7, 9, 12, 14)$$
$$f_2 = X_3 X_2(\overline{X_4} + X_1) + \overline{X_2}(\overline{X_3}X_1 + \overline{X_4}X_3)$$
$$f_3 = \overline{X_2}\overline{X_1} + X_3 X_2 X_1 + \overline{X_4}X_3 X_2$$

4.2 Show that, for the programmed FPLA of Exercise 4.1, it is possible to accommodate a subsequent modification to f_3 so that it becomes:

$$f_3^* = X_4 \oplus X_3 \oplus X_4 X_3 X_2 X_1$$

X_4	X_3	X_2	X_1	f_1	f_2	f_3	f_4
0	0	0	0	0	0	0	1
0	0	0	1	0	0	1	0
0	0	1	0	0	0	0	1
0	0	1	1	0	1	0	1
0	1	0	0	0	0	0	0
0	1	0	1	1	0	1	0
0	1	1	0	0	0	0	0
0	1	1	1	1	1	1	1
1	0	0	0	1	1	0	1
1	0	0	1	1	1	1	0
1	0	1	0	0	1	0	1
1	0	1	1	0	0	0	0
1	1	0	0	1	1	1	0
1	1	0	1	1	1	1	1
1	1	1	0	0	1	1	0
1	1	1	1	1	0	1	0

Fig. 4.40 Example functions for Exercise 4.3.

4.3 Four functions of four variables are defined in the truth tables of Fig. 4.40. Indicate how these functions can be realized on:

a) a 64-bit ROM comprising an 8×8 array, six address lines and one output line;

b) a PLA which can provide four functions of four variables involving up to eight product terms in total.

Inputs X Y Z	Present state Sym. A B C				Next state Sym. NA NB NC				Outputs				
	Sym.	A	B	C	Sym.	NA	NB	NC	H.INC	H.DEC	H.CLR	H.LOD	H.TOT
0 − −	1	0	0	0	1	0	0	0	1	0	1	0	0
1 − −	1	0	0	0	2	0	0	1	1	0	1	0	0
− 0 −	2	0	0	1	4	1	1	1	0	0	0	1	0
− 1 −	2	0	0	1	3	1	0	1	1	0	0	1	0
− − −	3	1	0	1	5	1	1	0	0	0	0	1	0
− − 0	4	1	1	1	5	1	1	0	0	0	0	0	0
− − 1	4	1	1	1	6	0	1	1	0	1	0	0	0
0 − −	5	1	1	0	1	0	0	0	0	0	0	0	0
1 − −	5	1	1	0	7	0	1	0	0	0	0	0	0
− 1 −	6	0	1	1	7	0	1	0	0	0	0	1	0
− 0 −	6	0	1	1	4	1	1	1	0	0	0	1	0
− − −	7	0	1	0	1	0	0	0	1	0	0	0	1

Fig. 4.41 Example ASM table for Exercise 4.4.

4.4 Show how the ASM defined in Fig. 4.41 can be implemented with a PLA and D-type bistables using:

a) simplified system functions,
b) direct mapping of link paths.

4.5 Implement the ASM of Fig. 4.41 using a PLS structure which involves SR-bistables with active-high inputs.

4.6 Derive a ROM-based design for the ASM of Fig. 4.41 which employs D-type bistables and

a) a full decode of all system functions,
b) preselection of each state qualifier,
c) a ROM-word format with qualifier test and alternative link addresses.

4.7 Disregarding the conditional outputs of the ASM of Fig. 4.41, assume that the table represents a microprogram structure. The microinstruction format includes a qualifier index (wherein 00 indicates a direct transition, 01 indicates X, 10 indicates Y and 11 indicates Z), a jump if true or false indicator bit, a jump address and a command output list. Reassign the ASM to accommodate this structure and construct the microcode for this arrangement.

Chapter 5
Reed-Muller Algebraic Descriptions

5.1 INTRODUCTION

Up to this point we have considered only the design and implementation of switching circuits originating from, and synthesized according to, the description afforded by the connectives of Boolean algebra. In recent years an alternative form of description based on the operations of modulo-2 arithmetic has presented an attractive and rewarding field of investigation. The resulting algebra, being an example of a finite field, supports the familiar mathematical devices such as matrices, transforms, polynomials, etc., and these operations are especially suitable for computer implementation. As a result, CAD schemes for this algebraic regime are readily devised. The algebra can be used to describe and analyse an alternative form of both combinational and sequential circuits and an important subclass of these can be shown to exhibit linear properties. These latter types are particularly amenable to analysis and design. They are also important because they find widespread application in areas of digital communications such as coding schemes for error control and synchronization, or sequence generation for process identification and system testing. Furthermore, this alternative mode of representation extends easily to the description of multiple-valued switching circuits and therefore provides a useful avenue into this largely unexploited area. This chapter deals with the formulation of this algebraic description and presents some methods for the design and synthesis of combinational circuits expressed in this mode. Chapter 6 deals with some aspects of related sequential circuits.

The basic connectives of this modulo-2 algebra are those of modulo-2 addition and modulo-2 multiplication operating on the integers modulo-2, that is 0 and 1. Fig. 5.1 gives the arithmetic tables for these two operations together with their circuit symbols. When expressed in the form of truth tables we observe that modulo-2 addition is identical to the Boolean exclusive-OR operation (EOR) and modulo-2 multiplication is identical to the Boolean AND operation. Thus at least the basic connectives of this new algebra have a ready physical implementation in terms of familiar switching circuit components. However, it is convenient in this context to use the new symbolic form of circuit elements and we can be assured that a direct physical interpretation can always be made.

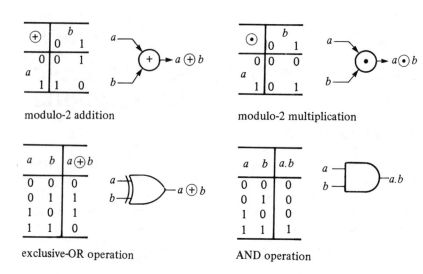

modulo-2 addition

modulo-2 multiplication

exclusive-OR operation

AND operation

Fig. 5.1 Basic connectives of modulo-2 algebra and their Boolean equivalents.

From these fundamental operation tables it would appear that the only difference between the modulo-2 description and that of Boolean algebra is that between the exclusive-OR operation and the inclusive-OR operation. This comes down to the fact that whereas $1 + 1 = 1$ in Boolean algebra, $1 \oplus 1 = 0$ in modulo-2 algebra. As we shall see, this apparently trivial variation leads to very significant differences in the resulting algebra, and consequently in the methods of design and implementation.

The basic requirements of any algebra employed to describe and manipulate switching circuit functions can be listed as follows:

1. *Functionally complete.* The algebra should be capable of providing a distinct algebraic representation or expression for each possible function of a given number of variables.

2. *Flexible.* The algebra should be amenable to manipulation so that design algorithms can be set up and employed with reasonable ease.

3. *Realizable.* The basic connectives and any higher-level functional operations should have simple and reliable physical switching circuit counterparts.

We have already observed that this last attribute is satisfied for this modulo-2 arithmetic. Before proceeding to discuss the other points it is worth noting here that this modulo-2 algebra will be found to be a special, and indeed the simplest, case of a type of algebra known as a finite field or Galois field algebra. In fact, it is very easy to extend all the concepts derived in this chapter to cover the situation of modulo-p arithmetic, where p is a prime integer. Unfortunately, when the modulus is composite, that is, non-prime, the corresponding arithmetic does not lead to a consistent and functionally complete algebra. However, it is possible in some non-prime situations to set up a perfectly consistent algebra with equivalent properties to the prime case. These finite or Galois fields exist whenever q, the number of values, is prime or the integer power of a single prime, i.e. $q = p^k$. These fields are symbolized as GF(q) and our simple modulo-2 case can be seen to be the field GF(2). In later chapters, where we consider future developments in multiple-valued switching circuits, it will be seen that the representation provided by GF(q) presents a very attractive alternative to those developed from a generalization of the Boolean-type algebras.

5.2 THE ALGEBRA OF GF(2)

If a, b and c are two-valued variables and $\oplus$ and $\odot$ represent modulo-2 addition and multiplication, we can establish the following from Fig. 5.1:

1. Closure laws $a \oplus b$ and $a \odot b$ are also two-valued
2. Associative laws $a \oplus (b \oplus c) = (a \oplus b) \oplus c = a \oplus b \oplus c$
$a \odot (b \odot c) = (a \odot b) \odot c = a \odot b \odot c$
3. Distributive laws $a \odot (b \oplus c) = a \odot b \oplus a \odot c$
4. Commutative laws $a \oplus b = b \oplus a$, $a \odot b = b \odot a$
5. Identities $a \oplus 0 = a$, $a \odot 1 = a$

Inspection of these properties reveals the similarities between this algebra and the algebra of real numbers. The latter is, in fact, an example of an infinite field and so the correspondence is not unexpected. Further properties result from the particular nature of modulo-2 arithmetic:

6. *Inverses.*   We have $a \oplus a = 0$, thus $a = -a$ and every element is its own additive inverse. This means that addition and subtraction are the same over GF(2). From this it follows that if $a \oplus b = c$, then

$$a = b \oplus c, \quad b = a \oplus c \text{ and } a \oplus b \oplus c = 0$$

Also, since $0 \odot 0 = 0$ and $1 \odot 1 = 1$ we have $a \odot a = a$.

It is obviously of interest to relate GF(2) algebra to Boolean algebra. From the basic connectives we know that

$$a \odot b = a . b \quad \text{and} \quad a \oplus b = a . \overline{b} + \overline{a} . b$$

The latter enables us to establish that

$$a \oplus 1 = a . \overline{1} + \overline{a} . 1 = a . 0 + \overline{a} = \overline{a}$$

Since, by de Morgan,

$$a + b = \overline{\overline{a} . \overline{b}}$$

we can establish that

$$a + b = \overline{(a \oplus 1) \odot (b \oplus 1)} \oplus 1 = a \odot b \oplus a \oplus b$$

Therefore, $= (a \oplus 1) \oplus$

$$a . b = a \odot b$$
$$a + b = a \odot b \oplus a \oplus b$$
$$\overline{a} = a \oplus 1$$

and all the connectives of Boolean algebra can be implemented in terms of modulo-2 components. As the former is a known functionally complete algebra, it follows that modulo-2 algebra is also functionally complete.

We now need to establish a general form of algebraic expression. From this point on we shall not distinguish between Boolean AND and modulo-2 multiplication and we shall use the same symbol or juxtaposition in algebraic expressions. The standard Boolean expression for one variable, x_1, may be written

$$f(x_1) = d_0 \overline{x_1} + d_1 x_1$$

where $d_i = 0$ or 1, are truth table values. Thus, by de Morgan,

$$f(x_1) = (\overline{d_0 \overline{x_1} . d_1 x_1})$$

Hence

$$f(x_1) = (d_0(x_1 \oplus 1) \oplus 1) . (d_1 x_1 \oplus 1) \oplus 1$$
$$= d_0 d_1 x_1 \oplus d_0 d_1 x_1 \oplus d_0 x_1 \oplus d_0 \oplus d_1 x_1$$
$$= d_0 \oplus (d_0 \oplus d_1) x_1$$
$$f(x_1) = c_0 \oplus c_1 x_1 \qquad \text{over GF(2), where } c_i = 0 \text{ or } 1$$

The coefficients of this new expression are not directly equal to the truth table values but may be related to the latter by means of a modulo-2 transform matrix.

$$\begin{bmatrix} c_0 \\ c_1 \end{bmatrix} = \begin{bmatrix} 1 & 0 \\ 1 & 1 \end{bmatrix} . \begin{bmatrix} d_0 \\ d_1 \end{bmatrix} \qquad \text{over GF(2)}$$

and all matrix multiplications and additions are performed modulo-2. Symbolically, we may write

$$c = T_1 d$$

and we can extend this concept to functions for two or more variables. For example, where $n = 2$ is the number of variables, x_1, x_2, the DCF is

$$f(x_2, x_1) = d_0.m_0 + d_1.m_1 + d_2.m_2 + d_3.m_3$$

Since the minterms are mutually exclusive in that $m_i.m_j = 0$ for all i, j with $i \neq j$, we may replace the inclusive-OR ($+$) by the exclusive-OR ($\oplus$) without altering the validity of the expression. Thus,

$$
\begin{aligned}
f(x_2, x_1) &= d_0 m_0 \oplus d_1 m_1 \oplus d_2 m_2 \oplus d_3 m_3 \\
&= d_0 \bar{x}_2 \bar{x}_1 \oplus d_1 \bar{x}_2 x_1 \oplus d_2 x_2 \bar{x}_1 \oplus d_3 x_2 x_1 \\
&= d_0 (x_2 \oplus 1)(x_1 \oplus 1) \oplus d_2 (x_2 \oplus 1) x_1 \oplus d_2 x_2 (x_1 \oplus 1) \oplus d_3 x_2 x_1 \\
&= d_0 \oplus (d_0 \oplus d_1) x_1 \oplus (d_0 \oplus d_2) x_2 \oplus (d_0 \oplus d_1 \oplus d_2 \oplus d_3) x_2 x_1
\end{aligned}
$$

Therefore

$$f(x_2, x_1) = c_0 \oplus c_1 x_1 \oplus c_2 x_2 \oplus c_3 x_2 x_1 \qquad \text{over GF(2)}$$

where

$$
\begin{pmatrix} c_0 \\ c_1 \\ c_2 \\ c_3 \end{pmatrix} =
\begin{pmatrix} 1 & 0 & 0 & 0 \\ 1 & 1 & 0 & 0 \\ 1 & 0 & 1 & 0 \\ 1 & 1 & 1 & 1 \end{pmatrix} \cdot
\begin{pmatrix} d_0 \\ d_1 \\ d_2 \\ d_3 \end{pmatrix}
$$

or

$$c = T_2.d \qquad \text{over GF(2)}$$

The transform matrix T_2 is seen to contain the one-variable transform in three places, so that T_2 can be partitioned as follows

$$T_2 = \begin{bmatrix} T_1 & 0 \\ T_1 & T_1 \end{bmatrix}$$

In general, the n-variable transform T_n is found to have a similar recursive structure, so that

$$T_n = \begin{bmatrix} T_{n-1} & 0 \\ T_{n-1} & T_{n-1} \end{bmatrix} \qquad \begin{array}{l} \text{for } n > 0 \\ \text{and } T_0 = [1] \end{array} \qquad \text{over GF(2)}$$

The general n-variable expression takes the form

$$
\begin{aligned}
F(x_n, x_{n-1}, \ldots, x_1) = {}& c_0 \oplus c_1 x_1 \oplus c_2 x_2 \oplus c_3 x_2 x_1 \oplus c_4 x_3 \oplus c_5 x_3 x_1 \oplus \ldots \\
& \oplus c_{2^n - 1} x_n x_{n-1} \ldots x_1 \qquad \text{over GF(2)}
\end{aligned}
$$

or

$$F(x_n, x_{n-1}, \ldots, x_1) = \sum_{i=0}^{2^n - 1} c_i x_n^{e_{i,n}} x_{n-1}^{e_{i,n-1}} \ldots x_1^{e_{i,1}}$$

Where Σ signifies summation over GF(2), the $e_{i,j}$ are 0 or 1 so that $x_k^0 = 1$, $x_k^1 = x_k$. This is a modulo-2 sum-of-products form known as the complement-free ring-sum or *Reed–Muller* expansion. In this form we have 2^n possible product terms selected from the n variables. We may refer to these as π-terms (or piterms) and symbolize them as π_i. The suffix i is the decimal equivalent of the binary number formed from the concatenation $e_{i,n}e_{i,n-1}\ldots e_{i,1}$ where $e_{i,1}$ is taken as the least significant bit. Thus,

$$x_6 x_3 x_1 = x_6{}^1 x_5{}^0 x_4{}^0 x_3{}^1 x_2{}^0 x_1{}^1 = \pi_{37}$$

and

$$\pi_{23} = x_5{}^1 x_4{}^0 x_3{}^1 x_2{}^1 x_1{}^1 = x_5 x_3 x_2 x_1$$

Note that $x_i = \pi_{2^{i-1}}$ and $\pi_0 = 1$. The shorthand notation of the RM expansion becomes

$$F(x_n, x_{n-1}, \ldots, x_1) = \sum_{i=0}^{2^n-1} c_i \pi_i \qquad \text{over GF(2)}$$

Each choice of coefficients c_i leads to a distinct expansion and therefore there are again 2^{2^n} expressions of this form.

5.3 THE OPERATIONAL AND FUNCTION DOMAINS

As the coefficients of the RM expansion are not directly equal to the truth table coefficients, this regime requires two forms of map representation. The truth table or Karnaugh map represents the operational behaviour of the function and therefore depicts the *operational domain*. Thus, the d_i coefficients can be plotted on an operational domain map identical in structure to an n-variable Karnaugh map. The coefficients of the RM expansion form the *function domain* description and can be depicted on a function domain map. The latter has similar structure to the equivalent Karnaugh map, but the labelling of the cells is different. The map is once again divided into two equal sets of cells in a different way for each variable. In one set, the cells correspond to piterms which contain the variable x_i; the other set covers cells whose piterms do not contain the variable, and thus x_i is weighted as 1 in the product. We can arrange therefore that minterms and piterms occur in the same relative positions on these two maps. Fig. 5.2 shows the structures for $n = 3$ and $n = 4$. Similar maps are easily constructed for larger numbers of variables. For the case $n = 3$ we illustrate the location of each minterm and piterm as deduced from the labelling on the edges of the map. This reveals the following notation:

i	0	1	2	3	4	5	6	7
m_i	$\bar{x}_3\bar{x}_2\bar{x}_1$	$\bar{x}_3\bar{x}_2 x_1$	$\bar{x}_3 x_2\bar{x}_1$	$\bar{x}_3 x_2 x_1$	$x_3\bar{x}_2\bar{x}_1$	$x_3\bar{x}_2 x_1$	$x_3 x_2\bar{x}_1$	$x_3 x_2 x_1$
π_i	1	x_1	x_2	$x_2 x_1$	x_3	$x_3 x_1$	$x_3 x_2$	$x_3 x_2 x_1$

$n = 3$:

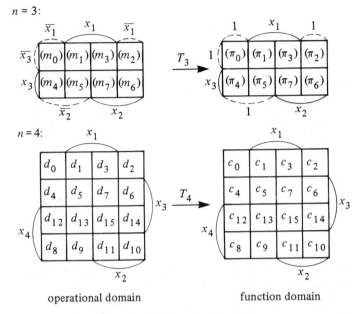

$n = 4$:

operational domain   function domain

Fig. 5.2   Operational domain and function domain maps.

In the case of the $n = 4$ maps we show the positions of the corresponding coefficients used to depict a function either in the operational domain (the d_i values) or the function domain (the c_i values). In each case the function domain map can be derived by applying the appropriate transform to the coefficients of the operational domain map. It is also important to establish the means whereby we may deduce the operational domain map or, equivalently, the truth table, for a given RM expansion. This would then furnish the inverse transform. For example, for $n = 2$ we have

$$f(x_2, x_1) = c_0 \oplus c_1 x_1 \oplus c_2 x_2 \oplus c_3 x_2 x_1$$

Now,

$$d_0 = f(0, 0) = c_0$$
$$d_1 = f(0, 1) = c_0 \oplus c_1$$
$$d_2 = f(1, 0) = c_0 \oplus c_2$$
$$d_3 = f(1, 1) = c_0 \oplus c_1 \oplus c_2 \oplus c_3$$

so that

$$\begin{Bmatrix} d_0 \\ d_1 \\ d_2 \\ d_3 \end{Bmatrix} = \begin{bmatrix} 1 & 0 & 0 & 0 \\ 1 & 1 & 0 & 0 \\ 1 & 0 & 1 & 0 \\ 1 & 1 & 1 & 1 \end{bmatrix} \cdot \begin{Bmatrix} c_0 \\ c_1 \\ c_2 \\ c_3 \end{Bmatrix} \qquad \text{over GF(2)}$$

or

$$d = S_2 c$$

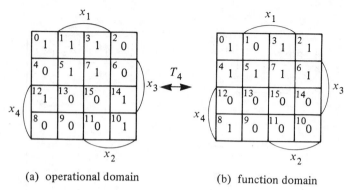

(a) operational domain   (b) function domain

Fig. 5.3 Example of transform process.

Clearly $S_2 = T_2^{-1} = T_2$ is the inverse transform. This relationship is true for all values of n for functions over GF(2). That is,

$$S_n = T_n^{-1} = T_n \qquad \text{over GF(2)}$$

and so the transform is identical in both directions. As an example of these relationships consider the four-variable function defined on the four-variable operational domain map of Fig. 5.3a. The coefficients d_i can be extracted to form the d vector which when multiplied by the appropriate transform T_4 will yield the coefficients c_i for the function domain map of Fig. 5.3b. Thus

$$T_4 d = c$$

or

$$
\begin{pmatrix}
1 & 0 & 0 & 0 & 0 & 0 & 0 & 0 & 0 & 0 & 0 & 0 & 0 & 0 & 0 & 0 \\
1 & 1 & 0 & 0 & 0 & 0 & 0 & 0 & 0 & 0 & 0 & 0 & 0 & 0 & 0 & 0 \\
1 & 0 & 1 & 0 & 0 & 0 & 0 & 0 & 0 & 0 & 0 & 0 & 0 & 0 & 0 & 0 \\
1 & 1 & 1 & 1 & 0 & 0 & 0 & 0 & 0 & 0 & 0 & 0 & 0 & 0 & 0 & 0 \\
1 & 0 & 0 & 0 & 1 & 0 & 0 & 0 & 0 & 0 & 0 & 0 & 0 & 0 & 0 & 0 \\
1 & 1 & 0 & 0 & 1 & 1 & 0 & 0 & 0 & 0 & 0 & 0 & 0 & 0 & 0 & 0 \\
1 & 0 & 1 & 0 & 1 & 0 & 1 & 0 & 0 & 0 & 0 & 0 & 0 & 0 & 0 & 0 \\
1 & 1 & 1 & 1 & 1 & 1 & 1 & 1 & 0 & 0 & 0 & 0 & 0 & 0 & 0 & 0 \\
1 & 0 & 0 & 0 & 0 & 0 & 0 & 0 & 1 & 0 & 0 & 0 & 0 & 0 & 0 & 0 \\
1 & 1 & 0 & 0 & 0 & 0 & 0 & 0 & 1 & 1 & 0 & 0 & 0 & 0 & 0 & 0 \\
1 & 0 & 1 & 0 & 0 & 0 & 0 & 0 & 1 & 0 & 1 & 0 & 0 & 0 & 0 & 0 \\
1 & 1 & 1 & 1 & 0 & 0 & 0 & 0 & 1 & 1 & 1 & 1 & 0 & 0 & 0 & 0 \\
1 & 0 & 0 & 0 & 1 & 0 & 0 & 0 & 1 & 0 & 0 & 0 & 1 & 0 & 0 & 0 \\
1 & 1 & 0 & 0 & 1 & 1 & 0 & 0 & 1 & 1 & 0 & 0 & 1 & 1 & 0 & 0 \\
1 & 0 & 1 & 0 & 1 & 0 & 1 & 0 & 1 & 0 & 1 & 0 & 1 & 0 & 1 & 0 \\
1 & 1 & 1 & 1 & 1 & 1 & 1 & 1 & 1 & 1 & 1 & 1 & 1 & 1 & 1 & 1
\end{pmatrix}
\cdot
\begin{pmatrix}
1 \\ 1 \\ 0 \\ 1 \\ 0 \\ 1 \\ 0 \\ 1 \\ 0 \\ 0 \\ 1 \\ 0 \\ 1 \\ 0 \\ 1 \\ 0
\end{pmatrix}
=
\begin{pmatrix}
1 \\ 0 \\ 1 \\ 1 \\ 1 \\ 1 \\ 1 \\ 1 \\ 1 \\ 0 \\ 0 \\ 0 \\ 0 \\ 0 \\ 0 \\ 0
\end{pmatrix}
$$

and the function is

$$f(x_4, x_3, x_2, x_1) = \pi_0 \oplus \pi_2 \oplus \pi_3 \oplus \pi_4 \oplus \pi_5 \oplus \pi_6 \oplus \pi_7 \oplus \pi_8$$
$$= 1 \oplus x_2 \oplus x_2 x_1 \oplus x_3 \oplus x_3 x_1 \oplus x_3 x_2 \oplus x_3 x_2 x_1 \oplus x_4$$

It is not always convenient to employ the full matrix multiplication to compute the transform and there are a number of ways of speeding up this process and reducing the computational task. One method which is suitable for manual transformation of small problems involving up to, say, six variables, relies on the transformation of each minterm or piterm of the function taken individually. We can then combine these to form the complete transform. This technique is therefore particularly useful for sparse functions. To understand the process we begin by deriving the expansion of each possible minterm for, say, four variables. We find that

$$m_{15} = x_4 x_3 x_2 x_1 = \pi_{15}$$
$$m_{14} = x_4 x_3 x_2 \bar{x}_1 = x_4 x_3 x_2 (x_1 \oplus 1) = x_4 x_3 x_2 \oplus x_4 x_3 x_2 x_1 = \pi_{14} \oplus \pi_{15}$$

and similarly

$$m_{13} = \pi_{13} \oplus \pi_{15}$$
$$m_{12} = \pi_{12} \oplus \pi_{13} \oplus \pi_{14} \oplus \pi_{15}$$
$$m_{11} = \pi_{11} \oplus \pi_{15}$$
$$m_{10} = \pi_{10} \oplus \pi_{11} \oplus \pi_{14} \oplus \pi_{15}$$
$$m_9 = \pi_9 \oplus \pi_{11} \oplus \pi_{13} \oplus \pi_{15}$$
$$m_8 = \pi_8 \oplus \pi_9 \oplus \pi_{10} \oplus \pi_{11} \oplus \pi_{12} \oplus \pi_{13} \oplus \pi_{14} \oplus \pi_{15}$$
$$m_7 = \pi_7 \oplus \pi_{15}$$
$$m_6 = \pi_6 \oplus \pi_7 \oplus \pi_{14} \oplus \pi_{15}$$
$$m_5 = \pi_5 \oplus \pi_7 \oplus \pi_{13} \oplus \pi_{15}$$
$$m_4 = \pi_4 \oplus \pi_5 \oplus \pi_6 \oplus \pi_7 \oplus \pi_{12} \oplus \pi_{13} \oplus \pi_{14} \oplus \pi_{15}$$
$$m_3 = \pi_3 \oplus \pi_7 \oplus \pi_{11} \oplus \pi_{15}$$
$$m_2 = \pi_2 \oplus \pi_3 \oplus \pi_6 \oplus \pi_7 \oplus \pi_{10} \oplus \pi_{11} \oplus \pi_{14} \oplus \pi_{15}$$
$$m_1 = \pi_1 \oplus \pi_3 \oplus \pi_5 \oplus \pi_7 \oplus \pi_9 \oplus \pi_{11} \oplus \pi_{13} \oplus \pi_{15}$$
$$m_0 = \pi_0 \oplus \pi_1 \oplus \pi_2 \oplus \pi_3 \oplus \pi_4 \oplus \pi_5 \oplus \pi_6 \oplus \pi_7 \oplus \pi_8 \oplus \pi_9 \oplus \pi_{10} \oplus \pi_{11} \oplus \pi_{12} \oplus$$
$$\pi_{13} \oplus \pi_{14} \oplus \pi_{15}$$

As the inverse transform is identical we can immediately rewrite these equations to relate each piterm as a combination of minterms. If we plot the transform of each minterm (or piterm) on a piterm (or minterm) map we obtain the structures of Fig. 5.4. We observe that the transform of m_i (π_i) consists of all the piterms (minterms) included in the smallest group of 1, 2, 4, 8, etc., adjacent cells which also includes both π_i (m_i) and π_{15} (m_{15}). We can transform each minterm (piterm) of the function by using an intermediate map to

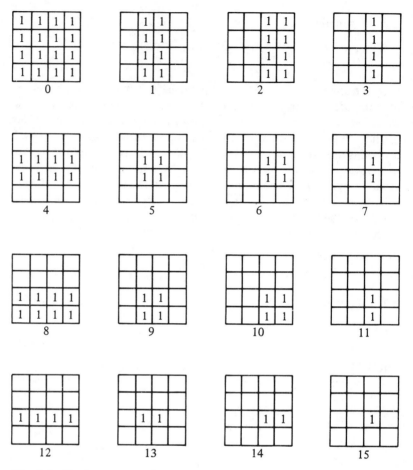

Fig. 5.4 Single-term transforms for $n = 4$.

record the number of occurrences of each piterm (minterm) in the transformed function. To transform m_i (π_i) we write a 1 in the cells corresponding to π_i (m_i) and π_{15} (m_{15}). We also write a 1 in every cell inside the smallest group of 2, 4, 8, etc., adjacent cells containing both of the first two cells. When all minterms (piterms) of the function have been transformed in this way we then count up the number of occurrences of each piterm (minterm) on the intermediate map. Cells holding an even number of marks will resolve to zero as these terms will disappear from the function and so a 0 is recorded in these positions on the final map. Cells which have an odd number of marks resolve to just one occurrence of these terms and a 1 is entered in the corresponding positions of the final map. Fig. 5.5 illustrates this procedure for the previous example.

Another simple method for performing these transforms follows

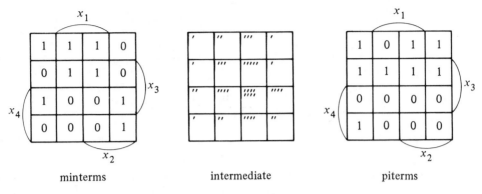

minterms   intermediate   piterms

Fig. 5.5   Transform by combining single-term transforms.

from the triangular structure of the transform matrix. We can construct another triangular array rather in the manner of an inverted
Pascal triangle as depicted in Fig. 5.6. We begin by listing the 2^n
coefficients (in this case $n = 3$) in sequence along the first row of the
array. The next row is formed by taking the pairwise modulo-2 sum
of the coefficients immediately above. This is repeated for each row
of the array until only one value is left. On inspection of the
complete triangle we observe that the left-most element of each row
is computed in exactly the same way as the corresponding coefficient
of the transformed function. Fig. 5.7 illustrates this process for an
example function.

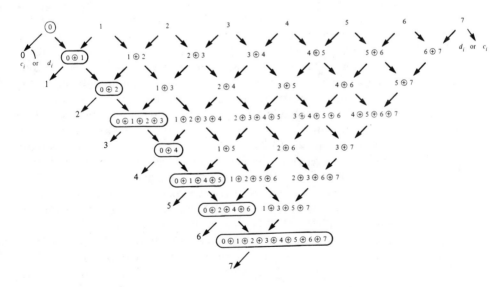

Fig. 5.6   Triangular transform method.

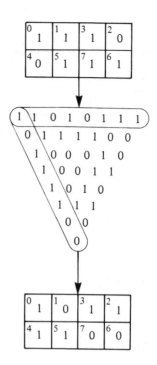

Fig. 5.7 Example of a triangular transform method.

5.4 GENERALIZED REED–MULLER EXPANSIONS

The Reed–Muller expansion as defined previously represents a modulo-2 sum-of-products canonical form of expression. However, this is not the only possible form. In fact, we may substitute for any x_i its complement $\bar{x}_i$ and still retain a canonical form. As there are n variables we have 2^n possible substitutions giving rise to an equal number of possible expansions. These are termed the generalized Reed–Muller (GRM) expansions and each one may be identified by means of a *polarity* number. This number is computed by taking the decimal equivalent of the n-bit binary number formed by writing a 0 or a 1 for each variable according to whether it is employed in true or complemented form respectively. The original RM expansion can therefore be regarded as the GRM expansion with zero polarity because it employs uncomplemented variables throughout. It may also be referred to as the positive RM expansion.

One way to derive these GRM expansions would be to set up individual transforms for each polarity to act on the operational domain coefficients. However, it is more useful to regard each polarity expansion as a further transformation on the zero polarity expansion. The latter can be regarded as an identity transform on the RM expansion. Thus, when expanding a GRM form with a set of coefficients c_i, using a particular polarity, the terms $\bar{x}_i$ can be replaced by $x_i \oplus 1$ and multiplied out to produce another RM form without complemented variables, but with a different set of coefficients a_i. The a_i can then be regarded as a transform on the c_i.

For example, when $n = 1$ we can write the GRM form as

$$f(\dot{x}_1) = c_0 \oplus c_1 \dot{x}_1$$

where $\dot{x}_1$ is either x_1 or $\bar{x}_1$ but not both. Let $\dot{x}_1 = x_1$, thus

$$f(\dot{x}_1) = c_0 \oplus c_1 x_1$$
$$= a_0 \oplus a_1 x_1$$

where $a_0 = c_0$, $a_1 = c_1$, so that the zero polarity GRM expansion is an identity transform on the original form:

$$\begin{bmatrix} a_0 \\ a_1 \end{bmatrix} = \begin{bmatrix} 1 & 0 \\ 0 & 1 \end{bmatrix} \begin{bmatrix} c_0 \\ c_1 \end{bmatrix}$$

or

$$a = Z_0 c$$

Now, if $\dot{x}_1 = \bar{x}_1 = x_1 \oplus 1$

$$f(\dot{x}_1) = c_0 \oplus c_1 \bar{x}_1$$
$$= c_0 \oplus c_1(x_1 \oplus 1) = c_0 \oplus c_1 \oplus c_1 x_1$$
$$= a_0 \oplus a_1 x_1$$

and a_0, a_1 are related to c_0 and c_1 by the transform process:

$$\begin{bmatrix} a_0 \\ a_1 \end{bmatrix} = \begin{bmatrix} 1 & 1 \\ 0 & 1 \end{bmatrix} \begin{bmatrix} c_0 \\ c_1 \end{bmatrix}$$

or

$$a = Z_1 c$$

which can be regarded as a transform Z_1 on the zero polarity form c. Next, consider $n = 2$, where there are now four cases.

1. $\dot{x}_2 \rightarrow x_2$; $\dot{x}_1 \rightarrow x_1$, i.e. polarity $= 0$
$$f(\dot{x}_2, \dot{x}_1) = f(x_2, x_1) = c_0 \oplus c_1 x_1 \oplus c_2 x_2 \oplus c_3 x_2 x_1$$
$$= a_0 \oplus a_1 x_1 \oplus a_2 x_2 \oplus a_3 x_2 x_1$$

2. $\dot{x}_2 \rightarrow x_2$; $\dot{x}_1 \rightarrow \bar{x}_1$, i.e. polarity $= 1$
$$f(\dot{x}_2, \dot{x}_1) = f(x_2, \bar{x}_1) = c_0 \oplus c_1 \bar{x}_1 \oplus c_2 x_2 \oplus c_3 x_2 \bar{x}_1$$
$$= c_0 \oplus c_1(x_1 \oplus 1) \oplus c_2 x_2 \oplus c_3 x_2(x_1 \oplus 1)$$
$$= (c_0 \oplus c_1) \oplus c_1 x_1 \oplus (c_2 \oplus c_3) x_2 \oplus c_3 x_2 x_1$$
$$= a_0 \oplus a_1 x_1 \oplus a_2 x_2 \oplus a_3 x_2 x_1$$

3. $\dot{x}_2 \to \bar{x}_2$; $\dot{x}_1 \to x_1$, i.e. polarity $= 2$

$$\begin{aligned}
f(\dot{x}_2, \dot{x}_1) = f(\bar{x}_2, x_1) &= c_0 \oplus c_1 x_1 \oplus c_2 \bar{x}_2 \oplus c_3 \bar{x}_2 x_1 \\
&= (c_0 \oplus c_2) \oplus (c_1 \oplus c_3) x_1 \oplus c_2 x_2 \oplus c_3 x_2 x_1 \\
&= a_0 \oplus a_1 x_1 \oplus a_2 x_2 \oplus a_3 x_2 x_1
\end{aligned}$$

4. $\dot{x}_2 \to \bar{x}_2$; $\dot{x}_1 \to \bar{x}_1$, i.e. polarity $= 3$

$$\begin{aligned}
f(\dot{x}_2, \dot{x}_1) = f(\bar{x}_2, \bar{x}_1) &= c_0 \oplus c_1 \bar{x}_1 \oplus c_2 \bar{x}_2 \oplus c_3 \bar{x}_2 \bar{x}_1 \\
&= (c_0 \oplus c_1 \oplus c_2 \oplus c_3) \oplus (c_1 \oplus c_3) x_1 \\
&\quad \oplus (c_2 \oplus c_3) x_2 \oplus c_3 x_2 x_1 \\
&= a_0 \oplus a_1 x_1 \oplus a_2 x_2 \oplus a_3 x_2 x_1
\end{aligned}$$

The coefficients a_i are of course different in each case and we can devise a transform matrix to relate them to the coefficients c_i.

1. $P = 0$

$$Z_{00} = \begin{pmatrix} 1 & 0 & 0 & 0 \\ 0 & 1 & 0 & 0 \\ 0 & 0 & 1 & 0 \\ 0 & 0 & 0 & 1 \end{pmatrix} = \begin{pmatrix} Z_0 & 0 \\ 0 & Z_0 \end{pmatrix}$$

2. $P = 1$

$$Z_{01} = \begin{pmatrix} 1 & 1 & 0 & 0 \\ 0 & 1 & 0 & 0 \\ 0 & 0 & 1 & 1 \\ 0 & 0 & 0 & 1 \end{pmatrix} = \begin{pmatrix} Z_1 & 0 \\ 0 & Z_1 \end{pmatrix}$$

3. $P = 2$

$$Z_{10} = \begin{pmatrix} 1 & 0 & 1 & 0 \\ 0 & 1 & 0 & 1 \\ 0 & 0 & 1 & 0 \\ 0 & 0 & 0 & 1 \end{pmatrix} = \begin{pmatrix} Z_0 & Z_0 \\ 0 & Z_0 \end{pmatrix}$$

4. $P = 3$

$$Z_{11} = \begin{pmatrix} 1 & 1 & 1 & 1 \\ 0 & 1 & 0 & 1 \\ 0 & 0 & 1 & 1 \\ 0 & 0 & 0 & 1 \end{pmatrix} = \begin{pmatrix} Z_1 & Z_1 \\ 0 & Z_1 \end{pmatrix}$$

We observe that in each case these matrices may be partitioned into combinations of the one-variable transforms Z_0 and Z_1.

Now, the Krönecker product of two matrices, A, B, where

$$A = \begin{pmatrix} a_{11} & a_{12} \dots a_{1q} \\ a_{21} & a_{22} \dots a_{2q} \\ \cdot & \cdot \quad \cdot \\ \cdot & \cdot \quad \cdot \\ \cdot & \cdot \quad \cdot \\ a_{p1} & a_{p2} \dots a_{pq} \end{pmatrix} \quad \text{and} \quad B = \begin{pmatrix} b_{11} & b_{12} \dots b_{1s} \\ b_{21} & b_{22} \dots b_{2s} \\ \cdot & \cdot \quad \cdot \\ \cdot & \cdot \quad \cdot \\ \cdot & \cdot \quad \cdot \\ b_{r1} & b_{r2} \dots b_{rs} \end{pmatrix}$$

Reed–Muller Algebraic Descriptions **145**

is defined as $A*B$ and

$$A*B = \begin{bmatrix} a_{11}[B] & a_{12}[B] \ldots a_{1q}[B] \\ a_{21}[B] & a_{22}[B] \ldots a_{2q}[B] \\ \cdot & \cdot & \cdot \\ \cdot & \cdot & \cdot \\ \cdot & \cdot & \cdot \\ a_{p1}[B] & a_{p2}[B] \ldots a_{pq}[B] \end{bmatrix}$$

Thus, if A is a $(p \times q)$ matrix and B is an $(r \times s)$ matrix, then $A*B$ will have dimension $(pr \times qs)$. The $*$ operation is associative but not commutative. That is,

$$A*(B*C) = (A*B)*C = A*B*C$$
$$A*B \neq B*A$$

This operation is useful for describing the recursive matrix formations encountered in this regime. For example, the basic inter-domain transform T_n can be described in terms of the Krönecker product as

$$T_n = T_1*T_{n-1} = T_1*T_1*T_{n-2}$$
$$= T_1*T_1*\ldots*T_1 \quad n \text{ times}$$

and similarly for S_n. In the case of the GRM transform matrices derived earlier we find

$$Z_{00} = Z_0*Z_0$$
$$Z_{01} = Z_0*Z_1$$
$$Z_{10} = Z_1*Z_0$$
$$Z_{11} = Z_1*Z_1$$

This result generalizes to n variables, so that for polarity $P = i$

$$Z_{e_n e_{n-1} \ldots e_1} = Z_{\langle i \rangle} = Z_{e_n}*Z_{e_{n-1}}*\ldots*Z_{e_1}$$

where $e_i = 0$ or 1, and the decimal equivalent of $e_n e_{n-1} \ldots e_1 = i$. Thus,

$$Z_{e_j} = Z_0 \text{ or } Z_1$$

is the modification to x_j.

As an example, suppose $n = 4$ and we wish to deduce the GRM expansion of polarity 13. We require to set up the transform matrix $Z_{\langle 13 \rangle} = Z_{1101}$ where

$$Z_{1101} = Z_1 * Z_1 * Z_0 * Z_1$$
$$= \begin{bmatrix} 1 & 1 \\ 0 & 1 \end{bmatrix} * \begin{bmatrix} 1 & 1 \\ 0 & 1 \end{bmatrix} * \begin{bmatrix} 1 & 0 \\ 0 & 1 \end{bmatrix} * \begin{bmatrix} 1 & 1 \\ 0 & 1 \end{bmatrix}$$

$$= \begin{bmatrix} 1 & 1 \\ 0 & 1 \end{bmatrix} * \begin{bmatrix} 1 & 1 \\ 0 & 1 \end{bmatrix} * \begin{bmatrix} 1 & 1 & 0 & 0 \\ 0 & 1 & 0 & 0 \\ 0 & 0 & 1 & 1 \\ 0 & 0 & 0 & 1 \end{bmatrix}$$

$$= \begin{bmatrix} 1 & 1 \\ 0 & 1 \end{bmatrix} * \begin{bmatrix} 1 & 1 & 0 & 0 & 1 & 1 & 0 & 0 \\ 0 & 1 & 0 & 0 & 0 & 1 & 0 & 0 \\ 0 & 0 & 1 & 1 & 0 & 0 & 1 & 1 \\ 0 & 0 & 0 & 1 & 0 & 0 & 0 & 1 \\ 0 & 0 & 0 & 0 & 1 & 1 & 0 & 0 \\ 0 & 0 & 0 & 0 & 0 & 1 & 0 & 0 \\ 0 & 0 & 0 & 0 & 0 & 0 & 1 & 1 \\ 0 & 0 & 0 & 0 & 0 & 0 & 0 & 1 \end{bmatrix}$$

$$Z_{\langle 13 \rangle} = \begin{bmatrix}
1 & 1 & 0 & 0 & 1 & 1 & 0 & 0 & 1 & 1 & 0 & 0 & 1 & 1 & 0 & 0 \\
0 & 1 & 0 & 0 & 0 & 1 & 0 & 0 & 0 & 1 & 0 & 0 & 0 & 1 & 0 & 0 \\
0 & 0 & 1 & 1 & 0 & 0 & 1 & 1 & 0 & 0 & 1 & 1 & 0 & 0 & 1 & 1 \\
0 & 0 & 0 & 1 & 0 & 0 & 0 & 1 & 0 & 0 & 0 & 1 & 0 & 0 & 0 & 1 \\
0 & 0 & 0 & 0 & 1 & 1 & 0 & 0 & 0 & 0 & 0 & 0 & 1 & 1 & 0 & 0 \\
0 & 0 & 0 & 0 & 0 & 1 & 0 & 0 & 0 & 0 & 0 & 0 & 0 & 1 & 0 & 0 \\
0 & 0 & 0 & 0 & 0 & 0 & 1 & 1 & 0 & 0 & 0 & 0 & 0 & 0 & 1 & 1 \\
0 & 0 & 0 & 0 & 0 & 0 & 0 & 1 & 0 & 0 & 0 & 0 & 0 & 0 & 0 & 1 \\
0 & 0 & 0 & 0 & 0 & 0 & 0 & 0 & 1 & 1 & 0 & 0 & 1 & 1 & 0 & 0 \\
0 & 0 & 0 & 0 & 0 & 0 & 0 & 0 & 0 & 1 & 0 & 0 & 0 & 1 & 0 & 0 \\
0 & 0 & 0 & 0 & 0 & 0 & 0 & 0 & 0 & 0 & 1 & 1 & 0 & 0 & 1 & 1 \\
0 & 0 & 0 & 0 & 0 & 0 & 0 & 0 & 0 & 0 & 0 & 1 & 0 & 0 & 0 & 1 \\
0 & 0 & 0 & 0 & 0 & 0 & 0 & 0 & 0 & 0 & 0 & 0 & 1 & 1 & 0 & 0 \\
0 & 0 & 0 & 0 & 0 & 0 & 0 & 0 & 0 & 0 & 0 & 0 & 0 & 1 & 0 & 0 \\
0 & 0 & 0 & 0 & 0 & 0 & 0 & 0 & 0 & 0 & 0 & 0 & 0 & 0 & 1 & 1 \\
0 & 0 & 0 & 0 & 0 & 0 & 0 & 0 & 0 & 0 & 0 & 0 & 0 & 0 & 0 & 1
\end{bmatrix}$$

and the corresponding polarity expansion is found from the relationship

$$a = Z_{\langle 13 \rangle} \cdot c$$

where c is the column vector comprising the coefficients of the GRM of polarity zero. For example, consider the function of Fig. 5.3b. When we use this to form the column vectors c, we obtain

$$f(\bar{x}_4, \bar{x}_3, x_2, \bar{x}_1) = \bar{x}_1 \oplus \bar{x}_3 \bar{x}_1 \oplus \bar{x}_3 x_2 \bar{x}_1 \oplus \bar{x}_4$$

as the GRM expansion of polarity $P = 13$. This will have the same operational behaviour as the zero polarity expansion in terms of the original input variables. This polarity expansion is clearly a simpler expression than the original even when the extra cost of inverting three of the input variables is taken into account. This points the way to the consideration of design and simplification techniques for this Reed–Muller regime.

5.5 DESIGN METHODS

Unfortunately, there is no counterpart of the Boolean reduction formulae $ab + a\bar{b} = a$, or $a\bar{b} + b = a + b$, available in this modulo-2 regime. Simplification of expressions is therefore not possible by this means. The only direct form of simplification is that which may result from algebraic factorization. However, this can only be performed on certain functions and at the expense of increasing the number of levels. For example, the circuit of Fig. 5.8a corresponds to the direct implementation of the previous example of a four-variable function. That is,

$$f(x_4, x_3, x_2, x_1) = 1 \oplus x_2 \oplus x_2 x_1 \oplus x_3 \oplus x_3 x_1 \oplus x_3 x_2 \oplus x_3 x_2 x_1 \oplus x_4$$

which can be factorized as follows:

$$f(x_4, x_3, x_2, x_1) = 1 \oplus x_2(1 \oplus x_1) \oplus x_3(1 \oplus x_1) \oplus x_3 x_2(1 \oplus x_1) \oplus x_4$$
$$= 1 \oplus (1 \oplus x_1)(x_2 \oplus x_3 \oplus x_3 x_2) \oplus x_4$$

and this can be synthesized as in Fig. 5.8b.

A more systematic procedure is required to enable any arbitrary function to be simplified. One such method arises from the use of GRM expansions and the employment of the most 'economic' polarity expansion. The problem of predicting the optimum polarity

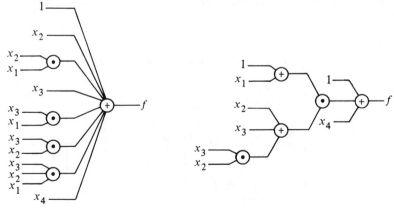

(a) two-level representation   (b) factorized multi-level representation

Fig. 5.8 Simplification by factorization.

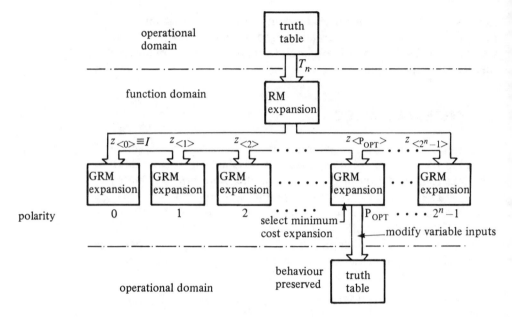

Fig. 5.9   Outline of a simplification process based on GRM transforms.

for a given function remains unsolved and some form of search procedure is required. However, for small values of n it is possible to test all possible polarities together with some cost function in order to locate the best form. The technique is outlined in Fig. 5.9. A given truth table behaviour is used to define the operational domain coefficients which are then transformed into the function domain by the appropriate matrix. This is then used to form all

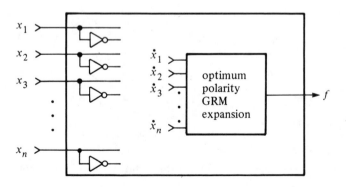

Fig. 5.10   Preserving original behaviour by inverting selected inputs.

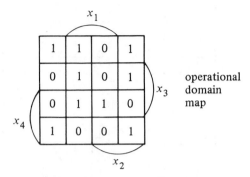

Fig. 5:11 Example function for GRM search technique.

other polarity GRM transforms and from these the optimum according to some cost function is selected. This function is then implemented together with extra inverters to modify the input variables in order to re-establish the original truth table behaviour as indicated in Fig. 5.10. As an example, consider the function defined by the operational domain map of Fig. 5.11. The 16 possible GRM expansions are given in Fig. 5.12.

The zero polarity expansion is obtained by transforming the operational domain map with T_4. Thus, for $P = 0$, we have

$$f(x_4, x_3, x_2, x_1) = 1 \oplus x_2 x_1 \oplus x_3 \oplus x_3 x_1 \oplus x_3 x_2 \oplus x_3 x_2 x_1 \oplus x_4 x_1 \oplus x_4 x_2 x_1$$
$$\oplus x_4 x_3 x_1 \oplus x_4 x_3 x_2 \oplus x_4 x_3 x_2 x_1$$

The remaining polarity expansion can be deduced by transforming this function with the appropriate matrices $Z_{\langle 1 \rangle}, Z_{\langle 2 \rangle}, \ldots, Z_{\langle 2^n - 1 \rangle}$.

The selection of the optimum polarity expansion is highly dependent on the choice of costing function. The costings shown in Fig. 5.12 are based on the assumption that synthesis is made by using just three types of circuit element:

1. the inverter   1 cost unit
2. the two-input adder   3 cost units
3. the two-input multiplier 2 cost units

Direct synthesis of the zero polarity expansion requires 10 adders, 15 multipliers and no inverters, giving a total cost of 60 units. The optimum cost polarity occurs when $P = 11$ or 15. The polarity 11 expansion requires 5 adders, 7 multipliers and 3 inverters giving a total cost of 32. The corresponding expansion is

$$f(\bar{x}_4, x_3, \bar{x}_2, \bar{x}_1) = \bar{x}_1 \oplus x_3 \oplus \bar{x}_4 \bar{x}_2 \oplus \bar{x}_4 \bar{x}_2 \bar{x}_1 \oplus \bar{x}_4 x_3 \oplus \bar{x}_4 x_3 \bar{x}_2 \bar{x}_1$$

$P = 0; C = 60$ $P = 1; C = 62$ $P = 2; C = 49$ $P = 3; C = 43$

$P = 4; C = 52$ $P = 5; C = 46$ $P = 6; C = 49$ $P = 7; C = 35$

$P = 8; C = 42$ $P = 9; C = 44$ $P = 10; C = 36$ $P = 11; C = 32$

$P = 12; C = 33$ $P = 13; C = 35$ $P = 14; C = 35$ $P = 15; C = 32$

Fig. 5.12   16 GRM expansions of the function of Fig. 5.11. P = polarity, C = cost.

Other costing functions allied to alternative forms of synthesis may yield a different choice of optimum polarity.

It is clearly inconvenient to perform an exhaustive search through all polarity transforms by building each individual transform by the Krönecker product process and then performing the matrix product. Inspection of the four transforms for the case $n = 2$ reveals the following relationships:

$$Z_{\langle 1 \rangle} . Z_{\langle 2 \rangle} = Z_{01} . Z_{10} = \begin{bmatrix} 1 & 1 & 0 & 0 \\ 0 & 1 & 0 & 0 \\ 0 & 0 & 1 & 1 \\ 0 & 0 & 0 & 1 \end{bmatrix} . \begin{bmatrix} 1 & 0 & 1 & 0 \\ 0 & 1 & 0 & 1 \\ 0 & 0 & 1 & 0 \\ 0 & 0 & 0 & 1 \end{bmatrix}$$

$$= \begin{bmatrix} 1 & 1 & 1 & 1 \\ 0 & 1 & 0 & 1 \\ 0 & 0 & 1 & 1 \\ 0 & 0 & 0 & 1 \end{bmatrix}$$

$$= Z_{11} = Z_{\langle 3 \rangle}$$

and we find

$$Z_{01} . Z_{01} = Z_{10} . Z_{10} = Z_{00}$$

and the complete product table is given in Fig. 5.13. We observe that the operation of product formation between any pair of these matrices is commutative. These relationships lead to the general result that

$$Z_{\langle i \rangle} . Z_{\langle j \rangle} = Z_{\langle j \rangle} . Z_{\langle i \rangle} = Z_{\langle k \rangle}$$

and k is derived from the bit-by-bit modulo-2 sum of the binary forms of i and j. This permits us to generate all the transforms by forming the products of a suitable subset. Thus, if we set up all the matrices $Z_{\langle s \rangle}$ for $s = 1, 2, 4$, etc., we can derive the remainder by forming the appropriate products of these basic types. For example, consider the case $n = 3$. We can set up the three basic transforms:

$$Z_{\langle 1 \rangle} = Z_{001} = Z_0 * Z_0 * Z_1$$
$$Z_{\langle 2 \rangle} = Z_{010} = Z_0 * Z_1 * Z_0$$
$$Z_{\langle 4 \rangle} = Z_{100} = Z_1 * Z_0 * Z_0$$

Then the remaining transforms follow from:

$$Z_{\langle 3 \rangle} = Z_{011} = Z_{010} . Z_{001} = Z_{\langle 2 \rangle} . Z_{\langle 1 \rangle}$$
$$Z_{\langle 5 \rangle} = Z_{101} = Z_{100} . Z_{001} = Z_{\langle 4 \rangle} . Z_{\langle 1 \rangle}$$
$$Z_{\langle 6 \rangle} = Z_{110} = Z_{100} . Z_{010} = Z_{\langle 4 \rangle} . Z_{\langle 2 \rangle}$$
$$Z_{\langle 7 \rangle} = Z_{111} = Z_{100} . Z_{010} . Z_{001} = Z_{\langle 4 \rangle} . Z_{\langle 2 \rangle} . Z_{\langle 1 \rangle} = Z_{\langle 6 \rangle} Z_{\langle 1 \rangle}$$

For larger values of n we can always arrange to generate each transform from the previous one with one matrix product provided we follow the Gray code sequence for the polarity numbers. For example, when $n = 4$ we preform $Z_{\langle 1 \rangle}$, $Z_{\langle 2 \rangle}$, $Z_{\langle 4 \rangle}$ and $Z_{\langle 8 \rangle}$. Then

$\cdot$	Z_{00}	Z_{01}	Z_{10}	Z_{11}
Z_{00}	Z_{00}	Z_{01}	Z_{10}	Z_{11}
Z_{01}	Z_{01}	Z_{00}	Z_{11}	Z_{10}
Z_{10}	Z_{10}	Z_{11}	Z_{00}	Z_{01}
Z_{11}	Z_{11}	Z_{10}	Z_{01}	Z_{00}

Fig. 5.13   Relationship between the GRM transform matrices.

$$Z_{\langle 0 \rangle} = Z_{0000} = \text{identity matrix}$$
$$Z_{\langle 1 \rangle} = Z_{0001} = Z_{\langle 0 \rangle} \cdot Z_{\langle 1 \rangle} \quad (\text{or } Z_{\langle 1 \rangle} = Z_0 * Z_0 * Z_0 * Z_1)$$
$$Z_{\langle 3 \rangle} = Z_{0011} = Z_{\langle 1 \rangle} \cdot Z_{\langle 2 \rangle}$$
$$Z_{\langle 2 \rangle} = Z_{0010} = Z_{\langle 3 \rangle} \cdot Z_{\langle 1 \rangle} \quad (\text{or } Z_{\langle 2 \rangle} = Z_0 * Z_0 * Z_1 * Z_0)$$
$$Z_{\langle 6 \rangle} = Z_{0110} = Z_{\langle 2 \rangle} \cdot Z_{\langle 4 \rangle}$$
$$Z_{\langle 7 \rangle} = Z_{0111} = Z_{\langle 6 \rangle} \cdot Z_{\langle 1 \rangle}$$
$$Z_{\langle 5 \rangle} = Z_{0101} = Z_{\langle 7 \rangle} \cdot Z_{\langle 2 \rangle}$$
$$Z_{\langle 4 \rangle} = Z_{0100} = Z_{\langle 5 \rangle} \cdot Z_{\langle 1 \rangle} \quad (\text{or } Z_{\langle 4 \rangle} = Z_0 * Z_1 * Z_0 * Z_0)$$
$$Z_{\langle 12 \rangle} = Z_{1100} = Z_{\langle 4 \rangle} \cdot Z_{\langle 8 \rangle}$$
$$Z_{\langle 13 \rangle} = Z_{1101} = Z_{\langle 12 \rangle} \cdot Z_{\langle 1 \rangle}$$
$$Z_{\langle 15 \rangle} = Z_{1111} = Z_{\langle 13 \rangle} \cdot Z_{\langle 2 \rangle}$$
$$Z_{\langle 14 \rangle} = Z_{1110} = Z_{\langle 15 \rangle} \cdot Z_{\langle 1 \rangle}$$
$$Z_{\langle 10 \rangle} = Z_{1010} = Z_{\langle 14 \rangle} \cdot Z_{\langle 4 \rangle}$$
$$Z_{\langle 11 \rangle} = Z_{1011} = Z_{\langle 10 \rangle} \cdot Z_{\langle 1 \rangle}$$
$$Z_{\langle 9 \rangle} = Z_{1001} = Z_{\langle 11 \rangle} \cdot Z_{\langle 2 \rangle}$$
$$Z_{\langle 8 \rangle} = Z_{1000} = Z_{\langle 9 \rangle} \cdot Z_{\langle 1 \rangle} \quad (\text{or } Z_{\langle 8 \rangle} = Z_1 * Z_0 * Z_0 * Z_0)$$

These relationships mean that we can also generate the GRM forms in sequence. If c_i, $0 < i < 2^n - 1$, represents the coefficients of the polarity $P = i$ expansion then we can generate the following sequence of forms beginning with c_0:

$$c_0$$

$c_1 = Z_{\langle 1 \rangle} \cdot c_0$	$c_3 = Z_{\langle 2 \rangle} \cdot c_1$	$c_2 = Z_{\langle 1 \rangle} \cdot c_3$
$c_6 = Z_{\langle 4 \rangle} \cdot c_2$	$c_7 = Z_{\langle 1 \rangle} \cdot c_6$	$c_5 = Z_{\langle 2 \rangle} \cdot c_7$
$c_4 = Z_{\langle 1 \rangle} \cdot c_5$	$c_{12} = Z_{\langle 8 \rangle} \cdot c_4$	$c_{13} = Z_{\langle 1 \rangle} \cdot c_{12}$
$c_{15} = Z_{\langle 2 \rangle} \cdot c_{13}$	$c_{14} = Z_{\langle 1 \rangle} \cdot c_{15}$	$c_{10} = Z_{\langle 4 \rangle} \cdot c_{14}$
$c_{11} = Z_{\langle 1 \rangle} \cdot c_{10}$	$c_9 = Z_{\langle 2 \rangle} \cdot c_{11}$	$c_8 = Z_{\langle 1 \rangle} \cdot c_9$

In fact, the process can be speeded up even more because all these matrices are triangular and most of the products in the matrix product process involve zeros and need not be carried out. If we restrict our attention to the $n = 3$ case again, we note that the three fundamental transforms $Z_{\langle 1 \rangle}$, $Z_{\langle 2 \rangle}$ and $Z_{\langle 4 \rangle}$ performed on the coefficients of c give the following:

$$a = Z_{\langle 1 \rangle} \cdot c \quad \text{or} \quad a = Z_{\langle 2 \rangle} \cdot c \quad \text{or} \quad a = Z_{\langle 4 \rangle} \cdot c$$

where

$$a_0 = c_0 \oplus c_1 \quad \text{or} \quad a_0 = c_0 \oplus c_2 \quad \text{or} \quad a_0 = c_0 \oplus c_4$$
$$a_1 = c_1 \qquad\qquad\quad a_1 = c_1 \oplus c_3 \qquad\quad a_1 = c_1 \oplus c_5$$
$$a_2 = c_2 \oplus c_3 \qquad\quad a_2 = c_2 \qquad\qquad\quad a_2 = c_2 \oplus c_6$$

$$a_3 = c_3 \qquad\qquad a_3 = c_3 \qquad\qquad a_3 = c_3 \oplus c_7$$
$$a_4 = c_4 \oplus c_5 \qquad a_4 = c_4 \oplus c_6 \qquad a_4 = c_4$$
$$a_5 = c_5 \qquad\qquad a_5 = c_5 \oplus c_7 \qquad a_5 = c_5$$
$$a_6 = c_6 \oplus c_7 \qquad a_6 = c_6 \qquad\qquad a_6 = c_6$$
$$a_7 = c_7 \qquad\qquad a_7 = c_7 \qquad\qquad a_7 = c_7$$

Fig. 5.14 demonstrates how these three processes can be regarded as three types of manipulation on the set of coefficients and can be performed by a simple algorithm or, indeed, circuit. By performing a sequence of these manipulations on the set of coefficients representing the zero polarity expansion, we can generate each GRM form in turn but in Gray code order as indicated previously. Fig. 5.15 illustrates the complete process for the three-variable case.

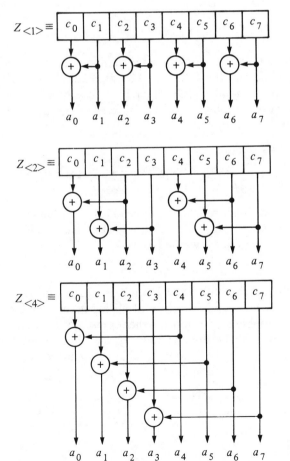

Fig. 5.14 The three fundamental transforms for three variables.

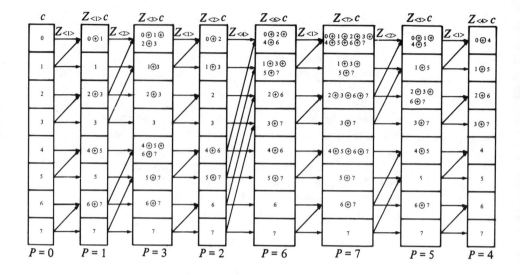

As an alternative to, or in combination with, the direct factorization method and the GRM method of circuit design, synthesis by means of the general multilevel circuit tree may prove more attractive than in the Boolean case. We have seen that the RM canonical forms can be written as

$$F_1 = c_0 \oplus c_1 x_1$$
$$F_2 = c_0 \oplus c_1 x_1 \oplus c_2 x_2 \oplus c_3 x_2 x_1 = (c_0 \oplus c_1 x_1) \oplus (c_2 \oplus c_3 x_1) x_2$$
$$= F_1 \oplus F_1^* . x_2$$

where F_1 and F_2 are functions of one and two variables respectively, and F_1^* is similar in structure to F_1 but has a different set of coefficients. In general we find

$$F_n = F_{n-1} \oplus F_{n-1}^* . x_n$$

F_{n-1} and F_{n-1}^* can both be replaced by similar expressions involving F_{n-2}, F_{n-2}^*, etc., and so on, until all inputs are coefficients. The basic one-variable expression and the representation of the n-variable function can both be implemented by the same circuit module, as illustrated in Fig. 5.16. The n-variable case can be expanded using

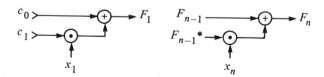

Fig. 5.16 One-variable circuit module.

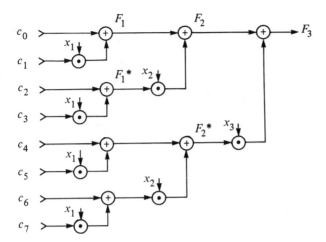

Fig. 5.17 Three-variable circuit tree.

similar modules to produce the tree structure given in Fig. 5.17 for the case $n = 3$. This structure has the universal property in that it can mechanize any RM (or GRM) expansion of three variables by applying the appropriate function domain coefficients to the inputs. However, for a particular function, some of the individual gates may be redundant and may be removed from the structure without affecting the operation. For example, it will always be possible to remove the set of modules at the inputs and replace them with the residue functions of the first variable. Consider any one of these first modules. The four possible combinations of input values are shown in Fig. 5.18. In each case the output is a trivial residue function and the complete module can be eliminated. This elimination process can sometimes be extended further into the tree structure and the technique represents a straightforward method for obtaining a multilevel synthesis directly from the function domain description. Fig. 5.19a defines the function domain map for a three-variable function. Fig. 5.19b shows the synthesis procedure based on the general three-variable tree. The final representation, after elimination of redundant gates, is depicted in Fig. 5.19c. As in the

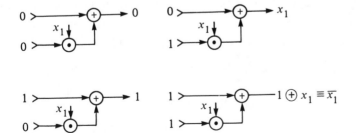

Fig. 5.18 Four basic configurations of a one-variable module.

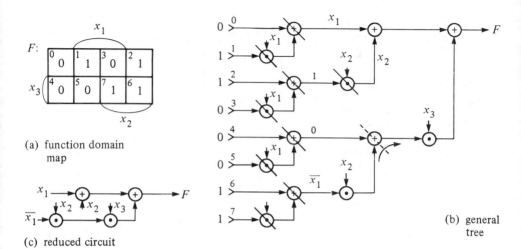

(a) function domain map

(c) reduced circuit

(b) general tree

Fig. 5.19 Demonstration of tree-circuit simplification and synthesis.

Boolean case, this type of universal structure leads on to the consideration of multiplexer-type implementations. The Reed–Muller expansion equivalent of a 4:1 MUX employed as a ULM could be defined as in Fig. 5.20. Note that the data inputs are the function domain coefficients and not those of the operational domain. This structure can directly synthesize any RM expression of two variables. As x_1 and x_2 take on their four possible combinations of values, the output follows the operational domain behaviour of the function. Thus, when

$$x_2 = 0 \text{ and } x_1 = 0 \quad \text{then} \quad F_2 = c_0 = d_0$$
$$x_2 = 0 \text{ and } x_1 = 1 \quad \qquad F_2 = c_0 \oplus c_1 = d_1$$
$$x_2 = 1 \text{ and } x_1 = 0 \quad \qquad F_2 = c_0 \oplus c_2 = d_2$$
$$x_2 = 1 \text{ and } x_1 = 1 \quad \qquad F_2 = c_0 \oplus c_1 \oplus c_2 \oplus c_3 = d_3$$

However, this RM device can also support functions of three variables if we are prepared to employ the residue functions of a third variable rather than the raw coefficients. Thus, the 4:1 RM device can support any function of three variables and is therefore an RM-ULM$_3$. Now,

$$\begin{aligned}
F(x_3, x_2, x_1) &= c_0 \oplus c_1 x_1 \oplus c_2 x_2 \oplus c_3 x_2 x_1 \oplus c_4 x_3 \oplus c_5 x_3 x_1 \\
&\quad \oplus c_6 x_3 x_2 \oplus c_7 x_3 x_2 x_1 \\
&= (c_0 \oplus c_4 x_3) \oplus (c_1 \oplus c_5 x_3) x_1 \oplus (c_2 \oplus c_6 x_3) x_2 \\
&\quad \oplus (c_3 \oplus c_7 x_3) x_2 x_1 \\
&= f_0 \oplus f_1 x_1 \oplus f_2 x_2 \oplus f_3 x_2 x_1
\end{aligned}$$

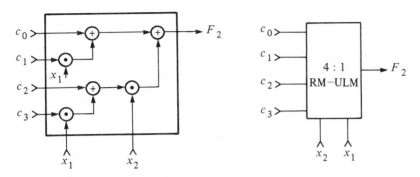

Fig. 5.20   The construction of a Reed–Muller 4:1 selector.

and each of the functions $f_i = c_j \oplus c_k x_3$ resolves to 0, 1, x_3 or $\bar{x}_3$. We could equally well have selected x_2 or x_1 to form the residue functions. In each case the process is equivalent to compressing the function domain map to obtain a lower-order map with map-entered variables. This is an equivalent process to that observed in Chapter 3 for the Boolean regime. However, in the Reed–Muller case the rules for deducing the residues are slightly different. Fig. 5.21 illustrates the process of compressing a three-variable map into a two-variable map with one map-entered variable. The form of the one-variable function dictates that $1 \oplus 1 . x_3$ resolves to $1 \oplus x_3 = \bar{x}_3$ and $1 \oplus 0 . x_3$ resolves to 1 whereas

$$1 . \bar{x}_3 + 1 . x_3 = \bar{x}_3 + x_3 = 1$$

and

$$1 . \bar{x}_3 + 0 . x_3 = \bar{x}_3$$

so the situation is the reverse of the Boolean case. Having derived the compressed maps we can then deduce the inputs to the RM-ULM as indicated in Fig. 5.22. Obviously, the principles can be extended to larger functions and ULMs, and the techniques described

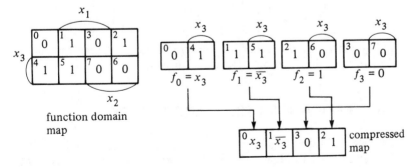

Fig. 5.21   Compressing function domain map with map-entered variables.

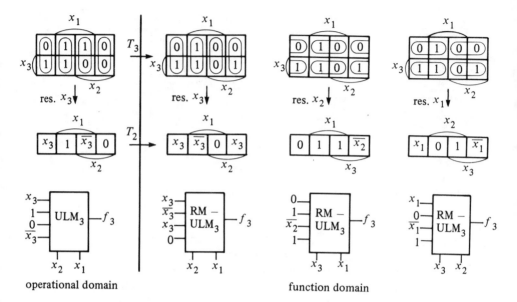

Fig. 5.22 Synthesis by means of Reed–Muller ULMs.

for the Boolean regime have their counterparts here in suitably modified form.

The use of maps with map-entered variables can also speed up the transform processes defined earlier because by compressing the operational domain map by entering one variable we can use a lower-order transform to deduce the function domain map. Thus, instead of transforming the full three-variable operational domain map with T_3 to obtain the full function domain map we can use the reduced map with T_2 to derive the compressed function map. Thus, for the example of Fig. 5.22, we have:

$$\begin{bmatrix} 1 & 0 & 0 & 0 \\ 1 & 1 & 0 & 0 \\ 1 & 0 & 1 & 0 \\ 1 & 1 & 1 & 1 \end{bmatrix} \cdot \begin{bmatrix} x_3 \\ 1 \\ 0 \\ \bar{x}_3 \end{bmatrix} = \begin{bmatrix} x_3 \\ x_3 \oplus 1 \\ x_3 \\ x_3 \oplus 1 \oplus x_3 \oplus 1 \end{bmatrix} = \begin{bmatrix} x_3 \\ \bar{x}_3 \\ x_3 \\ 0 \end{bmatrix}$$

and similarly for the other map-entered forms. We can also adopt similar procedures in the GRM design technique.

5.6 APPLICATIONS TO CODING THEORY

The Reed–Muller algebraic descriptions clearly provide an alternative to the Boolean algebraic approach for the description, design and synthesis of general combinational switching functions.

However, this regime also includes an important subclass of circuits which have a linear property and as such have found application in coding techniques, especially those concerned with group or block codes for error control.

If the switching function is such that its RM expansion does not include any product terms of the primary input variables then the function has a linear property. Thus, a linear function can be implemented using only modulo-2 adders, although it is convenient also to include a scalar or constant multiplier in the general descriptions. As the constant can only be 0 or 1, this latter device is synthesized as an open or closed connection respectively and therefore does not correspond to a circuit device. A general linear expression involving n variables would therefore take the form

$$f(x_n, x_{n-1}, \ldots, x_1) = b_n x_n \oplus b_{n-1} x_{n-1} \oplus \ldots \oplus b_1 x_1 \quad \text{over GF(2)}$$

where $b_i = 0$ or 1. The response to a set of input values $X_i = X_n$, $X_{n-1}, \ldots, X_1$ would be:

$$f(X_n, X_{n-1}, \ldots, X_1) = b_n X_n \oplus b_{n-1} X_{n-1} \oplus \ldots \oplus b_1 X_1$$

and to a different set $Y_i = Y_n$, $Y_{n-1}, \ldots, Y_1$ would be:

$$f(Y_n, Y_{n-1}, \ldots, Y_1) = b_n Y_n \oplus b_{n-1} Y_{n-1} \oplus \ldots \oplus b_1 Y_1$$

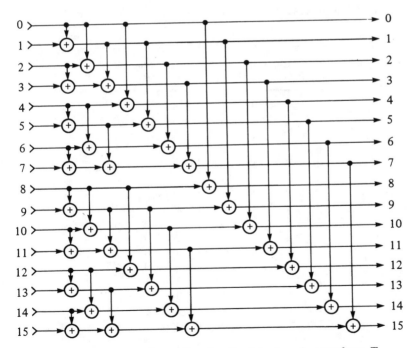

Fig. 5.23 Linear circuit for performing the interdomain transform T_4.

Now consider a third set of inputs $Z_i = Z_n, Z_{n-1}, \ldots, Z_1$ in which $Z_i = X_i \oplus Y_i$; that is, $Z_n = X_n \oplus Y_n$, $Z_{n-1} = X_{n-1} \oplus Y_{n-1}$, etc. The output will be:

$$
\begin{aligned}
f(Z_n, Z_{n-1}, \ldots, Z_1) &= b_n Z_n \oplus b_{n-1} Z_{n-1} \oplus \ldots \oplus b_1 Z_1 \\
&= b_n(X_n \oplus Y_n) \oplus b_{n-1}(X_{n-1} \oplus Y_{n-1}) \oplus \ldots \\
&\quad \oplus b_1(X_1 \oplus Y_1) \\
&= b_n X_n \oplus b_{n-1} X_{n-1} \oplus \ldots \oplus b_1 X_1 \oplus b_n Y_n \\
&\quad \oplus b_{n-1} Y_{n-1} \oplus \ldots \oplus b_1 Y_1 \\
&= f(X_n, X_{n-1}, \ldots, X_1) \oplus f(Y_n, Y_{n-1}, \ldots, Y_1)
\end{aligned}
$$

and the response to a composite input is the sum of the responses to the components taken individually. In other words, superposition holds and the process is linear.

The interdomain transforms T_n can be seen to be examples of linear functions since each coefficient can be expressed as a linear combination of coefficients of the original description. The linear circuit of Fig. 5.23 mechanizes this transform process for four-variable functions. If one set of coefficients is applied to the inputs, the equivalent set of transformed coefficients is obtained from the outputs.

Another simple example is provided by the Gray code-to-binary conversion process. Fig. 5.24 lists a 4-bit unit-distance or Gray code

Gray code				Binary code			
G_1	G_2	G_3	G_4	B_1	B_2	B_3	B_4
0	0	0	0	0	0	0	0
0	0	0	1	0	0	0	1
0	0	1	1	0	0	1	0
0	0	1	0	0	0	1	1
0	1	1	0	0	1	0	0
0	1	1	1	0	1	0	1
0	1	0	1	0	1	1	0
0	1	0	0	0	1	1	1
1	1	0	0	1	0	0	0
1	1	0	1	1	0	0	1
1	1	1	1	1	0	1	0
1	1	1	0	1	0	1	1
1	0	1	0	1	1	0	0
1	0	1	1	1	1	0	1
1	0	0	1	1	1	1	0
1	0	0	0	1	1	1	1

Fig. 5.24 Four-bit Gray code and its pure binary equivalent.

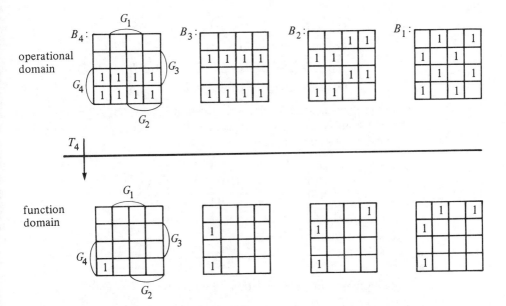

Fig. 5.25 Operational and function domain maps for Gray-to-binary code conversion.

together with its pure binary equivalent. This multiple-output truth table enables us to set up the four operational domain maps for the individual components of each codeword. These can then be converted to the function domain maps as indicated in Fig. 5.25 which reveal that each function is a linear combination of Gray-code digits. We find that

$$B_4 = G_4$$
$$B_3 = G_3 \oplus G_4$$
$$B_2 = G_2 \oplus G_3 \oplus G_4$$
$$B_1 = G_1 \oplus G_2 \oplus G_3 \oplus G_4$$

and the corresponding circuit is given in Fig. 5.26a. We can use GF(2) algebra to manipulate these equations, thereby obtaining the inverse binary-to-Gray code conversion:

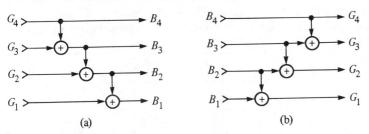

Fig. 5.26 Linear circuits for Gray code conversion.

$$G_4 = B_4$$
$$G_3 = B_3 \oplus G_4 = B_3 \oplus B_4$$
$$G_2 = B_2 \oplus G_3 \oplus G_4 = B_2 \oplus B_3 \oplus B_4 \oplus B_4 = B_2 \oplus B_3$$
$$G_1 = B_1 \oplus G_2 \oplus G_3 \oplus G_4 = B_1 \oplus B_2$$

and the corresponding circuit is given in Fig. 5.26b. Alternatively, as the system is linear, we can regard the code conversions as matrix transform operations. Thus,

$$\begin{pmatrix} B_4 \\ B_3 \\ B_2 \\ B_1 \end{pmatrix} = \begin{pmatrix} 1 & 0 & 0 & 0 \\ 1 & 1 & 0 & 0 \\ 1 & 1 & 1 & 0 \\ 1 & 1 & 1 & 1 \end{pmatrix} \begin{pmatrix} G_4 \\ G_3 \\ G_2 \\ G_1 \end{pmatrix} \quad \text{over GF(2)}$$

or

$$B = T.G$$

Multiplying both sides of this equation by T^{-1} would give us

$$T^{-1}.B = T^{-1}.T.G = G$$

and so reveals the inverse operation. Thus we can find the inverse transform by inverting the matrix T, using GF(2) arithmetic. In order for this inverse transform to exist the determinant $|T|$ must not equal zero. In GF(2) this implies $|T| = 1$ and this is found to be the case here. Performing the matrix inversion reveals that

$$T^{-1} = \begin{pmatrix} 1 & 0 & 0 & 0 \\ 1 & 1 & 0 & 0 \\ 0 & 1 & 1 & 0 \\ 0 & 0 & 1 & 1 \end{pmatrix}$$

which concurs with the results derived by algebraic means.

This possibility of employing matrix operations is of great importance in the implementation of error-detecting and error-correcting codes. The familiar technique of the simple parity check which provides error detection by ensuring that all codewords have the same parity, that is, the same number of 1s, can also be implemented with a linear circuit. The arrangement of Fig. 5.27 adds an even parity check digit to a 4-bit word. If a single error occurs in this

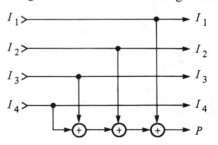

Fig. 5.27 Linear circuit for simple parity-check encoder.

word during transmission the resulting received word will exhibit an odd number of ones and so the parity will have changed. This can be checked with a similar circuit and if failure occurs the system can be prevented from using the corrupted information. The Hamming codes extend this principle by having multiple parity checks each covering a different combination of message digits. A single error in a codeword will cause one or more of these parity checks to fail. The pattern of parity check failures can be used to locate the position of the error providing the checking domains of each parity digit have been chosen correctly. Locating the position of an error in a binary message is sufficient for correction because we only need to invert the digit found at this location. The encoding and decoding circuits for these single-error correcting Hamming codes can be performed by linear combinational circuits. Fig. 5.28 shows the encoder circuit for a 7-bit Hamming code.

Another well known class of error control codes are the Reed-Muller codes and in fact these represent the origin of the Reed-Muller expansion itself. The RM expansion leads to a construction of codes which are capable of detecting and correcting multiple errors. The encoding and decoding circuits for these codes can be described in terms of general circuits represented in RM expansion form.

Circuits derived from Reed-Muller expansions are found to be particularly amenable to automatic testing and fault-location procedures as described in Chapter 7. As we shall also observe later, the generalization of the Reed–Muller approach enables a useful description of multiple-valued switching circuits to be formulated.

Whereas the general sequential circuit design techniques described in earlier chapters could equally well employ RM expansions for the description and synthesis of the combinational functions involved, a special class of linear sequential circuits which combine the linear aspects noted above with a sequential operation

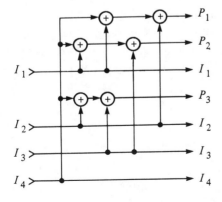

Fig. 5.28 Encoder for 7-bit Hamming code.

is another important departure. Chapter 6 investigates the properties and applications of this important subclass of sequential circuits.

5.7 BIBLIOGRAPHICAL NOTES

The Reed–Muller expansion evolves from the original structures described by Reed (1954) and Muller (1954) for error control codes. Mukhopadhyay and Schmitz (1970) and Green and Dimond (1970) are early papers relating to design methods for RM expansions. Green and Edkins (1978), Wu *et al.* (1982) and Besslich (1983) are papers dealing with RM and GRM design methods. Applications of the linear circuits to coding theory are well documented in the standard texts such as Peterson and Weldon (1972) and MacWilliams and Sloane (1977).

5.8 EXERCISES

5.1 Find the Reed–Muller expansion of the following Boolean switching functions:

a) $f(X_3, X_2, X_1) = X_1(X_2 + \overline{X_3}) + X_3\overline{X_2}\,\overline{X_1}$

b) $f(X_4, X_3, X_2, X_1) = \overline{X_4}\,\overline{X_3}X_1 + X_3\overline{X_1} + X_4(\overline{X_2}X_1 + X_2\overline{X_1})$

5.2 Construct the transform matrix for the polarity 9 GRM expansion of a four-variable Reed–Muller expression. Derive the polarity 9 expansion for the function of Exercise 5.1b.

5.3 Given that the polarity 11 expansion of a four-variable function is:

$$f(X_4, X_3, X_2, X_1) = \overline{X_4} \oplus \overline{X_2} \oplus X_3\overline{X_1} \oplus \overline{X_4}X_3\overline{X_1} \oplus \overline{X_2}\,\overline{X_1} \oplus \overline{X_4}X_3\overline{X_2}\,\overline{X_1}$$

deduce the polarity 9 expression.

5.4 Construct the transform matrix to derive the polarity 9 GRM expansion for a four-variable function directly from the operational domain description. Verify your answers by using the operational domain equivalent of the function of Exercise 5.1b.

5.5 Derive a simplified circuit tree for the function:

$$f(X_3, X_2, X_1) = X_3(1 \oplus X_2) \oplus X_2X_1(1 \oplus X_3)$$

5.6 Synthesize the following using RM-ULM$_3$ components:

$$f(X_5, X_4, X_3, X_2, X_1) = 1 \oplus X_3 \oplus X_3X_2 \oplus X_3X_2X_1 \oplus X_4X_1 \oplus X_5X_3$$
$$\oplus X_5X_3X_1$$

Chapter 6
Linear Sequential Circuits

6.1 INTRODUCTION

We now turn to the study of a subclass of synchronous binary sequential circuits which have many interesting properties and a linear operation. These circuits employ only modulo-2 adders and unit delay elements. Typically, EOR gates and D-type bistables are employed in the synthesis of these circuits. The simplest types have a single input and a single output and may be regarded as binary 'filters' operating on input sequences of binary digits to produce a modified output sequence. In this form they find many applications in coding and digital communications systems. The delay element has the property that after each clock pulse command its output takes on the value of the previous input, i.e. that existing at the time of applying the clock pulse, during the previous clock interval. It is assumed that all inputs, delay elements and outputs are synchronized to the same clock and therefore we need only concern ourselves with the behaviour during the clock intervals. These periods have been called discrete intervals of time or 'dits'. Symbolically, we can represent the behaviour of the delay element by means of an operator D so that the output $Z = D.X$ and $D.X$ is the previous value of the input X. We also adopt the convention that $D(D.X) = D^2X$, $D(D^2X) = D^3X$, etc., and for convenience we take $D^0X = IX = X$, where I is an identity operator.

6.2 FEEDFORWARD FILTERS

Consider the simple arrangement of Fig. 6.1. Here we assume that each stage, the source of the input digits and the destination of the

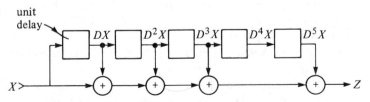

Fig. 6.1 Example of a feedforward linear filter.

output digits are all synchronized to the same timing clock. Using our notation for the D operator we can establish the relationship between the output and input of this circuit to be

$$Z = X \oplus DX \oplus D^2X \oplus D^3X \oplus D^5X$$

Thus the output is computed from the present input and certain past values of the input. The circuit remembers these past values by storing them in the delay elements and it has a memory span of 5 dits into the past. This is an example of a feedforward circuit because all information flow is in the forward direction from input towards the output through either the delay elements or the delay-free adder chain. Thus

$$Z = X(I \oplus D^2 \oplus D^3 \oplus D^4 \oplus D^5)$$

or

$$Z/X = I \oplus D \oplus D^2 \oplus D^3 \oplus D^5 = H(D)$$

The function $H(D)$, in this case a polynomial in D of degree five, which relates the output digit to the input digit during each dit, is a form of filter 'transfer' function, and is characteristic of the particular filter. As in conventional electrical filters, we can define particular inputs which reveal certain properties of the circuit. Fig. 6.2 shows the digital equivalent of the 'impulse' input (in this case a sequence consisting of a single 1 preceded and followed by an infinite string of 0s) and the 'step' input (which is an infinite string of 1s preceded by an infinite string of zeros). We may also like to picture these sequences as 'waveforms'.

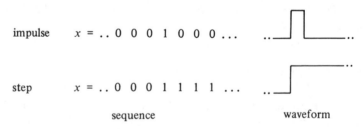

impulse $x = .. 0 \ 0 \ 0 \ 1 \ 0 \ 0 \ 0 \ ...$

step $x = .. 0 \ 0 \ 0 \ 1 \ 1 \ 1 \ 1 \ ...$

sequence   waveform

Fig. 6.2 Sequence equivalents of impulse and step inputs.

Consider the response of the previous five-stage filter to the impulse sequence. When the impulse is applied to the input all the delays will be holding 0 and the output will be 0. The X becomes a 1 so that Z also becomes 1. On the next clock the input returns to zero but now DX, as held in the first delay element, becomes a 1 and thus the output Z remains at 1. On successive clock pulses the single 1 passes down the delay chain and if the particular stage is

$X = \ldots 0\ 0\ 0\ 1\ 0\ 0\ 0\ \ldots$

$Z = \ldots 0\ 0\ 0\ 1\ 1\ 1\ 1\ 0\ 1\ 0\ 0\ \ldots$

Fig. 6.3 Impulse response of circuit of Fig. 6.1.

connected to the adder chain the output will be a 1, otherwise the output will be a 0. After 5 dits the 1 passes out of the delays and the output returns to 0 and remains there. Fig. 6.3 shows the complete response both as a digit sequence and as a waveform. In electrical filters the impulse response and transfer function are related by the Laplace transform, whereas in this discrete two-valued regime there is a direct relationship. The 1s in the impulse response can be regarded as coefficients of the powers of D in the transfer function polynomial $H(D)$. We can use similar arguments to establish the step response of our filter as given in Fig. 6.4. As we may expect from a linear system when disturbed from rest, it exhibits a transient behaviour before entering another steady-state condition. Further, as we are operating with a linear system we can also use super-position to deduce the step response from the impulse response. Fig. 6.5a demonstrates that we can represent the step input as a superposition of an infinite series of impulse inputs, each delayed by one dit. Thus, the step response can be found by the superposition of an infinite series of impulse responses as indicated in Fig. 6.5b. Here are obvious parallels with the process of convolution in the continuous world. Furthermore, the particular nature of modulo-2 addition permits us to represent the impulse input as the summation of just two step inputs delayed by one dit as shown in Fig. 6.6a. Hence the impulse response can be deduced from the step response as indicated in Fig. 6.6b. This process enables us to determine the response to any input sequence since we can always represent it by a series of delayed impulse inputs and hence deduce the output by summing the equivalent impulse responses. Consider the response

$X = \ldots 0\ 0\ 0\ 1\ 1\ 1\ 1\ \ldots$

$Z = \ldots 0\ 0\ 0\ 1\ 0\ 1\ 0\ 0\ 1\ 1\ 1\ \ldots$

Fig. 6.4 Step response of circuit of Fig. 6.1.

$$
\begin{array}{cc}
\ldots 0001000\ldots & \ldots 00011110100\ldots \\
\ldots 0001000\ldots & \ldots 00011110100\ldots \\
\ldots 0001000\ldots & \ldots 00011110100\ldots \\
\ldots 0001000\ldots & \ldots 00011110100\ldots \\
\cdot & \cdot \\
\cdot & \cdot \\
\cdot & \cdot \\
\end{array}
$$

$\oplus$

$$
\begin{array}{cc}
\ldots 0001111\ldots & \ldots 000101001111\ldots \\
\text{(a)} & \text{(b)}
\end{array}
$$

Fig. 6.5 Deriving step response from superposition of impulse responses.

of our filter to the input sequence of seven digits preceded and followed by 0s:

$$X = \ldots 0001010011000\ldots$$

We can break this down into a series of impulses as follows:

$$
X = \oplus \begin{array}{l}
\ldots 00010000\ldots \\
\ldots 0000010000\ldots \\
\ldots 0000000010000\ldots \\
\ldots 00000000010000\ldots
\end{array}
$$

Each of these will set off an impulse response and the total response Z will be the sum of all these responses:

$$
Z = \oplus \begin{array}{l}
\ldots 0001111010000\ldots \\
\ldots 000001111010000\ldots \\
\ldots 000000001111010000\ldots \\
\ldots 0000000001111010000\ldots
\end{array}
$$

and therefore

$$Z = \ldots 000110011010111000\ldots$$

We can perform this same process algebraically by representing the input sequence as a polynomial in D, i.e. $X(D)$, so that the output sequence, also represented as a polynominal in D, i.e. $Z(D)$, will result from the relationship.

$$
\begin{array}{cc}
\ldots 0001111\ldots & \ldots 00010100111\ldots \\
\ldots 0001111\ldots & \ldots 00010100111\ldots \\
\hline
\ldots 0001000\ldots & \ldots 00011110100\ldots \\
\text{(a)} & \text{(b)}
\end{array}
$$

Fig. 6.6 Deriving impulse response from superposition of step responses.

$$Z(D)/X(D) = H(D)$$

or

$$Z(D) = H(D)X(D)$$

If the previous input sequence is represented as the polynomial

$$X(D) = I \oplus D^2 \oplus D^5 \oplus D^6$$

then

$$Z(D) = (I \oplus D \oplus D^2 \oplus D^3 \oplus D^5) \cdot (I \oplus D^2 \oplus D^5 \oplus D^6)$$
$$= I \oplus D \oplus D^4 \oplus D^5 \oplus D^7 \oplus D^9 \oplus D^{10} \oplus D^{11}$$

which gives the polynomial form of the response to $X(D)$. We can now see that the representation of the impulse function is $X_i(D) = I$ so the impulse response $Z_i(D)$ is given by

$$Z_i(D) = H(D) \cdot X_i(D) = H(D) \cdot I = H(D)$$

as we noted previously. Also, the step input $X_s(D)$ can be represented as

$$X_s(D) = I \oplus D \oplus D^2 \oplus D^3 \oplus \ldots \rightarrow \infty$$

so that the step response $Z_s(D)$ is given by

$$\begin{aligned} Z_s(D) &= H(D) \cdot X_s(D) \\ &= H(D) \cdot (I \oplus D \oplus D^2 \oplus D^3 \oplus \ldots) \\ &= H(D) \oplus H(D)(D \oplus D^2 \oplus D^3 \oplus \ldots) \\ &= H(D) \oplus DH(D)(I \oplus D \oplus D^2 \oplus D^3 \oplus \ldots) \\ &= H(D) \oplus D \cdot Z_s(D) \end{aligned}$$

Therefore

$$\begin{aligned} Z_s(D) &= H(D)/(I \oplus D) = (I \oplus D \oplus D^2 \oplus D^3 \oplus D^5)/(I \oplus D) \\ &= I \oplus D^2 \oplus D^5 \oplus D^6 \oplus D^7 \oplus \ldots \end{aligned}$$

and

$$Z = \ldots 0001010111 \ldots \text{ as before}$$

Also

$$Z_s(D)(I \oplus D) = H(D) = Z_i(D)$$
$$Z_i(D) = (I + D)(I \oplus D^2 \oplus D^5 \oplus D^6 \oplus D^7 \oplus \ldots)$$
$$= I \oplus D \oplus D^2 \oplus D^3 \oplus D^5$$

Other input sequences are of interest, such as the square-wave input

$$X_{sq} = \ldots 00010101010 \ldots$$

or

$$X_{sq}(D) = I \oplus D^2 \oplus D^4 \oplus D^6 \oplus \ldots$$

Thus

$$Z_{sq}(D) = H(D).X_{sq}(D)$$
$$= H(D)(I \oplus D^2 \oplus D^4 \oplus D^6 \oplus \ldots)$$
$$= H(D) \oplus D^2 H(D)(I \oplus D^2 \oplus D^4 \oplus D^6 \oplus \ldots)$$
$$= H(D) \oplus D^2 Z_{sq}(D)$$

or

$$Z_{sq}(D) = H(D)/(I \oplus D^2)$$

For our example,

$$Z_{sq}(D) = (I \oplus D \oplus D^2 \oplus D^3 \oplus D^5)/(I \oplus D^2)$$
$$= I \oplus D \oplus D^5 \oplus D^7 \oplus D^9 \oplus \ldots$$

and Fig. 6.7 illustrates this square-wave response. In fact, for any infinite periodic input which is made up of periodic extensions of a finite sequence $f(D)$ of length k dits, i.e.

$$X(D) = f(D) \oplus D^k f(D) \oplus D^{2k} f(D) \oplus \ldots \rightarrow \infty$$

It is easily shown that

$$Z(D) = [H(D).f(D)]/(I \oplus D^k)$$

For example, let

$$X(D) = \ldots 000111001110011100 \ldots \text{ etc.}$$

so $f(D) = I \oplus D \oplus D^2$ and $k = 5$. The corresponding response is given by

$$Z(D) = [H(D).(I \oplus D \oplus D^2)]/(I \oplus D^5)$$

and, for our example filter, we have

$$Z(D) = [(I \oplus D \oplus D^2 \oplus D^3 \oplus D^5)(I \oplus D \oplus D^2)]/(I \oplus D^5)$$
$$= (I \oplus D^2 \oplus D^3 \oplus D^6 \oplus D^7)/(I \oplus D^5)$$
$$= 1 \oplus D^2 \oplus D^3 \oplus D^5 \oplus D^6 \oplus D^8 \oplus D^{10} \oplus$$
$$D^{11} \oplus D^{13} \oplus D^{15} \oplus D^{16} \oplus \ldots$$

$$X_{sq} = \ldots 0 0 0 1 0 1 0 1 0 1 0 \ldots$$

$$Z_{sq} = \ldots 0 0 0 1 1 0 0 0 1 0 1 0 \ldots$$

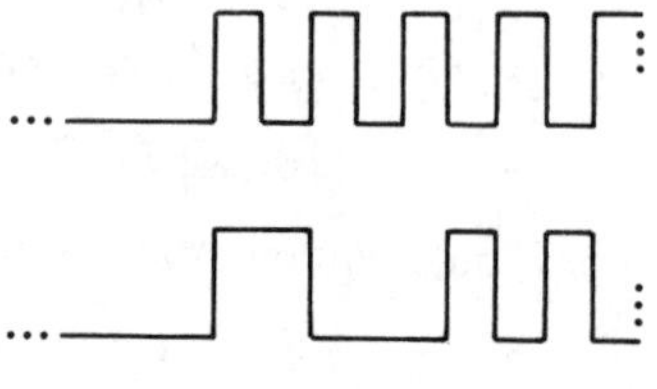

Fig. 6.7 Square-wave response of the filter of Fig. 6.1.

and

$$Z = \ldots 0001011011010110110 \ldots$$

and the output also becomes periodic ultimately.

We can also deduce a non-trivial input sequence which will produce an all-0 output. Each new digit X_0 in such a sequence must be such that

$$H(D).X_0 = 0$$

Therefore

$$(I \oplus D \oplus D^2 \oplus D^3 \oplus D^5).X_0 = 0$$

or

$$X_0 = (D \oplus D^2 \oplus D^3 \oplus D^5).X_0 = D.X_0 \oplus D^2 X_0 \oplus D^3 X_0 \oplus D^5 X_0$$

That is, we make each new input digit equal to the modulo-2 sum of selected previous input digits. As long as each new input digit 'matches' the pattern held in the memories, the output will be maintained at zero. The sequence of input digits so formed is termed a *null sequence*.

Strictly speaking, the only true null sequence is the all-0 input sequence because we should always begin with the filter at rest, i.e. all memories holding 0s. In such a situation a 1 applied to the input will cause the output to rise to a 1 thus violating the null output condition. However, we can limit the output to be a single 1 followed thereafter by 0s for all time. That is, we can make the output $Z(D) = I$, the impulse sequence. Thus, if $X_0(D)$ is the 'null' sequence which produces the impulse sequence output

$$I = H(D)X_0(D)$$
$$X_0(D) = I/H(D)$$

For example, if $H(D) = 1 \oplus D \oplus D^3$ then

$$X_0(D) = I/(I \oplus D \oplus D^3) = 1 \oplus D \oplus D^2 \oplus D^4 \oplus D^7 \oplus D^8 \oplus \ldots \text{ etc.}$$

That is,

$$X = \ldots 00011101001110100 \ldots \qquad \text{repeating sequence}$$
$$Z = \ldots 00010000000000000 \ldots$$

If we attempt this with our original example we find the null sequence is a repeating sequence of 31 digits. The null sequences are clearly related to the structure of $H(D)$ and are therefore characteristic of the particular filter. In a sense, the filter may be regarded as 'tuned' to its null sequences, as any other input sequences will pass through the filter after being scrambled.

6.3 ARRANGEMENTS OF FILTERS

We can deduce the behaviour of certain arrangements of individual filters by deriving an equivalent single filter.

Series or cascade connection

Consider an arrangement of k separate but synchronized linear filters in which the input is applied to the first filter, its output is used as the input to the second, and so on, so that the overall output is taken from the output of the kth filter. This arrangement of k filters in cascade is depicted in Fig. 6.8a. We wish to find an equivalent single filter with transfer function $H_{\text{eff}}(D)$ as given in Fig. 6.8b. Now, in the first arrangement,

$$Z_1(D) = H_1(D).X(D)$$
$$Z_2(D) = H_2(D).Z_1(D) = H_2(D).H_1(D).X(D)$$
$$Z_k(D) = H_k(D)Z_{k-1}(D) = H_k(D)H_{k-1}(D)...H_1(D)X(D)$$
$$Z(D)\ = H_{\text{eff}}(D).X(D)$$

Thus the cascade connection leads to a product of the individual transfer functions. For example, when $k = 3$, let

$$H_1(D) = I{\oplus}D^2, H_2(D) = I{\oplus}D^3$$

and

$$H_3(D) = I{\oplus}D{\oplus}D^2$$

The cascade arrangement of these three filters is shown in Fig. 6.9a. Now

$$H_{\text{eff}}(D) = (I{\oplus}D^2)(I{\oplus}D^3)(I{\oplus}D{\oplus}D^2) = I{\oplus}D{\oplus}D^6{\oplus}D^7$$

and this single filter equivalent is shown in Fig. 6.9b. Note that the number of delays is the same in both cases and is the sum of the

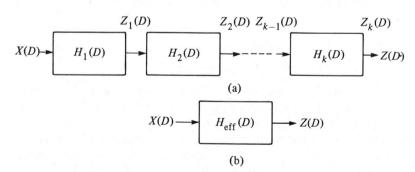

(a)

(b)

Fig. 6.8 Series connection of linear filters.

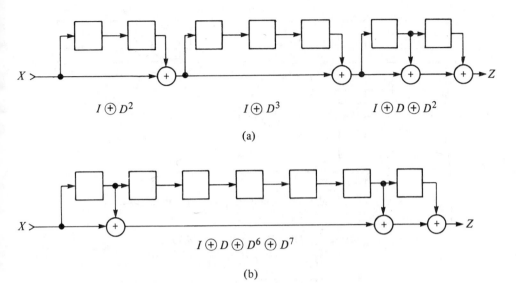

(a)

$$I \oplus D \oplus D^6 \oplus D^7$$

(b)

Fig. 6.9 Cascade of filters and equivalent single filter.

delays in each factor. However, the number of adders may vary. We can now determine the response of either arrangement to any input sequence $X(D)$ from

$$Z(D) = H_{\text{eff}}(D) . X(D)$$

Parallel connection

Here the input is applied to the k filters simultaneously and the output is formed from the sum of the filter outputs as shown in Fig. 6.10. Thus,

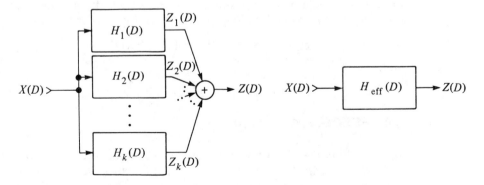

Fig. 6.10 Parallel connections of filters.

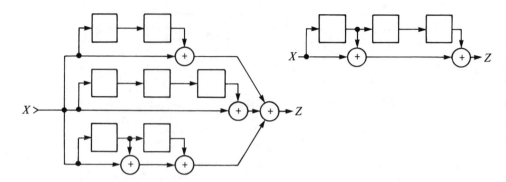

Fig. 6.11 Parallel filters and their equivalent single filter.

$$Z(D) = Z_1(D) \oplus Z_2(D) \oplus \ldots \oplus Z_k(D)$$
$$= H_1(D).X(D) \oplus H_2(D).X(D) \oplus \ldots \oplus H_k(D).X(D)$$
$$= [H_1(D) \oplus H_2(D) \oplus \ldots \oplus H_k(D)].X(D)$$
$$= H_{\text{eff}}(D).X(D)$$

and thus the parallel connection leads to the sum of the individual transfer functions. For example, if the three previous filters are connected in parallel, we have:

$$H_{\text{eff}}(D) = I \oplus D^2 \oplus I \oplus D^3 \oplus I \oplus D \oplus D^2 = I \oplus D \oplus D^3$$

and the two arrangements are shown in Fig. 6.11. Note that the number of delays in $H_{\text{eff}}(D)$ is equal to the number of delays in the largest factor.

Series/parallel connection

We can also envisage combinations of the previous arrangements as indicated in Fig. 6.12. To reduce to an effective single filter we need to replace parallel paths by adding and series paths by multiplying the individual transfer functions. Thus, in the two cases illustrated,

$$H_{\text{eff}}(D) = [H_1(D) \oplus H_2(D)].H_3(D)$$

and

$$H_{\text{eff}}(D) = H_1(D).H_2(D) \oplus H_3(D)$$

6.4 FEEDBACK FILTERS

All the filters described thus far have been feedforward types. We can also describe filters with feedback paths which involve information flow in two directions. Consider the simple arrangement of Fig. 6.13. Here the output Z is formed from the present input X and

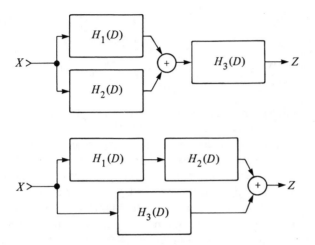

Fig. 6.12 Series/parallel arrangements of filters.

certain past values of the output. The latter are stored in the delay chain and here again the memory span is 5 dits. We can write

$$Z = X \oplus DZ \oplus D^2Z \oplus D^3Z \oplus D^5Z$$

or

$$X = Z \oplus DZ \oplus D^2Z \oplus D^3Z \oplus D^5Z$$
$$= Z(I \oplus D \oplus D^2 \oplus D^3 \oplus D^5)$$
$$Z/X = H(D) = I/(I \oplus D \oplus D^2 \oplus D^3 \oplus D^5)$$
$$= I/F(D)$$

So the transfer function in this case is the inverse of that of the previous example. Once again we can treat inputs and outputs as polynomials in D, so that

$$Z(D) = H(D).X(D) = X(D)/F(D)$$

In particular, if $X(D) = I$, i.e. the impulse sequence, we have

$$Z(D) = H(D).I = I/F(D)$$

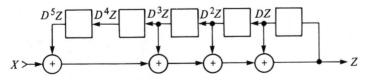

Fig. 6.13 Example of a feedback filter.

For example, if $H(D) = I/(I \oplus D \oplus D^3)$, we have

$$Z(D) = I/(I \oplus D \oplus D^3) = I \oplus D \oplus D^2 \oplus D^4 \oplus D^7 \oplus D^8 \oplus \ldots \text{ etc.}$$

Thus, when $X = \ldots 00010000\ldots$,

$$Z = \ldots 00011101001110100\ldots \text{ repeating}$$

So the impulse response of this filter is the null sequence of the inverse filter $H(D) = I \oplus D \oplus D^3$. As the output is a repeating sequence, once started by the single 1 input, it continues without further input. In practice the circuit may produce this output on switching on because some non-zero condition may be present in the delay elements. If the filter is started from rest, we can only trigger this sequence by applying a 1 to the input or by imposing some other non-zero state on the memory elements. The circuit can be regarded as the discrete equivalent of an 'oscillator' which may require triggering in order to set off the oscillation. The sequences produced in the absence of any input can be regarded as the unforced or natural modes of oscillation. It is in this autonomous mode that these filters are better known as feedback shift registers (FSRs) and are a rich source of sequences with many interesting properties and applications.

Of course, the feedback filters can also operate in the forced mode and in fact will 'unscramble' the sequence produced at the output of the inverse feedforward filter to restore the original input sequence. Consider the arrangement of Fig. 6.14 and assume that $X(D) = X_0(D)$, the null sequences of $H(D)$. This will ensure that $Z(D) = I$, the impulse sequence. This impulse applied to the inverse filter will reproduce the null sequences of the first filter at the output. Once initiated, the second filter effectively operates in the autonomous mode since its input remains at zero, and so the connection between the two filters can be removed and the input sequence of the first filter still appears at the output of the second! Of course this trick only works for the null sequence input. Any other input sequences will result in non-zero intermediate sequences and so the connection must be maintained in order to recover the original sequences from the second filter.

This arrangement of the two related filters forms the basis of a number of coding schemes for error control and data encryption.

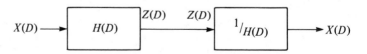

Fig. 6.14 Linear sequential filter cascaded with its inverse.

6.5 AUTONOMOUS FEEDBACK SEQUENTIAL CIRCUITS

Autonomous sequential feedback filters represent an important subclass better known as feedback shift register sequence generators. They exhibit a fascinating behaviour and are a rich source of sequences employed in coding techniques and digital communications. They are conveniently described in terms of the algebra of GF(2) and represent an important application of this approach. In this autonomous mode it is more useful to regard these devices as finite-state machines rather than filters with a transfer function. The collection of delays is termed a shift register and we now regard the adder chain as supplying the feedback round the register. This slightly modified viewpoint leads us to represent the FSR in the manner of Fig. 6.15 which shows the general n-stage version. The coefficients a_i are 0 or 1 and act as scalar multipliers to pick off the required feedback taps. For a particular register these will resolve to open or closed connections. The output can be regarded as originating from the feedback path at the point where it enters the register. The same values will ultimately appear in all stages of the register and also at the output of the delay chain and sometimes it is convenient to recognize this point as the 'output' of the circuit.

Consider the simple example when $n = 4$. Let $\langle x_i \rangle$ represent the new or next value of variable x_i. Thus writing $\langle x_i \rangle = x_j$ is equivalent to the assignment $x_i := x_j$. We can write, for the FSR of Fig. 6.15 with $n = 4$,

$$\langle x_4 \rangle = x_3$$
$$\langle x_3 \rangle = x_2$$
$$\langle x_2 \rangle = x_1$$
$$\langle x_1 \rangle = a_4 x_4 \oplus a_3 x_3 \oplus a_2 x_2 \oplus a_1 x_1$$

The first three equations describe the shift action and the fourth

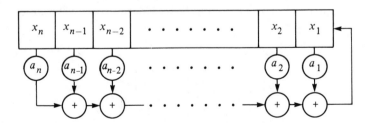

Fig. 6.15   General n-stage feedback shift register.

describes the linear feedback. We can also represent these equations in matrix form as

$$\begin{pmatrix} \langle x_4 \rangle \\ \langle x_3 \rangle \\ \langle x_2 \rangle \\ \langle x_1 \rangle \end{pmatrix} = \begin{bmatrix} 0 & 1 & 0 & 0 \\ 0 & 0 & 1 & 0 \\ 0 & 0 & 0 & 1 \\ a_4 & a_3 & a_2 & a_1 \end{bmatrix} \cdot \begin{pmatrix} x_4 \\ x_3 \\ x_2 \\ x_1 \end{pmatrix} \qquad \text{over GF(2)}$$

or

$$\langle X \rangle = T.X$$

where X represents the present state, $\langle X \rangle$ the next state and T a transition matrix which connects the two. Thus, the succession of states of this system can be regarded as X, $T.X$, $T(TX) = T^2 X$, $T^3 X$, etc. Now the process of generating the next state is purely deterministic, and there is only a finite number of possible states: in this case, $2^4 = 16$; in general, 2^n. Thus, this sequence must ultimately become periodic; that is, for some k, $T^k X = X$ for all X. This implies that $T^k = I$, the identity matrix, and it is of interest to deduce the value of k, the period, for a given system. We begin by deriving the characteristic equation $\phi(s)$ of the transition matrix. This can be defined as

$$\phi(s) = |T - sI| = |T \oplus sI| \qquad \text{over GF(2)}$$

$$\phi(s) = \begin{bmatrix} s & 1 & 0 & 0 \\ 0 & s & 1 & 0 \\ 0 & 0 & s & 1 \\ a_4 & a_3 & a_2 & a_1 \oplus s \end{bmatrix} = s \begin{bmatrix} s & 1 & 0 \\ 0 & s & 1 \\ a_3 & a_2 & a_1 \oplus s \end{bmatrix} \oplus \begin{bmatrix} 0 & 1 & 0 \\ 0 & s & 1 \\ a_4 & a_2 & a_1 \oplus s \end{bmatrix}$$

$$= s^4 \oplus a_1 s^3 \oplus a_2 s^2 \oplus a_3 s \oplus a_4$$

and $\phi(s)$ is seen to be a polynomial of degree 4 with coefficients which are identical to those of the feedback circuit but taken in reverse order. In general, an n-stage FSR will give rise to a characteristic polynomial of degree n whose coefficients are the reverse of those in the feedback equation. Thus $\phi(s)$ can be derived by inspection of the circuit, thereby avoiding the need to expand the determinant. The structure of $\phi(s)$ determines the sequential behaviour of the corresponding FSR. Consider the example of Fig.

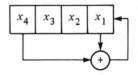

Fig. 6.16 Example of four-stage FSR.

6.16, from which we can determine the feedback equation to be

$$\langle x_4 \rangle = 1.x_4 \oplus 0.x_3 \oplus 0.x_2 \oplus 1.x_1$$

and the corresponding polynomial is

$$\phi(s) = s^4 \oplus 1.s^3 \oplus 0.s^2 \oplus 0.s \oplus 1$$
$$= s^4 \oplus s^3 \oplus 1 \qquad \text{over GF(2)}$$

Now any square matrix satisfies its own characteristic polynomial so we can write

$$\phi(T) = T^4 \oplus T^3 \oplus I = 0$$

or

$$T^4 = T^3 \oplus I$$

Thus

$$(T^4)^4 = (T^3 \oplus I)^4$$
$$T^{16} = T^{12} \oplus I$$

also

$$T^4 . T^{12} = (T^3 \oplus I)T^{12}$$
$$T^{16} = T^{15} \oplus T^{12}$$

Therefore,

$$T^{15} = I$$

and so the period of the system is predicted to be 15. We can verify this by computing each state by applying the transform matrix to the previous one. We find that the sequence of states is

   0001, 0011, 0111, 1111, 1110, 1101, 1010, 0101, 1011,
   0110, 1100, 1001, 0010, 0100, 1000 and back to 0001

confirming that the period is 15. Due to the shift action, the first three digits of each new state are the same as the last three digits of the previous state. We can compress this sequence of states into a sequence of digits with the same period by writing only the new digit created at each dit. Thus we obtain

   0001, 1, 1, 1, 0, 1, 0, 1, 1, 0, 0, 1, 0, 0, 0, 1, etc.

or

   000111101011001, 00011110... etc.

a repeating sequence of 15 digits. Contained in this sequence are all the possible states or combinations of four bits, with the exception of the all-zero state. The latter, used as a starting state, would clearly result in an all-zero output sequence. This FSR is an example of a maximum length linear FSR sequence or *m-sequence* and these arise from characteristic polynomials which cannot be factorized and are therefore irreducible. Associated with each irreducible polynomial is an *exponent* which is the smallest integer e such that $\phi(s)$ divides $s^e \oplus 1$ exactly. It turns out that e must be an integer which is a divisor of $2^n - 1$, n being the degree of $\phi(s)$. The maximum value of e is therefore $2^n - 1$, and any irreducible polynomial with maximum exponent is termed *primitive*. Maximum-length sequences arise from FSRs with primitive characteristic polynomials. If $\phi(s)$ is a non-primitive irreducible polynomial, that is, if $e < 2^n - 1$, then instead of delivering one cycle of states of length $2^n - 1$, the corresponding FSR has m cycles of e states where $m \cdot e = 2^n - 1$. We can therefore represent the collection of sequences of states for an irreducible polynomial of degree n as $\{1, m(e)\}$. That is, the *cycle set* for an FSR with an irreducible characteristic polynomial can be written as $\{1, m(e)\}$, which can be interpreted as 1 cycle of length 1, the all-zero sequence, and m cycles of length e, where $m \cdot e = 2^n - 1$. The FSR of Fig. 6.17 has characteristic polynomial

$$\phi(s) = s^4 \oplus s^3 \oplus s^2 \oplus s \oplus 1$$

which is irreducible but non-primitive. In fact its exponent $e = 5$ and so its cycle set is $\{1, 3(5)\}$. The three sequences generated by this FSR are

$$1\ 1\ 1\ 1\ 0,\ 1\ 1\ 1\ 1\ 0 \text{ etc.}$$
$$1\ 1\ 0\ 0\ 0,\ 1\ 1\ 0\ 0\ 0 \text{ etc.}$$
$$1\ 0\ 1\ 0\ 0,\ 1\ 0\ 1\ 0\ 0 \text{ etc.}$$

We can also easily predict the cycle set for certain polynomials which are not irreducible. In the case of non-repeated irreducible factors, when

$$\phi(s) = \phi_1(s)\phi_2(s)\ldots\phi_k(s)$$

we can derive the cycle set of $\phi(s)$ from the interaction of cycles of the k factor polynomials. Each of these acting alone will have a cycle set $\{1, m_i(e_i)\}$ where

$$m_i \cdot e_i = 2^{n_i} - 1$$

e_i is the exponent and n_i is the degree of $\phi_i(s)$.

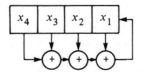

Fig. 6.17 FSR with non-primitive characteristic polynomial.

The interaction of two of these cycle sets, $\{1, m_i(e_i)\}$ and $\{1, m_j(e_j)\}$, produces a new cycle set containing the cycles of the factors together with new cycles generated by the product. The new cycle set takes the form

$$\{1, m_i(e_i), m_j(e_j), m(e)\}$$

where $m = m_i . m_j$. highest common factor (e_i, e_j) and $e =$ lowest common multiple (e_i, e_j).

The complete cycle set of $\phi(s)$ can be found by applying these rules for each new factor. For example, consider the example

$$\begin{aligned} \phi(s) &= s^5 \oplus s^4 \oplus 1 \\ &= (s^3 \oplus s \oplus 1)(s^2 \oplus s \oplus 1) \qquad \text{over GF(2)} \\ &= \phi_1(s) . \phi_2(s) \end{aligned}$$

Where both factors are irreducible and primitive, so $m_1 = m_2 = 1$ and $e_1 = 7$, $n_1 = 3$, $e_2 = 3$, $n_2 = 2$. The individual cycle sets are $\{1, 1(7)\}$ and $\{1, 1(3)\}$. The cycle set of the composite polynomial $\phi(s)$ is $\{1, 1(7), 1(3), 1(21)\}$. The corresponding FSR is depicted in Fig. 6.18a and the output sequences at point Z are confirmed to be

111110101001100010000, 11111 etc.	length 21
1110010, 11100 etc.	length 7
110, 11011 etc.	length 3
0, 00000 etc.	length 1

The shorter cycles are observed to be identical to the autonomous sequences of the factor FSRs acting alone as in Fig. 6.18b. Furthermore, when these two minor cycles are added modulo-2 they produce a shifted version of the major cycle of length 21. This gives a clue to one possible way of reproducing the overall behaviour from just the factor FSRs. Fig. 6.19 shows this arrangement and it is easily verified that as the two factors operate in their autonomous cycle sets the overall output at point Z is equivalent to that of the single composite FSR. We can also reproduce this behaviour by employing a cascade connection, in which one factor is forced by the autonomous sequences of the other. Each of the arrangements of Fig. 6.20 is also equivalent to the single FSR.

The behaviour resulting from composite polynomials with

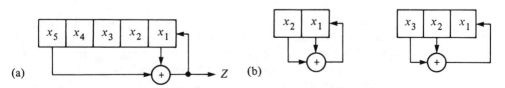

(a) (b)

Fig. 6.18 (a) FSR with composite characteristic polynomial, (b) FSRs corresponding to the factors of (a).

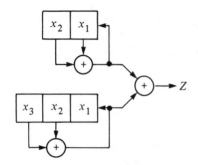

Fig. 6.19 Equivalent arrangement of factor FSRs.

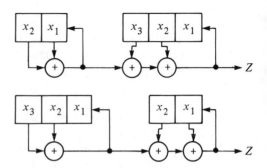

Fig. 6.20 Cascade equivalents of composite FSR.

repeated factors is more complicated but can be explained in terms of the theory of polynomials with coefficients from finite fields.

The most important types of FSR are those which give rise to m-sequences. These sequences can be exploited because of their discrete autocorrelation function which can be approximated to that of white noise. For this reason m-sequences are also referred to as pseudorandom binary sequences (PRBS). Tables of irreducible polynomials and their exponents have been available for many years and these enable us to construct FSRs which are capable of generating extremely long sequences of pseudorandom digits. Fig. 6.21 lists some primitive polynomials and the corresponding feedback connections for their related FSRs. We can also generalize the feedback functions to include products of the register stages. The feedback function can then be regarded as a general Reed–Muller expansion in n variables and many of the techniques described for this regime can be applied to the study of these non-linear forms. This general class includes those FSRs which generate a truly maximal length cycle of 2^n digits so that the all-zero state is included in the single cycle. Such a device is obviously self-starting for no matter what the initial state of the FSR the same output sequence results.

6.6 APPLICATIONS TO CODING THEORY

In contrast to the block or group coding approach which essentially involves a parallel encoding and decoding process, the cyclic codes adopt a serial mode of operation. In such a scheme the codewords are regarded as sequences which are encoded and decoded by passing them through linear sequential filters. As we have seen, these filters can represent the process of polynomial multiplication

n	$\phi(s)$	Feedback taps
2	$s^2 \oplus s \oplus 1$	$x_2 \oplus x_1$
3	$s^3 \oplus s^2 \oplus 1$	$x_3 \oplus x_1$
4	$s^4 \oplus s^3 \oplus 1$	$x_4 \oplus x_1$
5	$s^5 \oplus s^3 \oplus 1$	$x_5 \oplus x_2$
6	$s^6 \oplus s^5 \oplus 1$	$x_6 \oplus x_1$
7	$s^7 \oplus s^6 \oplus 1$	$x_7 \oplus x_1$
8	$s^8 \oplus s^6 \oplus s^5 \oplus s^4 \oplus 1$	$x_8 \oplus x_4 \oplus x_3 \oplus x_2$
9	$s^9 \oplus s^5 \oplus 1$	$x_9 \oplus x_4$
10	$s^{10} \oplus s^7 \oplus 1$	$x_{10} \oplus x_3$
11	$s^{11} \oplus s^9 \oplus 1$	$x_{11} \oplus x_2$
12	$s^{12} \oplus s^{11} \oplus s^{10} \oplus s^2 \oplus 1$	$x_{12} \oplus x_{10} \oplus x_2 \oplus x_1$
13	$s^{13} \oplus s^{12} \oplus s^{11} \oplus s \oplus 1$	$x_{13} \oplus x_{12} \oplus x_2 \oplus x_1$
14	$s^{14} \oplus s^{13} \oplus s^{12} \oplus s^2 \oplus 1$	$x_{14} \oplus x_{12} \oplus x_2 \oplus x_1$
15	$s^{15} \oplus s^{14} \oplus 1$	$x_{15} \oplus x_1$
16	$s^{16} \oplus s^{14} \oplus s^{13} \oplus s^{11} \oplus 1$	$x_{16} \oplus x_5 \oplus x_3 \oplus x_2$
17	$s^{17} \oplus s^{14} \oplus 1$	$x_{17} \oplus x_3$
18	$s^{18} \oplus s^{11} \oplus 1$	$x_{18} \oplus x_7$
19	$s^{19} \oplus s^{18} \oplus s^{17} \oplus s^{14} \oplus 1$	$x_{19} \oplus x_5 \oplus x_2 \oplus x_1$
20	$s^{20} \oplus s^{17} \oplus 1$	$x_{20} \oplus x_3$
23	$s^{23} \oplus s^{18} \oplus 1$	$x_{23} \oplus x_5$
31	$s^{31} \oplus s^{28} \oplus 1$	$x_{31} \oplus x_3$
35	$s^{35} \oplus s^{33} \oplus 1$	$x_{35} \oplus x_2$
40	$s^{40} \oplus s^{37} \oplus s^{36} \oplus s^{35} \oplus 1$	$x_{40} \oplus x_5 \oplus x_4 \oplus x_3$
60	$s^{60} \oplus s^{59} \oplus 1$	$x_{60} \oplus x_1$
63	$s^{63} \oplus s^{62} \oplus 1$	$x_{63} \oplus x_1$
70	$s^{70} \oplus s^{69} \oplus s^{67} \oplus s^{65} \oplus 1$	$x_{70} \oplus x_5 \oplus x_3 \oplus x_1$
80	$s^{80} \oplus s^{79} \oplus s^{78} \oplus s^{77} \oplus s^{75} \oplus s^{73} \oplus 1$	$x_{80} \oplus x_7 \oplus x_5 \oplus x_3 \oplus x_2 \oplus x_1$
90	$s^{90} \oplus s^{88} \oplus s^{87} \oplus s^{85} \oplus 1$	$x_{90} \oplus x_5 \oplus x_3 \oplus x_2$
100	$s^{100} \oplus s^{98} \oplus s^{93} \oplus s^{92} \oplus 1$	$x_{100} \oplus x_8 \oplus x_7 \oplus x_2$

Fig. 6.21 Some primitive polynomials and their corresponding FSRs.

and division. This happens to suit the mathematical structure of cyclic codes because the basic philosophy is to regard codewords as polynomials which are all multiples of one special polynomial called the code *generator* polynomial. Information, also regarded as a polynomial, is encoded by multiplying by the generator polynomial before transmission. If the codeword polynomial so formed is corrupted by noise during transmission then it will no longer be a multiple of the generator polynomial when it is received. This can be detected by dividing the received codeword by the generator polynomial. A non-zero remainder will indicate the presence of errors in the codeword. Familiar data transmission techniques such as the cyclic redundancy check (CRC) code operate with this principle. Furthermore, by carefully structuring the information and generator polynomials it is possible to use the results of the division to locate and correct the detected errors provided they do not exceed a predefined limit. Thus, it is possible to devise cyclic equivalents of the single-error correcting Hamming codes. This principle can also be extended to provide multiple-error correcting codes such as the Bose-Chaudhuri-Hocquenghem (BCH) codes.

The central requirement in all these schemes are circuits for performing polynomial multiplication and division and these can be furnished by linear sequential circuits. Consider the multiplication of any polynomial $a(x)$ by the fixed polynomial $b(x)$, where

$$a(x) = a_0 \oplus a_1 x \oplus a_2 x^2 \oplus \ldots \oplus a_{s-1} x^{s-1} \oplus a_s x^s \text{ degree } s$$
$$b(x) = b_0 \oplus b_1 x \oplus b_2 x^2 \oplus \ldots \oplus b_{r-1} x^{r-1} \oplus b_r x^r \text{ degree } r$$

Their product takes the form

$$
\begin{aligned}
c(x) &= a(x) \cdot b(x) \\
&= a_0 b_0 \oplus (a_0 b_1 \oplus a_1 b_0) x \oplus (a_0 b_2 \oplus a_1 b_1 \oplus a_2 b_0) x^2 \oplus \ldots \\
&\quad \oplus (a_{s-1} b_r \oplus a_s b_{r-1}) x^{s+r-1} \oplus a_s b_r x^{s+r}
\end{aligned}
$$

and has degree $s + r$. We can mechanize this product formation by means of the linear sequential circuit of Fig. 6.22 for binary polynomials. The operation can be described by Fig. 6.23 which records the input, the state of each memory element and the output after each clock pulse. Initially, the register holds all 0s and the coefficients of $a(x)$ are fed into the input high order first, and then followed by r 0s. We observe that at each shift of the register a new coefficient of the product polynomial $c(x)$ is delivered at the output. After $s + r + 1$ shifts the complete product has been formed and the register holds all 0s again so at this point the process can be

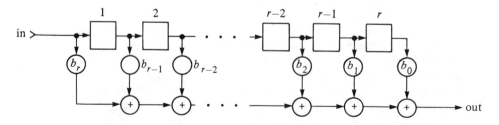

Fig. 6.22 Circuit for polynomial multiplication.

Time	Input	Register contents						Output
		1	2	· · ·	$r-2$	$r-1$	r	
0	a_s	0	0	· · ·	0	0	0	$a_s b_r$
1	a_{s-1}	a_s	0	· · ·	0	0	0	$a_{s-1}b_r \oplus a_s b_{r-1}$
2	a_{s-2}	a_{s-1}	a_s	· · ·	0	0	0	$a_{s-2}b_r \oplus a_{s-1}b_{r-1} \oplus a_s b_{r-2}$
·	·	·	·	·	·	·	·	·
·	·	·	·	·	·	·	·	·
·	·	·	·	·	·	·	·	·
$s+r-2$	0	0	0	· · ·	a_0	a_1	a_2	$a_0 b_2 \oplus a_1 b_1 \oplus a_2 b_0$
$s+r-1$	0	0	0	· · ·	0	a_0	a_1	$a_0 b_1 \oplus a_1 b_0$
$s+r$	0	0	0	· · ·	0	0	a_0	$a_0 b_0$

Fig. 6.23 Detailed operation of polynomial multiplier.

repeated for another input polynomial. This allows for a continuous process such as is required in a data transmission system wherein $a(x)$ would represent the information polynomial, $b(x)$ the generator polynomial, and $c(x)$ the codeword polynomial.

For a given polynomial $b(x)$ we can of course determine the pattern of pick-offs required in the circuit. For example, Fig. 6.24 shows the circuit for the multiplication of any input polynomial by the fixed polynomial

$$b(x) = 1 \oplus x^3 \oplus x^4 \oplus x^5 \oplus x^6.$$

In order to perform polynomial division it is necessary to employ linear sequential filters with feedback. Consider the division of any input dividend polynomial

$$d(x) = d_0 \oplus d_1 x \oplus d_2 x^2 \oplus \ldots \oplus d_s x^s$$

by the fixed divisor polynomial

$$g(x) = g_0 \oplus g_1 x \oplus g_2 x^2 \oplus \ldots \oplus g_r x^r$$

The result will be a quotient polynomial $q(x)$ of degree $s - r$ and possibly a remainder polynomial of degree less than r. The most

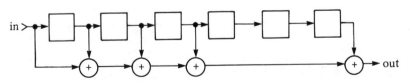

Fig. 6.24 Circuit to multiply and polynomial by the fixed polynomial $x^6 + x^5 + x^4 + x^3 + 1$ over GF(2).

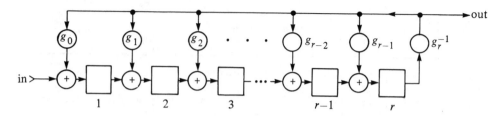

Fig. 6.25 Circuit for polynomial division.

significant terms of $q(x)$ will therefore be $q_{s-r}x^{s-r}$ and we can deduce q_{s-r} from the fact that

$$q_{s-r}x^{s-r} \cdot g_r x^r = d_s x^s$$

Thus,

$$q_{s-r} = d_s \cdot g_r^{-1}$$

In the long-division process performed by hand we continue by subtracting $d_s \cdot g_r^{-1} x^{s-r} \cdot g(x)$ from $d(x)$, thereby eliminating the term $d_s x^s$ and possibly several others. We then repeat this process by deducing the next coefficient in $q(x)$. For each new quotient coefficient q_i the polynomial $q_i \cdot g(x)$ is subtracted from the dividend and the process is repeated until no new terms of the quotient can be found. At this point there may be still some terms of the dividend and these form the remainder polynomial. The circuit of Fig. 6.25 performs this operation automatically when the dividend polynomial is fed in high order first. The memory elements initially hold all 0s. The output remains at 0 for the first r shifts, until the first input digit d_s reaches the end of the register. Then the first non-zero output coefficient appears, namely $d_s \cdot g_r^{-1}$. The feedback connections ensure that for each quotient coefficient q_i the polynomial $q_i \cdot g(x)$ is subtracted (by adding modulo-2) from the dividend held in the register. After $s+1$ shifts, the entire dividend polynomial has entered the register and the entire quotient has appeared at the output. The remainder polynomial is held in the register. For a given polynomial $g(x)$ we can resolve all the scalar multipliers into open or closed connections. Fig. 6.26 shows the circuit for the division of any polynomial by the fixed polynomial

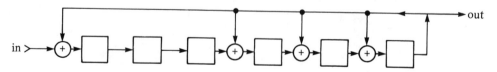

Fig. 6.26 Circuit to divide any polynomial by the fixed polynomial $1 + x^3 + x^4 + x^5 + x^6$ over GF(2).

Time	Input	Register contents						Output
		1	2	3	4	5	6	
0	1	0	0	0	0	0	0	0
1	1	1	0	0	0	0	0	0
2	0	1	1	0	0	0	0	0
3	1	0	1	1	0	0	0	0
4	1	1	0	1	1	0	0	0
5	0	1	1	0	1	1	0	0
6	1	0	1	1	0	1	1	1
7	0	0	0	1	0	1	0	0
8	0	0	0	0	1	0	1	1
9	0	1	0	0	1	0	1	1
10	1	1	1	0	1	0	1	1
11	—	0	1	1	1	0	1	

quotient $1 \oplus x \oplus x^2 \oplus x^4$

remainder $x \oplus x^2 \oplus x^3 \oplus x^5$

Fig. 6.27 Detailed operation of polynomial divider.

$x^6 \oplus x^5 \oplus x^4 \oplus x^3 \oplus 1$. Fig. 6.27 gives the detailed behaviour of the circuit when the input polynomial is $x^{10} \oplus x^9 \oplus x^7 \oplus x^6 \oplus x^4 \oplus 1$. This confirms that the result of this division is $x^4 \oplus x^2 \oplus x \oplus 1$ with a remainder of $x^5 \oplus x^3 \oplus x^2 \oplus x$.

As before, this process can be made continuous by clearing or shifting out the remainder from the register at the end of the division and before the application of the next input polynomial.

Other processes are also amenable to implementation by linear sequential circuits. In Chapter 5 we observed that the interdomain transforms could be implemented by combinational linear circuits giving a parallel mode of operation. We can also perform this, in a serial mode, by means of a linear sequential circuit. Fig. 6.28 shows the arrangement for T_2, the two-variable case. If the coefficients of one domain representation, say the d_i, are fed into the input, beginning with d_0, then after five shifts the coefficients of the other domain will be held in the delays. Fig. 6.29 illustrates the detailed operation of the circuit. The transformation of larger functions can

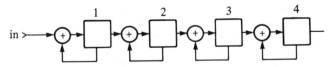

Fig. 6.28 Serial circuit for interdomain transform T_2.

Input	Contents of delays			
	1	2	3	4
d_0	0	0	0	0
d_1	d_0	0	0	0
d_2	$d_0 \oplus d_1$	d_0	0	0
d_3	$d_0 \oplus d_1 \oplus d_2$	d_1	d_0	0
—	$d_0 \oplus d_1 \oplus d_2 \oplus d_3 = c_3$	$d_0 \oplus d_2 = c_2$	$d_0 \oplus d_1 = c_1$	$d_0 = c_0$

Fig. 6.29 Detailed operation of the circuit of Fig. 6.28.

be made with longer versions of this filter. Thus, for the n-variable function we would require a chain of 2^n delays.

6.7 BIBLIOGRAPHICAL NOTES

Huffman (1956) and Elspas (1959) are early pioneering papers relating to linear sequential circuits. Kautz (1965) is a useful source which contains both the previous papers in addition to many others, and Gill (1966) is a definitive text on the subject. Golomb (1964, 1967) provide a fundamental study of FSR sequences and their applications. Berlekamp (1968), Peterson and Weldon (1972) and MacWilliams and Sloane (1977) are texts which all include comprehensive coverage of linear sequential circuits in coding theory applications.

6.8 EXERCISES

6.1 Find the impulse response, step response and null sequences of the linear sequential filter shown in Fig. 6.30.

6.2 When two linear sequential filters H_1 and H_2 are supplied with the same input sequence X, their output sequences are Z_1 and Z_2 respectively, where

$$X = \ldots 0001011000 \ldots$$
$$Z_1 = \ldots 00011101101000 \ldots$$
$$Z_2 = \ldots 00010110011101000 \ldots$$

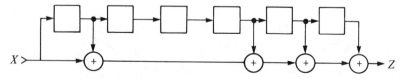

Fig. 6.30 Sequential filter for Exercise 6.1.

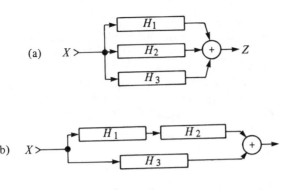

(a) X

H_1

H_2 $+$ Z

H_3

(b) X

H_1 H_2

$+$ Z

H_3

(c) X H_1 H_2 H_3 Z

Fig. 6.31 Filter arrangements for Exercise 6.3.

Deduce H_1 and H_2 and draw the circuit for each filter. These filters are then connected in cascade so that the output of H_1 is connected to the input of H_2. Find an equivalent single filter to this arrangement and determine its response to the input sequence:

$X = \ldots000111000\ldots$

6.3 Three sequential filters have transfer functions H_1, H_2 and H_3. When supplied with the same input sequence X, their outputs Z_1, Z_2 and Z_3 are as follows:

$X \ = \ \ldots000111000\ldots$
$Z_1 \ = \ \ldots0001011101000\ldots$
$Z_2 \ = \ \ldots000111111111000\ldots$
$Z_3 \ = \ \ldots0001101110101000\ldots$

Determine an equivalent single register filter for the arrangements shown in Fig. 6.31.

6.4 Find the autonomous sequences of the sequential filter given in Fig. 6.32. Determine the response of this filter to an input consisting of the periodic extensions of the sequence 101001011.

6.5 Deduce the cycle set of the FSR which has characteristic polynomial

$$\phi(s) = s^{11} \oplus s^{10} \oplus s^7 \oplus s \oplus 1$$

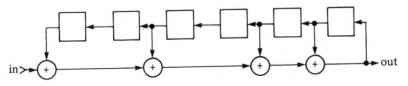

in> $+$

$+$ $+$ $+$ out

Fig. 6.32 Sequential filter for Exercise 6.4.

6.6 A certain FSR has a characteristic polynomial of degree 16 which can be factorized into three distinct irreducible factors with degrees 6, 6 and 4. If the exponents of these factors are 9, 21 and 5 respectively, find the cycle set of the FSR.

6.7 Construct circuits to (a) multiply and (b) divide any input polynomial by the fixed polynomial $x^8 \oplus x^4 \oplus x^3 \oplus x^2 \oplus 1$. Verify your designs by employing the input polynomial $x^{12} \oplus x^{11} \oplus x^5 \oplus x^3 \oplus x \oplus 1$.

Chapter 7
Further Topics

7.1 INTRODUCTION

The preceding chapters have covered the central problems concerned with the design and synthesis of switching circuits using
modern components. The alternative descriptions afforded by the
Reed–Muller expansions have also been considered and this has
enabled the study of the important subclasses of linear combinational
and sequential circuits together with their applications to digital
communications systems to be included. These subjects should form
the main core of any second-level course on logic design. This
chapter is devoted to a number of more advanced topics that could
be included in such a course where time permits or could form the
basis of an extended course or used to reinforce the subject taught
at postgraduate level. Just three topics are considered and these
represent three areas of rapid development and increasing importance which may well become common practice in the near future.

The first section deals with the important area of logic simulation,
which is becoming a vital phase of the design process. This enables a
thorough verification, evaluation and testing of a design to be
performed without the expensive and time-consuming process of
prototype manufacture. The related topic of circuit testing and fault
detection is considered in the next section. The process of fault
detection and location by observation of circuit outputs in response
to predetermined test input patterns is fast becoming a standard tool
in the logic designer's repertoire. As circuits increase in complexity
and are implemented in LSI and VLSI technologies, the traditional
forms of fault probing and monitoring are no longer appropriate,
and these non-intrusive automatic methods are preferred.

The final topic considered is that of multiple-valued logic design
and synthesis. Modern integrated circuit technologies may, at last,
make possible the mass production of cheap and reliable non-binary
switching elements. Such a possibility has many attractive ramifi-
cations for the logic designer which he must be ready to exploit. The
extension of the technique described for the binary components to
the multiple-valued regime is considered in some detail.

7.2 SIMULATION OF SWITCHING CIRCUITS

Logic simulation is becoming an increasingly important topic and can provide a useful contribution to the overall design of a digital system. The need to verify and evaluate the performance of initial designs is only partially satisfied by the expensive and time-consuming manufacture of prototype circuits. In a computer-aided design environment, logic simulation can replace much of this activity in a convenient and inexpensive manner. In addition, logic simulation can provide much more detailed and systematic information relating to circuit performance and the possible occurrence of races, hazards and the effects of propagation delays. The possibility of simulating fault conditions can also be of assistance in the development of test procedures for use on the final product. Logic simulation is obviously a vital adjunct to the design of gate-array circuits or fully customized VLSI circuits.

Simulation packages are becoming very sophisticated and permit the designer to study his design at many levels and enable the use of macros and predefined library procedures to build up simulations of modules and collections of units in addition to simple arrangements of discrete switching elements. However, to illustrate the technique we shall restrict our attention to the simulation of simple circuits.

The simplest type of simulator is one in which each gate is assigned an identifier or number and is listed together with all its individual connections. This coded information is then compiled into a set of executable instructions which are then processed by the simulator. In conjunction with the circuit description is an operational table which holds the current logic values of each line or node of the circuit. The simulation involves processing the description of the circuit using the operational table to derive the input values to each gate and to record the computed output values. This requires each gate to be scanned in turn and, if the circuit has been described in the correct order, it can be simulated for a given set of inputs by one pass through the table. For example, we could specify the circuit of Fig. 7.1 by a compound expression such as

$$L_6 := \text{OR}(\text{AND}(L_1, \text{NAND}(L_1, L_2)),$$
$$\text{AND}(L_2, \text{NAND}(L_1, L_2)))$$

or by the sequence of simple statements:

$$L_3 := \text{NAND}(L_1, L_2)$$
$$L_4 := \text{AND}(L_1, L_3)$$
$$L_5 := \text{AND}(L_2, L_3)$$
$$L_6 := \text{OR}(L_4, L_5)$$

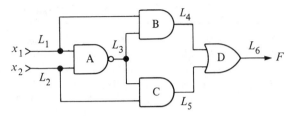

Fig. 7.1 Example circuit for logic simulation.

where NAND, AND and OR are assumed to be predefined functions in the appropriate programming language. More simply still, we could specify the circuit in tabular fashion as depicted in Fig. 7.2a, which could then be interpreted to enable the operation table to be deduced for a given set of input values. For example, Fig. 7.2b shows the state of this table for four sets of input values. In each case the condition is shown after the processing of each gate in the specified sequence of the description table. Clearly, if the logic description had been entered in some other order such as with gate B or gate C listed before gate A, then two passes would be required for each set of input conditions. Thus it is necessary to sort the gates into the optimum order for efficient one-pass simulation. This is usually a straightforward process for combinational circuits and we need to arrange that a gate is only processed when all its input values for the current pass have become available.

Sequential circuits inevitably involve several iterations at each simulation step because of the feedback connections. It is usually necessary to convert sequential circuits into equivalent combinational circuits by breaking the feedback loops thereby forming 'pseudo' inputs and outputs. Fig. 7.3 demonstrates this process for a simple circuit and shows how the table description can be formed. Simulation proceeds in the normal way but at the end of each pass the pseudo-outputs are compared to the corresponding pseudo-inputs and the values updated where necessary, and the process is repeated until a stable condition is reached.

The main drawback with this type of simulation is that of slow speed due to the fact that each gate has to be processed during each pass regardless of whether its inputs have changed from the previous condition. Also, it is usually difficult to incorporate things like hazard detection and propagation delays. As a result, this type of simulation is restricted to a logic verification role.

These problems are overcome with another type of simulation philosophy. In the table-driven simulators all data relevant to each

Gate	Inputs	Type	Output
A	L_1; L_2	NAND	L_3
B	L_1; L_3	AND	L_4
C	L_2; L_3	AND	L_5
D	L_4; L_5	OR	L_6

(a)

Pass	Step	L_1	L_2	L_3	L_4	L_5	L_6
1	new inputs	0	0	?	?	?	?
	gate A	0	0	1	?	?	?
	gate B	0	0	1	0	?	?
	gate C	0	0	1	0	0	?
	gate D	0	0	1	0	0	0
2	new inputs	0	1	(1)	(0)	(0)	(0)
	gate A	0	1	1	(0)	(0)	(0)
	gate B	0	1	1	0	(0)	(0)
	gate C	0	1	1	0	1	(0)
	gate D	0	1	1	0	1	1
3	new inputs	1	0	(1)	(0)	(1)	(1)
	gate A	1	0	1	(0)	(1)	(1)
	gate B	1	0	1	1	(1)	(1)
	gate C	1	0	1	1	0	(1)
	gate D	1	0	1	1	0	1
4	new inputs	1	1	(1)	(1)	(0)	(1)
	gate A	1	1	0	(1)	(0)	(1)
	gate B	1	1	0	0	(0)	(1)
	gate C	1	1	0	0	0	(1)
	gate D	1	1	0	0	0	0

(b)

Fig. 7.2 Circuit definition and operational table for the example of Fig. 7.1.

gate is stored in a table and includes as much detail as may be required. Thus gate type, rise and fall times, propagation delay, inputs and outputs are listed together with pointers linking each gate with others in the circuit arrangement. Thus we rely on a much more complex data structure than in the previous descriptions. This new form of description is used in conjunction with a timing mechanism which enables an 'event-scheduling' process to simulate only those gates whose inputs are changing state. The result is a

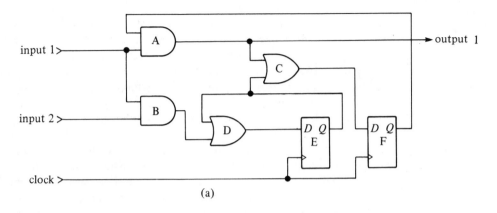

(a)

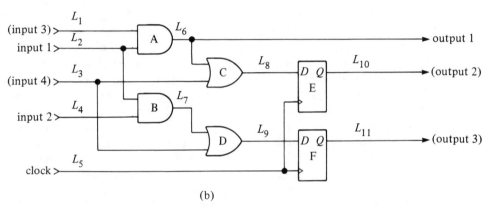

(b)

Gate	Level	Inputs	Type	Output
A	1	L_1; L_2	AND	L_6
B	1	L_2; L_4	AND	L_7
C	2	L_3; L_6	OR	L_8
D	2	L_3; L_7	OR	L_9
E	3	L_5; L_8	D-type	L_{10}
F	3	L_5; L_9	D-type	L_{11}

(c)

Fig. 7.3 (a) Example sequential circuit, (b) rearranged and levelized for simulation, and (c) tabular description.

much more meaningful simulation in terms of relative timings and delays within the circuits.

However, this requires a more structured operational table than in the compiled code simulators. Now we must have several levels on this table to represent different time slots. Each level will hold events which must become active at the relevant time. The basic time unit will be one pass through the simulation and the time slots must be capable of storing events to become active after the desired maximum number of units. This will determine one dimension of the operational table. The other dimension will depend on the likely number of events that will need to be scheduled for each time slot and this will be a function of circuit complexity. Thus the rows of the table are best implemented by some queue or file where events can be adjoined as they are generated elsewhere on the table. During each unit of simulated time the simulator processes the events scheduled on the current time-slot queue. This may generate other events which need to become active during some future time slot and so have to be scheduled by entering them in the queue of the appropriate time slot. Outputs from gates which were processed in previous time slots and are now due to become active also have to be processed during the current time slot. When all such tasks have been completed the simulation moves on to the next level and the old slot becomes available for storing future events. This enables a finite set of memory slots to be used over and over in a cyclic fashion during the course of a simulation. This rotating arrangement of time slots in a fixed section of store has been referred to as a *time wheel*. Fig. 7.4 depicts this arrangement and demonstrates the event scheduling mechanism.

Sometimes, due to the various delays being simulated, an event set to occur at some future time slot will have to be unscheduled because the conditions generating it have been subject to an intermediate development in the simulation. However, this means of storing events and their linking pointers included in their format can take account of these problems.

This manner of performing the simulation ensures that only those gates fed by active input lines are processed and the remainder will be considered during other time slots. In addition, the various delays associated with each type of circuit element are easily incorporated. Sequential circuits can be handled just as readily without the adjustments of the previous methods. All this makes for a more realistic simulation, but difficulties arise with initializing the model. This is especially the case with sequential circuits where the previous history of the circuit affects the present behaviour and if no previous history exists this has to be assumed or imposed on the simulation in some way. The great attraction of logic simulation performed by table-driven methods lies in the possibility of logic verification and design verification before construction commences. It also allows a detailed investigation of possible race and hazard conditions to be performed as well as the effect of tolerances on circuit element parameters.

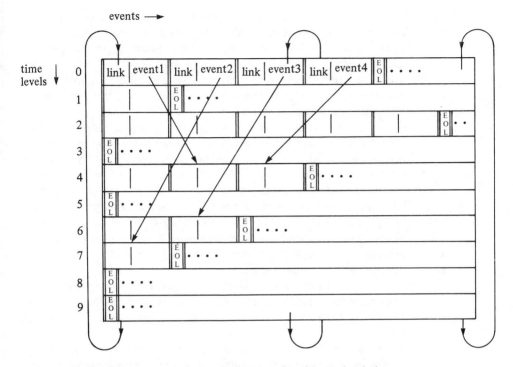

Fig. 7.4 Representation of event scheduling in table-driven simulation.

A further valuable role is that of predicting the behaviour of the circuit under various fault conditions. This enables efficient test procedures to be devised for use on the final implementation. This represents an increasingly important phase of the design process and the next section is devoted to the fundamental aspects of this technique.

7.3 AUTOMATIC TESTING OF SWITCHING CIRCUITS

The testing of switching circuits falls into two categories. First there is testing required for verification or to establish that the design conforms to the original specification. Second, there is testing to detect and possibly locate certain types of fault which may be present in the implemented circuit.

Traditionally, testing was performed by some form of exhaustive search procedure accompanied by probing with test equipment. As the implementations were in terms of discrete gates or small-scale integrated circuits this probing could be fairly intrusive and a large proportion of lines and nodes in the circuit could be physically contacted and monitored. With the more modern LSI and VLSI components this kind of probing is not possible on the physical circuit and thus testing must be confined to the inspection of the available output points to establish the response to chosen input conditions. The more intimate kind of inspection can be performed only on some form of simulation of the circuit where access to all points of the circuit can be arranged. However, this approach restricts the role of testing to that of design verification rather than operational validation of its physical implementations. As a result, interest has centred on deriving methods for the efficient automatic testing of switching circuits especially for use in volume production situations. Several techniques for the generation of test inputs to detect the presence of a single fault within a prescribed circuit have been evolved. Procedures have also been described for locating the position of a single fault and for the detection of multiple faults within a single circuit module.

As verification and testing of complex digital systems is of extreme importance, it is now recognized as essential that the design of such systems should involve ease of testability as a major design goal.

Fundamental to all these procedures is the need to generate a minimum test set of input vectors to detect the presence of a single fault within a combinational circuit by inspection of the output alone. Here the term 'fault' will be restricted to the situation where one line in the circuit remains permanently held at one of the logic levels. This identifies the so-called 'stuck-at-one' (s-a-1) and the 'stuck-at-zero' (s-a-0) faults.

There are three basic methods of test generation for such circumstances. These are based on:

1. the fault matrix,
2. Boolean differential calculus,
3. path sensitization.

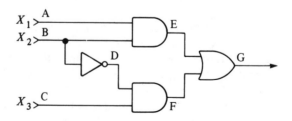

Fig. 7.5 Circuit for testing.

Tests Test No.	X_1 X_2 X_3	No fault f_0	A s-a-0 f_1	A s-a-1 f_2	B s-a-0 f_3	B s-a-1 f_4	C s-a-0 f_5	C s-a-1 f_6	D s-a-0 f_7	D s-a-1 f_8	E s-a-0 f_9	E s-a-1 f_{10}	F s-a-0 f_{11}	F s-a-1 f_{12}	G s-a-0 f_{13}	G s-a-1 f_{14}
T_0	0 0 0	0	0	0	0	0	0	1	0	0	0	1	0	1	0	1
T_1	0 0 1	1	1	1	1	0	0	1	0	1	1	1	0	1	0	1
T_2	0 1 0	0	0	1	0	0	0	0	0	0	0	1	0	1	0	1
T_3	0 1 1	0	0	1	1	0	0	0	0	1	0	1	0	1	0	1
T_4	1 0 0	0	0	0	0	1	0	1	0	0	0	1	0	1	0	1
T_5	1 0 1	1	1	1	1	1	0	1	0	1	1	1	0	1	0	1
T_6	1 1 0	1	0	1	0	1	1	1	1	1	0	1	1	1	0	1
T_7	1 1 1	1	0	1	1	1	1	1	1	1	0	1	1	1	0	1

Fig. 7.6 Initial form of fault matrix for the circuit of Fig. 7.5.

The fault matrix method is the most straightforward and most tedious method to set up. To be performed efficiently it really requires some form of logic simulator with a fault simulation capability. The matrix is an array wherein the rows consist of all the input test vectors and the columns list the output under all the fault conditions to be tested. The process of setting up and manipulating the fault matrix is best described by means of an example. Consider the simple circuit of Fig. 7.5. There are three primary inputs, X_1, X_2 and X_3, and thus an exhaustive test would involve eight distinct test input vectors, T_0, T_1,..., T_7. These form the rows of the initial matrix as indicated in Fig. 7.6. We can identify 15 different fault situations, including the no-fault condition, where one of the lines A, B,..., G is either s-a-0 or s-a-1. The outputs for each test input under each of these fault conditions form the columns of the matrix. Clearly, a test input is capable of detecting the presence of a given fault condition only when the output it produces is different from that of the fault-free condition. The matrix of Fig. 7.7 locates these

Test	f_1	f_2	f_3	f_4	f_5	f_6	f_7	f_8	f_9	f_{10}	f_{11}	f_{12}	f_{13}	f_{14}
T_0						1				1		1		1
T_1			1	1		1					1		1	
T_2		1								1		1		1
T_3		1	1					1		1		1		1
T_4				1		1				1		1		1
T_5					1	1					1		1	
T_6	1		1						1				1	
T_7	1								1				1	

Fig. 7.7 Fault detection cover of each test.

Test	f_1, f_9	f_2	f_3	f_4	f_5, f_7, f_{11}	f_6	f_8	f_{10}, f_{12}, f_{14}	f_{13}	
T_0						1		1		
T_1				1	1				1	←
T_2		1						1		
T_3		1	1				1	1		←
T_4				1		1		1		←
T_5					1				1	
T_6	1		1						1	←
T_7	1								1	

Fig. 7.8 Compressed fault matrix and selected tests.

differences on each column and is formed by adding modulo-2 the no-fault column to each fault column and then suppressing the zeros for clarity. We then discover that certain columns of this matrix are identical, which means that certain faults are indistinguishable from each other. This has consequences for fault location, but for now it enables us to compress the matrix by merging these identical columns, as shown in Fig. 7.8. The next step in the procedure is to select the minimum number of tests (rows) to cover all the required fault conditions (columns). Where there is only a single 1 in a column, as for f_8, the corresponding row indicates an 'essential' test which must be included in the test set as it represents the only way of covering the fault f_8. If the combination of all essential tests does not cover all the columns of the fault matrix, we must select from the remaining ones in order to complete this cover. In our example we find that one such test set is $\{T_2, T_4, T_5, T_7\}$ and thus we can test for all faults with just four tests rather than exhaustively with eight tests. Obviously, for more complex circuits, testing by this method could improve dramatically over exhaustive testing. However, the process of deriving this minimum test set is not trivial and the cost of setting this up must be offset against the savings during the actual testing.

The Boolean difference technique employs an algebraic method to derive the test inputs that will detect a specific fault in a circuit. The algebra is based on a Boolean form of differential calculus. Consider a Boolean expression given by

$$Z = z(X_1, X_2, \ldots, X_n)$$

where X_i are the primary inputs to the circuit. If X_k is in error, then a new function is defined as

$$Z_k = y(X_1, X_2, \ldots, \overline{X}_k, \ldots, X_n)$$

and X_k has been replaced by $\overline{X}_k$. The Boolean difference is defined as

$$dZ/dZ_k = Z \oplus Z_k = w(X_1, X_2, \ldots, X_n)$$

Consider the circuit used in the previous example. Thus

$$Z = X_1 X_2 + \overline{X}_2 X_3$$

if line A (X_1) is in error, we can define Z_1 as

$$Z_1 = \overline{X}_1 X_2 + \overline{X}_2 X_3$$
$$\begin{aligned} dZ/dZ_1 = Z \oplus Z_1 &= (X_1 X_2 + \overline{X}_2 X_3) \oplus (\overline{X}_1 X_2 + \overline{X}_2 X_3) \\ &= (X_1 X_2 \overline{X}_3 \oplus X_1 X_2 X_3 \oplus \overline{X}_1 \overline{X}_2 X_3 \oplus X_1 \overline{X}_2 X_3) \oplus \\ &\quad (\overline{X}_1 X_2 \overline{X}_3 \oplus \overline{X}_1 X_2 X_3 \oplus \overline{X}_1 \overline{X}_2 X_3 \oplus X_1 \overline{X}_2 X_3) \\ &= \overline{X}_1 X_2 \overline{X}_3 \oplus \overline{X}_1 X_2 X_3 \oplus X_1 X_2 \overline{X}_3 \oplus X_1 X_2 X_3 \end{aligned}$$

and these four minterms correspond to the test inputs T_2, T_3, T_6 and T_7. The Boolean difference covers all the input tests that will detect either an s-a-0 or an s-a-1 fault on one line of the circuit by computing the difference between the fault-free circuit and the faulty circuit. Thus, in our example, we have reproduced the entries in columns f_1 and f_2 of the fault matrix. Similarly, for line B, we find

$$\begin{aligned} dZ/dZ_2 = Z \oplus Z_2 &= (X_1 X_2 + \overline{X}_2 X_3) \oplus (X_1 \overline{X}_2 + X_2 X_3) \\ &= \overline{X}_1 \overline{X}_2 X_3 \oplus \overline{X}_1 X_2 X_3 \oplus X_1 \overline{X}_2 \overline{X}_3 \oplus X_1 X_2 \overline{X}_3 \\ &= T_1 + T_3 + T_4 + T_6 = f_2 + f_3 \end{aligned}$$

and for line C

$$\begin{aligned} dZ/dZ_3 = Z \oplus Z_3 &= \overline{X}_1 \overline{X}_2 \overline{X}_3 \oplus \overline{X}_1 \overline{X}_2 X_3 \oplus X_1 \overline{X}_2 \overline{X}_3 \oplus X_1 X_2 X_3 \\ &= T_0 + T_1 + T_4 + T_5 = f_4 + f_5 \end{aligned}$$

We can appreciate that each of these operations is essentially a transform on the original function. Thus, for the general three-variable function, let the truth table values be $d_0, d_1, \ldots, d_7$ and those of the Boolean difference be $c_0, c_1, \ldots, c_7$. It is easily verified that for a fault on line A, say, we can write

$$c_0 = d_0 \oplus d_4$$
$$c_1 = d_1 \oplus d_5$$
$$c_2 = d_2 \oplus d_6$$
$$c_3 = d_3 \oplus d_7$$
$$c_4 = d_4 \oplus d_0$$
$$c_5 = d_5 \oplus d_1$$
$$c_6 = d_6 \oplus d_2$$
$$c_7 = d_7 \oplus d_3$$

or

$$\begin{pmatrix} c_0 \\ c_1 \\ c_2 \\ c_3 \\ c_4 \\ c_5 \\ c_6 \\ c_7 \end{pmatrix} = \begin{pmatrix} 1 & 0 & 0 & 0 & 1 & 0 & 0 & 0 \\ 0 & 1 & 0 & 0 & 0 & 1 & 0 & 0 \\ 0 & 0 & 1 & 0 & 0 & 0 & 1 & 0 \\ 0 & 0 & 0 & 1 & 0 & 0 & 0 & 1 \\ 1 & 0 & 0 & 0 & 1 & 0 & 0 & 0 \\ 0 & 1 & 0 & 0 & 0 & 1 & 0 & 0 \\ 0 & 0 & 1 & 0 & 0 & 0 & 1 & 0 \\ 0 & 0 & 0 & 1 & 0 & 0 & 0 & 1 \end{pmatrix} \cdot \begin{pmatrix} d_0 \\ d_1 \\ d_2 \\ d_3 \\ d_4 \\ d_5 \\ d_6 \\ d_7 \end{pmatrix} \qquad \text{over GF(2)}$$

or

$$c = M_1 . d$$

The vector c reveals the test inputs which detect an s-a-0 or an s-a-1 fault on X_1. The transform matrix M_1 for a fault on line A is seen to be the product.

$$M_1 = \begin{bmatrix} 1 & 1 \\ 1 & 1 \end{bmatrix} * \begin{bmatrix} 1 & 0 \\ 0 & 1 \end{bmatrix} * \begin{bmatrix} 1 & 0 \\ 0 & 1 \end{bmatrix}$$

where $*$ is the Krönecker matrix product. By similar arguments we can establish that

$$M_2 = \begin{bmatrix} 1 & 0 \\ 0 & 1 \end{bmatrix} * \begin{bmatrix} 1 & 1 \\ 1 & 1 \end{bmatrix} * \begin{bmatrix} 1 & 0 \\ 0 & 1 \end{bmatrix}$$

and

$$M_3 = \begin{bmatrix} 1 & 0 \\ 0 & 1 \end{bmatrix} * \begin{bmatrix} 1 & 0 \\ 0 & 1 \end{bmatrix} * \begin{bmatrix} 1 & 1 \\ 1 & 1 \end{bmatrix}$$

and this reveals the general structure of these Boolean difference transforms. For the n-variable case we have a set of n matrices,

$$M_1 = \begin{bmatrix} 1 & 1 \\ 1 & 1 \end{bmatrix} * \begin{bmatrix} 1 & 0 \\ 0 & 1 \end{bmatrix} * \begin{bmatrix} 1 & 0 \\ 0 & 1 \end{bmatrix} * \ldots * \begin{bmatrix} 1 & 0 \\ 0 & 1 \end{bmatrix} \qquad \text{fault on line } X_1$$

$$M_2 = \begin{bmatrix} 1 & 0 \\ 0 & 1 \end{bmatrix} * \begin{bmatrix} 1 & 1 \\ 1 & 1 \end{bmatrix} * \begin{bmatrix} 1 & 0 \\ 0 & 1 \end{bmatrix} * \ldots * \begin{bmatrix} 1 & 0 \\ 0 & 1 \end{bmatrix} \qquad \text{fault on line } X_2$$

$$M_n = \begin{bmatrix} 1 & 0 \\ 0 & 1 \end{bmatrix} * \begin{bmatrix} 1 & 0 \\ 0 & 1 \end{bmatrix} * \begin{bmatrix} 1 & 0 \\ 0 & 1 \end{bmatrix} * \ldots * \begin{bmatrix} 1 & 1 \\ 1 & 1 \end{bmatrix} \qquad \text{fault on line } X_n$$

and each involves the Krönecker product of n factors.

The Boolean difference can also be applied to faults at other points in the circuit. Consider a fault on line D of our circuit. Now we can write:

$$Z = X_1 X_2 + D . X_3$$

where $D = \overline{X}_2$. Therefore,

$$Z_D = X_1 X_2 + \bar{D} X_3 = X_1 X_2 + X_2 X_3$$

and

$$\mathrm{d}Z/\mathrm{d}Z_\mathrm{D} = Z \oplus Z_\mathrm{D} = \overline{X}_1\overline{X}_2X_3 \oplus \overline{X}_1X_2X_3 \oplus X_1\overline{X}_2X_3$$
$$= T_1 + T_3 + T_5 = f_7 + f_8$$

Similarly, for line E,

$$Z = E + \overline{X}_2X_3$$
$$Z_\mathrm{E} = \overline{E} + \overline{X}_2X_3 = \overline{X}_1\overline{X}_2 + \overline{X}_2X_3$$

and

$$\mathrm{d}Z/\mathrm{d}Z_\mathrm{E} = Z \oplus Z_\mathrm{E} = \overline{X}_1\overline{X}_2\overline{X}_3 \oplus \overline{X}_1X_2\overline{X}_3 \oplus \overline{X}_1X_2X_3 \oplus X_1\overline{X}_2\overline{X}_3 \oplus$$
$$X_1X_2\overline{X}_3 \oplus X_1X_2X_3$$
$$= T_0 + T_2 + T_3 + T_4 + T_6 + T_7 = f_9 + f_{10}$$

and, for line F,

$$Z = X_1X_2 + F$$
$$Z_\mathrm{F} = X_1X_2 + \overline{F} = X_1X_2 + \overline{\overline{X}_2X_3}$$

and

$$\mathrm{d}Z/\mathrm{d}Z_\mathrm{F} = Z \oplus Z_\mathrm{F} = \overline{X}_1\overline{X}_2\overline{X}_3 \oplus \overline{X}_1\overline{X}_2X_3 \oplus \overline{X}_1X_2\overline{X}_3 \oplus$$
$$X_1\overline{X}_2\overline{X}_3 \oplus X_1\overline{X}_2X_3$$
$$= T_0 + T_1 + T_2 + T_3 + T_4 + T_5 = f_{11} + f_{12}$$

Obviously, as $Z = G$

$$Z_\mathrm{G} = \overline{G}$$

and

$$\mathrm{d}Z/\mathrm{d}Z_\mathrm{G} = Z \oplus Z_\mathrm{G} = G \oplus \overline{G} = 1$$
$$= T_0 + T_1 + T_2 + T_3 + T_4 + T_5 + T_6 + T_7 = f_{13} + f_{14}$$

We can also use the Karnaugh map to help in the identification of tests. For each fault line we add, on a cell-by-cell modulo-2 basis, the map of the original function to the map of the modified function. The result will be a map of the Boolean difference and will list the tests which detect an s-a-0 or an s-a-1 fault on the particular line. The modified function can be found algebraically as above or by manipulating the Karnaugh map of the original function. Fig. 7.9 demonstrates how the cells of a three-variable map should be interchanged for the cases of faults on the primary input lines. Other faults will require combinations of these manipulations. Fig. 7.10 shows how the complete test generation for the previous example can be performed using Karnaugh maps. These maps also make it easy to identify which tests in a set are for s-a-0 or s-a-1. The former will be those tests which lie in the area of the map

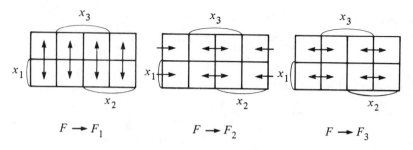

Fig. 7.9 Karnaugh map manipulation for forming Boolean differences.

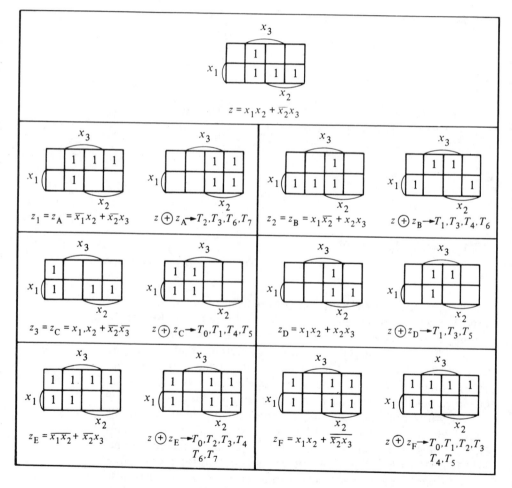

Fig. 7.10 Karnaugh map derivation of tests by Boolean differences.

where the fault variable is 1, and the latter are located where the fault variable is 0.

The path-sensitization method of test generation attempts to deduce a test to detect a specific fault by arranging that all gates on a path between the fault and a primary output are 'sensitized' and able to pass the fault on to the output where it can be observed. Thus, one path through an AND gate can be sensitized by ensuring all its other inputs are made logical 1, and for an OR gate all other inputs should be set to 0. Similar arrangements can be deduced for other gate types.

One-dimensional path sensitization requires setting up the conditions whereby just one path from fault to an output is sensitized. This is not always a straightforward procedure because although it is usually possible to assign values to sensitize the required path during the so-called 'forward-trace' phase inconsistencies may arise when attempting to assign values to the remaining circuit nodes, to sustain the original choices, during the 'backward-trace' phase. Thus, certain conditions required to support the sensitization of a particular gate may desensitize another. Under these circumstances, other possible paths should be investigated if they are available, otherwise no test for the particular fault can be found. These problems can sometimes by overcome by allowing for multiple-path sensitization through a circuit from fault to output.

The main method for generating these n-dimensional path sensitizations is due to Roth's D-algorithm. This is based on the algebra of D-cubes, where D stands for the discrepancy between the faulty and fault-free behaviour. Consider the two-input NAND gate of Fig. 7.11a, with inputs A, B, and output C. The normal truth table of Fig. 7.11b can be represented in the more compact form of

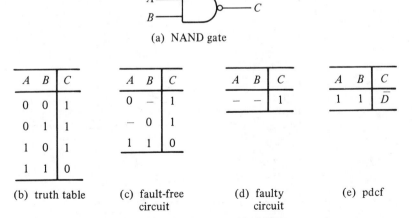

(a) NAND gate

A	B	C
0	0	1
0	1	1
1	0	1
1	1	0

(b) truth table

A	B	C
0	−	1
−	0	1
1	1	0

(c) fault-free circuit

A	B	C
−	−	1

(d) faulty circuit

A	B	C
1	1	D

(e) pdcf

Fig. 7.11 Primitive D-cube of failure for a NAND gate.

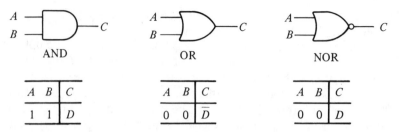

Fig. 7.12 Primitive D-cube of failure for other basic gates.

Fig. 7.11c for the fault-free condition. Suppose that the output becomes s-a-1, then the cover for the faulty circuit is that of Fig. 7.11d. The D-notation allows us to denote the discrepancy in operation between the correct and faulty circuit. Thus, we can write $11/\bar{D}$ to denote 11/0 for the correct and 11/1 for the faulty and $\bar{D}$ represents 0 in the correct and 1 in the fault condition. The $11/\bar{D}$ is called a primitive D-cube of failure or pdcf. Fig. 7.12 gives the pdcf's of some other simple logic elements.

In conjunction with Roth's algorithm, a method of labelling the nodes or lines of the circuit under test is usually adopted. We begin by labelling all primary inputs consecutively commencing at 1. Then we arrange that the number assigned to the output of each gate is higher than the numbers on its input lines. We can identify a gate by the number on its output line. The circuit of Fig. 7.13 is due to Schneider and was used by Roth to illustrate his algorithm. The lines have been labelled in the prescribed manner. Suppose we wish to devise a test for line 6 s-a-1. The pdcf of this gate must be $11/\bar{D}$ as indicated earlier, which requires us to make lines 2, 3 and 6 equal to 1, 1 and $\bar{D}$ respectively. In order to detect this fault we must force it to the output and this process is termed the 'D-drive'. This is done

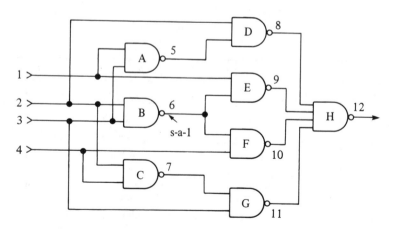

Fig. 7.13 Example circuit for D-algorithm analysis.

by defining the 'D-frontier' which is the set of gates which have a D or $\bar{D}$ on an input and unassigned outputs. In our example we have gates 9 and 10. To proceed we always select the lowest numbered gate and assess what is required to propagate the $\bar{D}$ on line 6 through this gate. Thus we are required to set line 1 to logical 1 so that line 9 will become D. This generates some implications because line 5 will become a 0 which in turn forces line 8 to a 1. We can keep track of all these conditions on a table similar to that of Fig. 7.14a, which summarizes the position so far. This reveals that several lines are still unassigned but no inconsistencies have arisen. These would be identified by conflicting entries in the same column of the table. We can therefore continue with the D-drive. The D-frontier now contains gates 10 and 12. Therefore we concentrate next on gate 10 and line 4 must be set to 1 to enable the $\bar{D}$ to be propagated. This implies that line 7 must be 0 and this forces line 11 to be 1. Again, fortunately, no inconsistencies have arisen and the D-drive is complete because line 12, the output, will become $\bar{D}$. Fig. 7.14b shows the complete assignment and this demonstrates that if the inputs are made 1 1 1 1 the fault on line 6 s-a-1 is observable at the output. In the fault-free circuit the output will be 0 and with line 6 s-a-1 the output will be 1.

If inconsistencies do arise during the D-drive it is necessary to backtrack to the previous decision and select a new gate for the D-drive. If after all possibilities have been tried there is still no consistent set of conditions then no test exists for the particular fault. Roth's algorithm guarantees to find a test if one exists.

Whereas the fault matrix reveals the 'fault cover' of each test, the Boolean difference and the path-sensitization methods do not directly indicate which other faults, if any, the test(s) may detect. However, in these cases it is fairly easy to deduce the fault cover of each test.

For example we have observed in Fig. 7.14, with the input condition 1 1 1 1, that the output is 0 in the fault-free condition. Any fault which causes the output to rise to 1 will be observable with this test. Thus if any of the inputs to gate 12 are s-a-0 the output will be forced to 1. Therefore this test also includes lines 8, 9, 10 or 11 s-a-0. Similarly, lines 8 and 11 could be s-a-0 because lines 5 or 7 were respectively s-a-1, so this test also covers these possible faults. Tracing even further back we can also deduce that this same test will detect any of the primary inputs s-a-0.

The Reed–Muller expansions of Chapter 5 produce circuits which are particularly amenable to test generation. The general three-variable expansion,

$$f(X_3, X_2, X_1) = c_0 \oplus c_1 X_1 \oplus c_2 X_2 \oplus c_3 X_2 X_1 \oplus c_4 X_3 \oplus$$
$$c_5 X_3 X_1 \oplus c_6 X_3 X_2 \oplus c_7 X_3 X_2 X_1$$

	Line numbers											
	1	2	3	4	5	6	7	8	9	10	11	12
pdcf		1	1			$\bar{D}$						
D-drive	1					$\bar{D}$			D			
Implication $\{$	1		1		0							
		1			0				1			
Summary	1	1	1	?	0	$\bar{D}$	?	1	D	?	?	?

(a)

	Line numbers											
	1	2	3	4	5	6	7	8	9	10	11	12
from (a)	1	1	1		0	$\bar{D}$		1	D			
D-drive				1		$\bar{D}$				D		
Implication $\{$				1			0				1	
								1	D	D	1	$\bar{D}$
Result	1	1	1	1	0	$\bar{D}$	0	1	D	D	1	$\bar{D}$

(b)

Fig. 7.14 Generation of test pattern for line 6 s-a-1.

could be synthesized by the arrangement of Fig. 7.15a. The specific function,

$$f(X_3, X_2, X_1) = 1 \oplus X_2 \oplus X_2 X_1 \oplus X_3 X_1 \oplus X_3 X_2 X_1$$

appears as in Fig. 7.15b. We assume that a single s-a-0 or s-a-1 fault occurs in the inputs or outputs of the multipliers or a single adder is faulty. The output of the faulty adder is allowed to be any one of the 15 two-variable functions other than the correct EOR operation. Also, we assume that the primary input rails are fault-free, although the inputs to individual gates may be faulty.

In order to detect a single fault in the cascade of adders it is necessary to apply a set of tests which will connect all possible input combinations to each unit of the chain. In fact this can be done with just four test patterns and these are listed for the three-variable case in test set 1 of Fig. 7.16a. The first test of all 0s will produce a 0 output under fault-free conditions, as inputs and outputs of all gates are 0s. In the third test $c_0 = 1$ and outputs of all multipliers will be 0 so the 1 propagates down the adder chain testing the $1 \oplus 0 = 1$ row

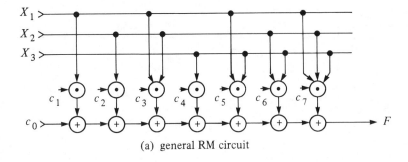

(a) general RM circuit

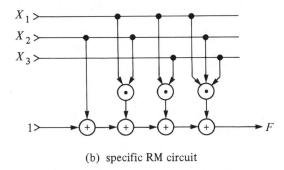

(b) specific RM circuit

Fig. 7.15 Direct cascade synthesis of RM expansions.

of the truth table in each case. For tests 2 and 4 all multipliers will have output 1 and with $c_0 = 0$ odd-numbered adders will be tested with $0 \oplus 1 = 1$ and even-numbered with $1 \oplus 1 = 0$. This situation is reversed when c_0 is made 1.

Now an s-a-0 fault at any multiplier input or output can be detected by applying all 1s to the variable inputs, with c_0 either 0 or 1, i.e. a don't care value. An s-a-1 fault on the output of any multiplier is detected by applying all 0s to the variable inputs with c_0 again a don't care. Both of these test patterns are included in the test set for the adder chain. An s-a-1 fault at any one of the inputs to the multipliers can be detected by one of three input vectors which places a 0 on just one input rail and 1s elsewhere as listed in test set 2 of Fig. 7.16a. An s-a-1 fault will cause the output of the corresponding multiplier to become 1 instead of 0 when the input vector has a 0 in the variable position of the fault. Thus the output of the complete network will become the inverse of the fault-free value.

These results generalize very readily to the n-variable case and Fig. 7.16a reveals that the complete circuit can be tested with just $n + 4$ tests, and furthermore these tests are identical for all n-variable

Test set 1	c_0	X_1	X_2	X_3
1	0	0	0	0
2	0	1	1	1
3	1	0	0	0
4	1	1	1	1

Test set 2	c_0	X_1	X_2	X_3
1	—	0	1	1
2	—	1	0	1
3	—	1	1	0

Test set 1	c_0	X_1	X_2	$X_3 \cdot \ \cdot \cdot X_n$
1	0	0	0	$0 \cdot \cdot \cdot 0$
2	0	1	1	$1 \cdot \cdot \cdot 1$
3	1	0	0	$0 \cdot \cdot \cdot 0$
4	1	1	1	$1 \cdot \cdot \cdot 1$

Test set 2	c_0	X_1	X_2	$X_3 \cdot \ \cdot \cdot X_n$
1	—	0	1	$1 \cdot \cdot \cdot 1$
2	—	1	0	$1 \cdot \cdot \cdot 1$
.	.	.	.	.
.	.	.	.	.
.	.	.	.	.
n	—	1	1	$1 \cdot \cdot \cdot 0$

Fig. 7.16 Test sets for circuits representing RM expansions with (a) three inputs, and (b) n inputs.

functions which makes the testing of RM expansions an attractive proposition.

If we wish to cover the possibility of faults on the primary inputs rails, in which case the rest of the circuit can be considered fault-free, we need to sensitize an odd number of paths from faulty input to the output because the nature of modulo-2 addition will cancel out an even number and appear to be fault-free. In some cases, where the input is used in an odd number of product terms, these faults will be detected by the tests in the test sets already specified. However, where primary inputs are used in an even number of product terms, such as X_3 in our example, we have to extend the test set by including extra test input vectors. These, of course, will be dependent on the particular function. We can also devise simple test procedures when circuits are represented in RM-tree form rather than this direct cascade arrangement.

The more difficult problem of fault location in general circuit implementations has also received much attention. Location of a single fault can sometimes be achieved by applying a series of tests and inspecting how the circuit fails. By comparing the pattern of failures with the test cover of each test it may be possible to isolate the single fault consistent with these results. Sometimes of course certain faults may be indistinguishable, such as either input of an AND gate s-a-0 or its output s-a-0. In these circumstances locating the faulty device is just as valid as isolating the particular fault. We can also extend the above principles to detect multiple errors. Also, more complex components such as multiplexers or even PLAs can be included in the test generation procedures. Techniques are also available for sequential circuits and here test input vectors are replaced with test input sequences and so the process becomes essentially a serial one.

7.4 MULTIPLE-VALUED SWITCHING CIRCUITS

Although much thought has been devoted by many workers during the past several years as to how the binary switching circuit regime might be extended to higher radices, contemporary technology has always precluded any significant advances on the practical applications front. This situation is rapidly changing, and the advent of LSI and VLSI techniques has made available a technology wherein highly complex circuits may be reproduced with relative ease and in an inexpensive and very compact physical form. Such a technology may soon make it possible to design and manufacture switching devices which operate with three, four or even more levels of logic values. One of the limiting factors in the development of conventional binary systems is concerned with the numbers of inputs and outputs required to communicate with the system modules. Thus, the complexity of the integrated circuitry within a LSI package is being limited by the mechanical problems associated with communication between circuits through input and output pins. In addition, a significant proportion of implementation costs of a digital system falls upon the wiring and routing for interconnecting the system modules both on the silicon wafer and at printed-circuit board, mother-board and subsystem levels. Furthermore, reliability of systems is also related to the number of external connections because there are sources of wiring errors and bad connections. One dramatic way to reduce the number of connections in a digital system is to allow each conductor to carry multiple-valued signals rather than the two-valued binary format. Thus, the adoption of a three-valued (ternary), four-valued (quaternary) or, in general, q-valued format enables n pins to pass 3^n, 4^n or q^n combinations of values, respectively, rather than just 2^n limited by the binary representation. Once this principle has been accepted, it becomes of interest to study the means whereby we may describe, design and synthesize systems which operate with multiple-valued signals.

The development of multiple-valued switching circuit theory has followed two main paths reflecting the dichotomy observed in the binary world. On the one hand we have a generalization of the familiar AND, OR and NOT binary Boolean connectives to their multiple-valued counterparts of *conjunction, disjunction* and *cycling* operations introduced by Post in 1920. On the other hand we have the extension of the modular approach first indicated by Bernstein in 1928, where the operations become modulo-p addition and multiplication on the integers modulo-p. Obviously, these early pioneers were not concerned with the development of switching algebras but rather with the description of formal logics. It was left to much later for other workers to recognize the importance of this early work in relation to multiple-valued switching circuits. This was also the case when Shannon first indicated the use of Boolean algebra to describe the action of relay circuits.

The familiar Boolean algebra on the values 0 and 1, which we can refer to as B(2), is just the simplest case of a whole family of algebras based on the abstract notion of a lattice. In fact we can construct a Boolean algebra for any number of values q which is also a power of two, i.e. $q = 2^k$. For example Fig. 7.17 shows the basic operations of B(4) on the set of 'values' (0, a, b, 1). Unfortunately, all Boolean algebras other than B(2) are found to be functionally incomplete and thus are of little use for the purpose of switching circuit design where we require a unique expression for each possible switching function. However, a different kind of generalization is provided by the Postian algebras. Here the basic connectives are taken as *conjunction* and *disjunction* which are provided by the min and max operations. These are defined as

$$x . y \quad = \min(x, y) \quad conjunction, \text{ result is minimum value of } x, y$$

$$x + y = \max(x, y) \quad disjunction, \text{ result is maximum value of } x, y$$

where x and y take values from the integers 0, 1, 2,..., $q - 1$ for a q-valued system. We can refer to the latter as P(q). In addition, there is a unary operation termed a *cycling* operation and x' is a cyclic shift of the values allotted to x. Alternatively, we could say $x' = x \oplus 1$ modulo-q. Fig. 7.18 gives the operational tables for the ternary and quaternary Postian algebras P(3) and P(4). The extension to other values of q is obvious and here we note that P(2) is

•	0	a	b	1
0	0	0	0	0
a	0	a	0	a
b	0	0	b	b
1	0	a	b	1

+	0	a	b	1
0	0	a	b	1
a	a	a	1	1
b	b	1	b	1
1	1	1	1	1

x	$\overline{x}$
0	1
a	b
b	a
1	0

Fig. 7.17 Operations of four-valued Boolean algebra B(4).

P(3):

•	0	1	2
0	0	0	0
1	0	1	1
2	0	1	2

ternary conjunction

+	0	1	2
0	0	1	2
1	1	1	2
2	2	2	2

ternary disjunction

x	x'	x''
0	1	2
1	2	0
2	0	1

ternary cycling

P(4):

•	0	1	2	3
0	0	0	0	0
1	0	1	1	1
2	0	1	2	2
3	0	1	2	3

quaternary
conjunction

+	0	1	2	3
0	0	1	2	3
1	1	1	2	3
2	2	2	2	3
3	3	3	3	3

quaternary
disjunction

x	x'	x''	x'''
0	1	2	3
1	2	3	0
2	3	0	1
3	0	1	2

quaternary
cycling

Fig. 7.18 Operations of ternary and quaternary Postian algebras.

identical to B(2). These tables reveal the following relationships, for P(3):

$$x.0 = 0.x = 0 \qquad x.2 = 2.x = x$$
$$x + 0 = 0 + x = x \qquad x + 2 = 2 + x = 2$$

so that 2 is the identity for conjunction. Also $1.x \neq x$ and $1.2 = 2.1 = 1$. As in the binary case, we can deduce the number of q-valued switching functions by enumerating the distinct 'truth tables'. Naturally, we now have to develop the multiple-valued counterpart of the truth table and we can regard this as a table showing the output value of the function corresponding to each possible combination of values of the q-valued inputs. For the n-variable function, there will be q^n rows, n input columns, and 1 output column on the table. Each output value can be selected in q ways giving a possibility of q^{q^n} different functions. Fig. 7.19 shows an example of a two-variable ternary truth table.

Unfortunately, it is not obvious how to construct an algebraic representation of this function using the P(3) operations. In the binary case this task was performed by assigning a unique product term to each row of the table which could then be selected using the output values as coefficients. This is not possible in P(3) unless we introduce some additional unary operations, because the basic product terms such as $x_2 x_1$ or $x_2' x_1$ have values on more than one

x_2	x_1	$f(x_2, x_1)$
0	0	0
0	1	0
0	2	2
1	0	0
1	1	0
1	2	2
2	0	1
2	1	1
2	2	2

Fig. 7.19   Example of a two-variable ternary function.

row of the truth table. One possible set of unary functions are the j-operators, symbolized as $j_i(x)$ and defined as follows, for $P(q)$:

$$j_i(x) = q - 1$$

when $x = i$ and $i = 0, 1, 2, \ldots, q - 1$; otherwise

$$j_i(x) = 0$$

Fig. 7.20 gives the truth table of the three j-operators for $P(3)$. These operators enable the equivalent of minterms to be defined. For $n = 1$ we note that

$$m_0 = j_0(x_1)$$
$$m_1 = j_1(x_1)$$

and

$$m_2 = j_2(x_1)$$

and observe that

$$m_0 + m_1 + m_2 = 2$$

Fig. 7.21 shows the nine minterms for two variables and each one is a combination of j-operators and has value 2 on one row of the truth

x	$j_0(x)$	$j_1(x)$	$j_2(x)$
0	2	0	0
1	0	2	0
2	0	0	2

Fig. 7.20   Definition of the ternary j-operators.

x_2 x_1	m_0 $j_0(x_2)j_0(x_1)$	m_1 $j_0(x_2)j_1(x_1)$	m_2 $j_0(x_2)j_2(x_1)$	m_3 $j_1(x_2)j_0(x_1)$	m_4 $j_1(x_2)j_1(x_1)$	m_5 $j_1(x_2)j_2(x_1)$	m_6 $j_2(x_2)j_0(x_1)$	m_7 $j_2(x_2)j_1(x_1)$	m_8 $j_2(x_2)j_2(x_1)$	$f(x_2, x_1)$
0 0	2	0	0	0	0	0	0	0	0	d_0
0 1	0	2	0	0	0	0	0	0	0	d_1
0 2	0	0	2	0	0	0	0	0	0	d_2
1 0	0	0	0	2	0	0	0	0	0	d_3
1 1	0	0	0	0	2	0	0	0	0	d_4
1 2	0	0	0	0	0	2	0	0	0	d_5
2 0	0	0	0	0	0	0	2	0	0	d_6
2 1	0	0	0	0	0	0	0	2	0	d_7
2 2	0	0	0	0	0	0	0	0	2	d_8

Fig. 7.21 The two-variable ternary minterms.

table and 0 elsewhere. This enables the disjunctive canonical form to be set up as

$$f(x_2, x_1) = d_0 j_0(x_2)j_0(x_1) + d_1 j_0(x_2)j_1(x_1) + d_2 j_0(x_2)j_2(x_1) +$$
$$d_3 j_1(x_2)j_0(x_1) + d_4 j_1(x_2)j_1(x_1) + d_5 j_1(x_2)j_2(x_1) +$$
$$d_6 j_2(x_2)j_0(x_1) + d_7 j_2(x_2)j_1(x_1) + d_8 j_2(x_2)j_2(x_1)$$

$$= \sum_{i=0}^{8} d_i m_i$$

where Σ is summation using the max operation. Thus, the term $d_i j_{c_2}(x_2)j_{c_1}(x_1) = d_i$ for $x_2 = c_2$ and $x_1 = c_1$, where $\langle i \rangle_{10} = \langle c_2, c_1 \rangle_3$, and zero otherwise. Therefore,

$$f(c_2, c_1) = d_i$$

and as $\langle c_2 c_1 \rangle$ goes through all ternary combinations from $\langle 00 \rangle$ to $\langle 22 \rangle$ the truth table values d_0 to d_8 are produced by the general expression. In conjunction with the truth table and canonical form we can also define ternary Karnaugh maps. Fig. 7.22a shows the general two-variable map which requires $3^2 = 9$ cells. The function defined by the truth table of Fig. 7.19 is depicted on the map of Fig. 7.22b.

The minterms m_2, m_5 and m_8 have coefficients equal to 2 and can be combined algebraically.

$$2.m_2 + 2.m_5 + 2.m_8 = 2j_0(x_2)j_2(x_1) + 2j_1(x_2)j_2(x_1) + 2j_2(x_2)j_2(x_1)$$
$$= 2j_2(x_1)[j_0(x_2) + j_1(x_2) + j_2(x_2)]$$
$$= 2j_2(x_1).2$$
$$= j_2(x_1)$$

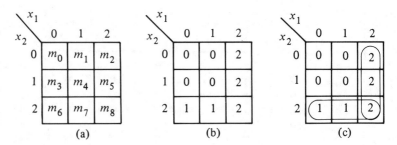

Fig. 7.22 General two-variable ternary map and example function with prime implicant selection.

The remaining minterms m_6, m_7 and m_8 can be combined

$$1.m_6 + 1.m_7 + m_8 \quad = 1.j_2(x_2).j_0(x_1) + 1.j_2(x_2)j_1(x_1) + j_2(x_2)j_2(x_1)$$
$$= 1.j_2(x_2)[j_0(x_1) + j_1(x_1) + j_2(x_1)]$$
$$= 1.j_2(x_2).2$$
$$= 1.j_2(x_2)$$

Therefore,

$$f(x_2, x_1) = j_2(x_1) + 1.j_2(x_2)$$

We can verify that this expression does in fact represent a simplification of the original canonical form by setting up the truth table of each term and the sum as demonstrated in Fig. 7.23. A typical realization of this reduced expression, in terms of ternary circuit components, is provided in Fig. 7.24. We can also appreciate that the same simplified expression could be derived by a looping process on the Karnaugh map as indicated in Fig. 7.22a. Here, we require to

x_2	x_1	a $j_2(x_1)$	b $1.j_2(x_2)$	$\Sigma a, b$	$f(x_2, x_1)$
0	0	0	0	0	0
0	1	0	0	0	0
0	2	2	0	2	2
1	0	0	0	0	0
1	1	0	0	0	0
1	2	2	0	2	2
2	0	0	1	1	1
2	1	0	1	1	1
2	2	2	1	2	2

Fig. 7.23 Verification of the simplification process.

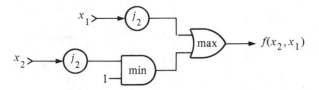

Fig. 7.24 Synthesis of the simplified function of Fig. 7.22.

locate groups of 1, 3, 9, etc., adjacent minterms on the map and each one will represent a prime implicant. If one or more of the values in the loop is equal to 1 then the term retains a coefficient of 1. A more complex example is given in Fig. 7.25. The simplification process yields the expression

$$f(x_2, x_1) = 1.j_0(x_1) + 1.j_1(x_2) + j_0(x_2)j_2(x_1) +$$
$$j_1(x_2)j_0(x_1) + j_2(x_2)j_1(x_1)$$

This demonstrates that design procedures can be set up for this and other Postian algebraic systems which are the counterparts of those devised for Boolean algebra. However, it is generally true that the manipulation of these algebraic descriptions becomes increasingly more difficult for higher values of q.

An alternative form of description is provided by the generalization of the modulo-2 arithmetic approach. For any $q = p$, a prime integer, we can employ modulo-p arithmetic on the integers modulo-p, i.e. 0, 1, 2,..., $p - 1$. Fig. 7.26 gives the arithmetic tables for the cases $p = 3$ and $p = 5$. As we observed in Chapter 5, this kind of algebraic structure is an example of a finite or Galois field and we would denote these two examples as GF(3) and GF(5).

The equivalent multiple-valued Reed–Muller expansion for a one-variable function over GF(p) can be expressed as

$$f(x_1) = c_0 \oplus c_1 x_1 \oplus c_2 x_1^2 \oplus \ldots \oplus c_{p-1} x_1^{p-1} \qquad \text{over GF}(p)$$

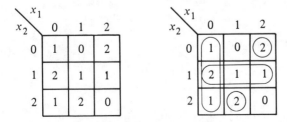

Fig. 7.25 Example of ternary function minimization.

GF(3):

$\odot$	0	1	2
0	0	0	0
1	0	1	2
2	0	2	1

modulo-3 multiplication

$\oplus$	0	1	2
0	0	1	2
1	1	2	0
2	2	0	1

modulo-3 addition

GF(5):

$\odot$	0	1	2	3	4
0	0	0	0	0	0
1	0	1	2	3	4
2	0	2	4	1	3
3	0	3	1	4	2
4	0	4	3	2	1

modulo-5 multiplication

$\oplus$	0	1	2	3	4
0	0	1	2	3	4
1	1	2	3	4	0
2	2	3	4	0	1
3	3	4	0	1	2
4	4	0	1	2	3

modulo-5 addition

Fig. 7.26   Arithmetic table for GF(3) and GF(5).

Thus for GF(3) this resolves to

$$f(x_1) = c_0 \oplus c_1 x_1 \oplus c_2 x_1^2 \qquad \text{over GF(3)}$$

Now from the arithmetic tables we observe that

$$x \oplus x = 2.x \quad \text{and} \quad x \oplus 2.x = 0$$

therefore

$$-x = 2.x$$

also

$$x.x = x^2 \quad \text{and} \quad x.x^2 = x^3 = x$$

The coefficients c_i are 0, 1 or 2 and can be related to the digits of the one-variable truth table as follows:

$$d_0 = f(0) = c_0$$
$$d_1 = f(1) = c_0 \oplus c_1 \oplus c_2$$
$$d_2 = f(2) = c_0 \oplus 2c_1 \oplus c_2$$

or, in matrix form, as

$$d = S_1.c$$

or

$$\begin{pmatrix} d_0 \\ d_1 \\ d_2 \end{pmatrix} = \begin{pmatrix} 1 & 0 & 0 \\ 1 & 1 & 1 \\ 1 & 2 & 1 \end{pmatrix} \cdot \begin{pmatrix} c_0 \\ c_1 \\ c_2 \end{pmatrix} \qquad \text{over GF(3)}$$

Thus, S_1 represents the ternary function domain to operational domain transform. We can derive the inverse transform $T_1 = S_1^{-1}$ as follows:

$$c_0 = d_0$$
$$d_0 \oplus d_1 \oplus d_2 = 2c_2$$

Therefore,

$$c_2 = 2d_0 \oplus 2d_1 \oplus 2d_2$$

and

$$c_1 = d_1 \oplus 2c_0 \oplus 2c_2 = d_1 \oplus 2d_0 \oplus d_0 \oplus d_1 \oplus d_2$$
$$= 2d_1 \oplus d_2$$

So that

$$c = T_1 . d$$

where

$$\begin{pmatrix} c_0 \\ c_1 \\ c_2 \end{pmatrix} = \begin{pmatrix} 1 & 0 & 0 \\ 0 & 2 & 1 \\ 2 & 2 & 2 \end{pmatrix} \cdot \begin{pmatrix} d_0 \\ d_1 \\ d_2 \end{pmatrix} \qquad \text{over GF(3)}$$

so T_1 represents the ternary operational domain to function domain transform and, unlike the GF(2) case, T_1 is not equal to S_1.

For two variables the ternary RM expansion is

$$f(x_2, x_1) = c_0 \oplus c_1 x_1 \oplus c_2 x_1^2 \oplus c_3 x_2 \oplus c_4 x_2 x_1 \oplus c_5 x_2 x_1^2 \oplus$$
$$c_6 x_2^2 \oplus c_7 x_2^2 x_1 \oplus c_8 x_2^2 x_1^2$$

and by similar arguments to the above we find that the corresponding transforms S_2 and T_2 take the form

$$S_2 = \begin{bmatrix} 1 & 0 & 0 & 0 & 0 & 0 & 0 & 0 & 0 \\ 1 & 1 & 1 & 0 & 0 & 0 & 0 & 0 & 0 \\ 1 & 2 & 1 & 0 & 0 & 0 & 0 & 0 & 0 \\ 1 & 0 & 0 & 1 & 0 & 0 & 1 & 0 & 0 \\ 1 & 1 & 1 & 1 & 1 & 1 & 1 & 1 & 1 \\ 1 & 2 & 1 & 1 & 2 & 1 & 1 & 2 & 1 \\ 1 & 0 & 0 & 2 & 0 & 0 & 1 & 0 & 0 \\ 1 & 1 & 1 & 2 & 2 & 2 & 1 & 1 & 1 \\ 1 & 2 & 1 & 2 & 1 & 2 & 1 & 2 & 1 \end{bmatrix} \quad \text{and} \quad T_2 = \begin{bmatrix} 1 & 0 & 0 & 0 & 0 & 0 & 0 & 0 & 0 \\ 0 & 2 & 1 & 0 & 0 & 0 & 0 & 0 & 0 \\ 2 & 2 & 2 & 0 & 0 & 0 & 0 & 0 & 0 \\ 0 & 0 & 0 & 2 & 0 & 0 & 1 & 0 & 0 \\ 0 & 0 & 0 & 0 & 1 & 2 & 0 & 2 & 1 \\ 0 & 0 & 0 & 1 & 1 & 1 & 2 & 2 & 2 \\ 2 & 0 & 0 & 2 & 0 & 0 & 2 & 0 & 0 \\ 0 & 1 & 2 & 0 & 1 & 2 & 0 & 1 & 2 \\ 1 & 1 & 1 & 1 & 1 & 1 & 1 & 1 & 1 \end{bmatrix}$$

As in the binary case these matrices exhibit a recursive structure so that

$$S_n = \begin{bmatrix} S_{n-1} & 0 & 0 \\ S_{n-1} & S_{n-1} & S_{n-1} \\ S_{n-1} & 2.S_{n-1} & S_{n-1} \end{bmatrix} \qquad \text{for } n > 0 \text{ and } S_0 = [1]$$

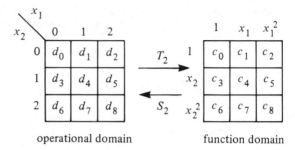

Fig. 7.27 Operational domain and function domain maps for GF(3).

and

$$T_n = \begin{bmatrix} T_{n-1} & 0 & 0 \\ 0 & 2T_{n-1} & T_{n-1} \\ 2T_{n-1} & 2T_{n-1} & 2T_{n-1} \end{bmatrix} \quad \text{for } n > 0 \text{ and } T_0 = [1]$$

Alternatively, we could express these in terms of the Krönecker matrix product

$$S_n = S_1 * S_{n-1}$$
$$= S_1 * S_1 * \ldots * S_1 \quad n \text{ times}$$

and

$$T_n = T_1 * T_{n-1}$$
$$= T_1 * T_1 * \ldots * T_1 \quad n \text{ times}$$

The two domains can be depicted by their respective maps as indicated in Fig. 7.27 for the two-variable case. We can employ the transform T_2 to derive the ternary Reed–Muller expansion of the function of Fig. 7.25 and the process is shown in Fig. 7.28. This reveals that the resulting expression is

$$f(x_2, x_1) = 1 \oplus 2x_1 \oplus 2x_2 \oplus x_2 x_1 \oplus x_2 x_1^2 \oplus 2x_2^2 \oplus x_2^2 x_1^2 \quad \text{over GF(3)}$$

Similar Reed–Muller expansions and transforms matrices are easily

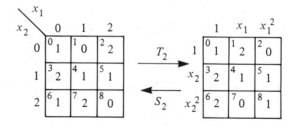

Fig. 7.28 Example of interdomain transformation.

$$S_1 = \begin{bmatrix} 1 & 0 & 0 & 0 & 0 \\ 1 & 1 & 1 & 1 & 1 \\ 1 & 2 & 4 & 3 & 1 \\ 1 & 3 & 4 & 2 & 1 \\ 1 & 4 & 1 & 4 & 1 \end{bmatrix} \qquad T_1 = \begin{bmatrix} 1 & 0 & 0 & 0 & 0 \\ 0 & 4 & 2 & 3 & 1 \\ 0 & 4 & 1 & 1 & 4 \\ 0 & 4 & 3 & 2 & 1 \\ 4 & 4 & 4 & 4 & 4 \end{bmatrix}$$

Fig. 7.29   Interdomain transforms for GF(5).

derived for other prime fields. For example, Fig. 7.29 gives the two transforms for one-variable functions over GF(5). Larger-dimension transforms can be built up using the Krönecker product.

Finite fields also exist for other non-prime values of q; to be precise, when $q = p^k$, where p is a prime and k is a positive integer. However, when $k > 1$ we cannot construct these fields by using the integers modulo-q with modulo-q arithmetic. For example, Fig. 7.30 gives the modulo-4 arithmetic tables. These do not form a field because the element 2 has no multiplicative inverse; that is, there is no element e such that $2.e = 1$ so that $e = 2^{-1}$. We require an inverse for every non-zero element so that we can also solve equations of the form $a.x + b = 0$, where a and b are elements at GF(q). Since $x = -b.a^{-1}$ for this situation we require an element for a^{-1}.

However, it can be shown that the elements of GF(q) where $q = p^k$ can be represented by k-digit numbers (k-tuples) made up from symbols of GF(p) and as such GF(p^k) is regarded as an *extension* field of GF(p). Of particular interest here are the extension fields of GF(2) since the elements of these fields will be k-bit binary numbers. Thus, GF(2^k) provides a way of adding and multiplying k-bit words treated as single entities.

Just as the prime fields GF(p) can be defined in terms of the addition and multiplication of integers modulo-(a prime integer), the composite extension fields GF(p^k) can be described in terms of addition and multiplication of polynomials modulo-(a prime

$\odot$	0	1	2	3
0	0	0	0	0
1	0	1	2	3
2	0	2	0	2
3	0	3	2	1

modulo-4 multiplication

$\oplus$	0	1	2	3
0	0	1	2	3
1	1	2	3	0
2	2	3	0	1
3	3	0	1	2

modulo-4 addition

Fig. 7.30   Modulo-4 arithmetic tables.

polynomial). In fact, the arithmetic of $GF(p^k)$ is that of polynomial addition and multiplication modulo-(a prime polynomial) of degree k over $GF(p)$.

Let $g(x)$ be a polynomial of degree k over $GF(p)$. That is,

$$g(x) = a_k x^k \oplus a_{k-1} x^{k-1} \oplus \ldots \oplus a_1 x \oplus a_0 \qquad \text{over } GF(p)$$

where a_i are elements of $GF(p)$. The values of x for which $g(x) = 0$ are called the *roots* of $g(x)$ and a degree k polynomial has k roots. However, these roots may or may not exist as elements of $GF(p)$. If they do exist in $GF(p)$ it implies that $g(x)$ is divisible over $GF(p)$ by a first-order factor of the form $x - \beta$, where β is the root. For then,

$$g(x) = (x - \beta)g'(x) \quad \text{and} \quad g(x) = 0 \qquad \text{when } x = \beta$$

By definition, the roots of an irreducible polynomial do not exist in the base field because there cannot be any factors. However, the roots of such polynomials do exist as elements of some extension field of $GF(p)$. In fact every element of $GF(p^k)$ is a root of some polynomial over $GF(p)$ of degree k or a divisor of k. Conversely, every irreducible polynomial over $GF(p)$ of degree k factorizes completely into first-degree factors over $GF(p^k)$. This process has a parallel in the case of the infinite real number field and its extension field of complex numbers; whereas a real polynomial of the form $x^2 + 1$ is irreducible and has no real roots, over the complex number field $x^2 + 1 = (x + j)(x - j)$, where $j^2 = -1$, and its roots exist, as imaginary numbers, in this extension field.

We can use these facts to obtain a representation of $GF(p^k)$ in terms of $GF(p)$ elements and arithmetic. Each non-zero element of $GF(p^k)$ has an *order* e, which is the smallest integer such that $\alpha^e = 1$. This value is either $p^k - 1$ or a divisor of $p^k - 1$. Elements with maximum order, $p^k - 1$, are called *primitive*. Primitive elements of $GF(p^k)$ are roots of primitive polynomials over $GF(p)$ of degree k. If we take all the powers of a primitive element of $GF(p^k)$, i.e. α^1, α^2, $\alpha^3, \ldots$, etc., we find these are distinct and because $\alpha^{p^k - 1} = 1$, $\alpha^{p^k} = \alpha$, the series repeats only at this stage. The sequence of powers of α will run through all the non-zero elements of $GF(p^k)$. Thus we can construct a representation of $GF(p^k)$ by taking a primitive polynomial of degree k over $GF(p)$ and deducing all the powers of a primitive root. We then resolve these modulo-(the generating polynomial). For example, we can construct a representation of $GF(8) = GF(2^3)$ given that $x^3 \oplus x \oplus 1$ is a degree-3 primitive polynomial over $GF(2)$. We argue as follows. Let α be a root of $x^3 \oplus x \oplus 1$. Therefore $\alpha^3 \oplus \alpha \oplus 1 = 0$ or $\alpha^3 = \alpha \oplus 1$ and α is a primitive element of $GF(8)$. Take all the powers of α and resolve into polynomials of degree 2 or less:

$$\alpha^0 = 1$$
$$\alpha^1 = \alpha$$
$$\alpha^2 = \alpha^2$$
$$\alpha^3 = \alpha \oplus 1$$
$$\alpha^4 = \alpha . \alpha^3 = \alpha(\alpha \oplus 1) = \alpha^2 \oplus \alpha$$
$$\alpha^5 = \alpha . \alpha^4 = \alpha^3 \oplus \alpha^2 = \alpha^2 \oplus \alpha \oplus 1$$
$$\alpha^6 = \alpha . \alpha^5 = \alpha^3 \oplus \alpha^2 \oplus \alpha = \alpha \oplus 1 \oplus \alpha^2 \oplus \alpha = \alpha^2 \oplus 1$$
$$\alpha^7 = \alpha . \alpha^6 = \alpha^3 \oplus \alpha = \alpha \oplus 1 \oplus \alpha = 1$$

and the process repeats here. We can show these elements in detached coefficients as:

	α^2	α	1
α^0	0	0	1
α^1	0	1	0
α^2	1	0	0
α^3	0	1	1
α^4	1	1	0
α^5	1	1	1
α^6	1	0	1

Thus, the elements of GF(8) can be regarded as 3-bit binary numbers. Addition over GF(8) can be seen to be equivalent to polynomial addition over GF(2)

$$\begin{array}{ccc} \alpha^3 \oplus \alpha^5 = & (\alpha \oplus 1) \oplus (\alpha^2 \oplus \alpha \oplus 1) = & \alpha^2 \\ \text{GF(8)} & \text{GF(2)} & \text{GF(8)} \end{array}$$

$\odot$	0	1	α	α^2	α^3	α^4	α^5	α^6
0	0	0	0	0	0	0	0	0
1	0	1	α	α^2	α^3	α^4	α^5	α^6
α	0	α	α^2	α^3	α^4	α^5	α^6	1
α^2	0	α^2	α^3	α^4	α^5	α^6	1	α
α^3	0	α^3	α^4	α^5	α^6	1	α	α^2
α^4	0	α^4	α^5	α^6	1	α	α^2	α^3
α^5	0	α^5	α^6	1	α	α^2	α^3	α^4
α^6	0	α^6	1	α	α^2	α^3	α^4	α^5

multiplication over GF(8)

$\oplus$	0	1	α	α^2	α^3	α^4	α^5	α^6
0	0	1	α	α^2	α^3	α^4	α^5	α^6
1	1	0	α^3	α^6	α	α^5	α^4	α^2
α	α	α^3	0	α^4	1	α^2	α^6	α^5
α^2	α^2	α^6	α^4	0	α^5	α	α^3	1
α^3	α^3	α	1	α^5	0	α^6	α^2	α^4
α^4	α^4	α^5	α^2	α	α^6	0	1	α^3
α^5	α^5	α^4	α^6	α^3	α^2	1	0	α
α^6	α^6	α^2	α^5	1	α^4	α^3	α	0

addition over GF(8)

Fig. 7.31 Operations of GF(8).

$\odot$	000 001 010 100 011 110 111 101	$\oplus$	000 001 010 100 011 110 111 101
000	000 000 000 000 000 000 000 000	000	000 001 010 100 011 110 111 101
001	000 001 010 100 011 110 111 101	001	001 000 011 101 010 111 110 100
010	000 010 100 011 110 111 101 001	010	010 011 000 110 001 100 101 111
100	000 100 011 110 111 101 001 010	100	100 101 110 000 111 010 011 001
011	000 011 110 111 101 001 010 100	011	011 010 001 111 000 101 100 110
110	000 110 111 101 001 010 100 011	110	110 111 100 010 101 000 001 011
111	000 111 101 001 010 100 011 110	111	111 110 101 011 100 001 000 010
101	000 101 001 010 100 011 110 111	101	101 100 111 001 110 011 010 000

multiplication over GF(2^3)   addition over GF(2^3)

Fig. 7.32   Operations of GF(8) interpreted as GF(2^3).

Multiplication over GF(8) is equivalent to polynomial multiplication modulo-$\alpha^3 \oplus \alpha \oplus 1$. Thus,

$$\alpha^3 . \alpha^5 = \alpha^8 = \alpha \qquad \text{since } \alpha^7 = 1$$

or

$$\alpha^3 . \alpha^5 = (\alpha \oplus 1)(\alpha^2 \oplus \alpha \oplus 1) = \alpha^3 \oplus 1$$
$$= \alpha \text{ modulo-}\alpha^3 \oplus \alpha \oplus 1$$

In this way, we can construct the operation tables for GF(8) as depicted in Fig. 7.31. Alternatively, we can represent these in terms of 3-bit numbers as in Fig. 7.32. For conciseness, it is convenient to represent the elements of GF(8), that is [0, 1, α, α^2, α^3, α^4, α^5, α^6], as 0, 1 and letters of the alphabet, in order to avoid confusion with the integers. Thus GF(8) = [0, 1, A, B, C, D, E, F]. In a similar way the smaller field GF(4) with elements [0, 1, A, B] can be constructed using $x^2 \oplus x \oplus 1$, which is a primitive polynomial over GF(2). This provides a consistent algebra for the quaternary field and the arithmetic tables are given in Fig. 7.33.

The Reed–Muller canonical form generalizes over the general field GF(q) to be, for one variable,

$\odot$	0	1	A	B		$\oplus$	0	1	A	B
0	0	0	0	0		0	0	1	A	B
1	0	1	A	B		1	1	0	B	A
A	0	A	B	1		A	A	B	0	1
B	0	B	1	A		B	B	A	1	0

GF(4) multiplication   GF(4) addition

Fig. 7.33   Operations of GF(4).

GF(4)

$$T_1 = \begin{pmatrix} 1 & 0 & 0 & 0 \\ 0 & 1 & B & A \\ 0 & 1 & A & B \\ 1 & 1 & 1 & 1 \end{pmatrix} \qquad S_1 = \begin{pmatrix} 1 & 0 & 0 & 0 \\ 1 & 1 & 1 & 1 \\ 1 & A & B & 1 \\ 1 & B & A & 1 \end{pmatrix}$$

GF(8)

$$T_1 = \begin{pmatrix} 1 & 0 & 0 & 0 & 0 & 0 & 0 & 0 \\ 0 & 1 & F & E & D & C & B & A \\ 0 & 1 & E & C & A & F & D & B \\ 0 & 1 & D & A & E & B & F & C \\ 0 & 1 & C & F & B & E & A & D \\ 0 & 1 & B & D & F & A & C & E \\ 0 & 1 & A & B & C & D & E & F \\ 1 & 1 & 1 & 1 & 1 & 1 & 1 & 1 \end{pmatrix} \qquad S_1 = \begin{pmatrix} 1 & 0 & 0 & 0 & 0 & 0 & 0 & 0 \\ 1 & 1 & 1 & 1 & 1 & 1 & 1 & 1 \\ 1 & A & B & C & D & E & F & 1 \\ 1 & B & D & F & A & C & E & 1 \\ 1 & C & F & B & E & A & D & 1 \\ 1 & D & A & E & B & F & C & 1 \\ 1 & E & C & A & F & D & B & 1 \\ 1 & F & E & D & C & B & A & 1 \end{pmatrix}$$

Fig. 7.34 One-variable interdomain transforms for GF(4) and GF(8).

$$f(x_1) = c_0 \oplus c_1 x_1 \oplus c_2 x_1^2 \oplus \ldots \oplus c_{q-1} x_1^{q-1} \qquad \text{over GF}(q)$$

This enables the interdomain transforms to be set up for these composite fields. Fig. 7.34 gives the transform pairs for GF(4) and GF(8).

We can devise similar design procedures for GF(q) to those described in Chapter 5 for GF(2). Thus, multiple-valued GRM expansions, modular circuit trees and other ULM techniques are available and can be employed with equal facility over these well behaved and flexible algebraic systems.

In particular, the multiple-valued equivalent of the multiplexer is a useful synthesis technique for both modes of algebraic representation. Such devices have been referred to as T-gates and Fig. 7.35 shows the arrangement and symbol for the simplest ternary device. The value applied to the control input x determines which of the three data inputs is connected to the output. Provided we can manufacture a physical device with these characteristics, we could use the T-gates to implement all the basic operations of either mode of representation. A single T-gate can implement any one-variable

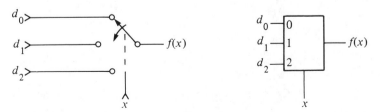

Fig. 7.35 Ternary T-gate and its mode of operation.

x	$j_0(x)$	$j_1(x)$	$j_2(x)$	x'	x''
0	2	0	0	1	2
1	0	2	0	2	0
2	0	0	2	0	1

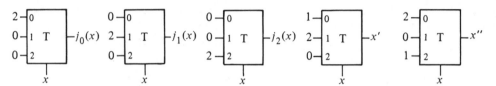

Fig. 7.36   T-gate implementation of ternary operations.

function. For example, the three Postian j-operators and cycling function could be implemented as in Fig. 7.36. Several T-gates can be used for the implementation of two-input operations. Fig. 7.37 gives representations of the Postian and GF(3) operations as well as the general two-variable implementation. Rules can be devised for simplifying these structures so that redundant T-gates can be removed.

It is a simple matter to extend these principles to higher values of q. In the case of $q = 2^k$ we also have the possibility of imple-

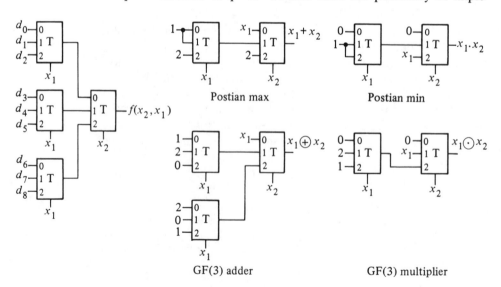

Fig. 7.37   T-gate implementation of some two-variable ternary functions.

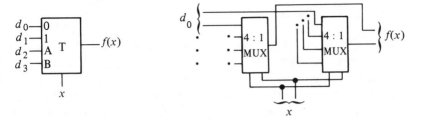

Fig. 7.38   Synthesis of a GF(4) T-gate from GF(2) components.

menting T-gates with GF(2) components used in parallel. Fig. 7.38 demonstrates how the $q = 4$ T-gate could be synthesized by using two 4:1 binary multiplexers.

We could obtain the four-level operation by interfacing inputs with 2-bit A-to-D converters and the output with a 2-bit D-to-A converter. Modern integrated circuit techniques may make it possible to implement 4- and 2^k-valued switching circuits by this method, in a reasonably inexpensive fashion.

7.5   BIBLIOGRAPHICAL NOTES

The simulation of digital systems has received widespread attention as a research topic and the literature is rapidly expanding. Blunden *et al.* (1977) and Chappell *et al.* (1977) represent early papers in this area. Breuer and Friedman (1976) and Lewin (1977) include coverage on logic simulation. Wilcox (1979) and Breuer and Friedman (1980) represent more recent contributions. Dimond (1983) provides a useful review of simulation techniques.

Roth (1980), Bennetts (1982, 1984) and Lala (1985) are comprehensive texts dealing with all aspects of automatic testing and design for testability. The paper by Reddy (1972) first drew attention to the testability of Reed–Muller expansion circuits. Jack (1983) gives a review of design for testability.

Much of multiple-valued switching circuit theory derives from the early papers of Post (1921) and Bernstein (1928). Green and Taylor (1974, 1976) discuss the generalization of Reed–Muller techniques to the multiple-valued case. Lee and Chen (1956) investigated the use of T-gates for ternary circuit synthesis. The compilation edited by Rine (1977) discusses the possible impact of multiple-valued logic on computer science. Davio *et al.* (1978) and Hurst (1978) both contain significant contributions on multiple-valued logics.

7.6 EXERCISES

7.1 Construct a tabular description of the circuit of Fig. 7.39 for use in a compiled-code simulation.

7.2 Set up an operation table for Exercise 7.1 and evaluate it for several passes using a different set of primary input values in each case.

7.3 Devise the fault matrix for the circuit of Fig. 7.39 and deduce a minimum set of tests to cover all faults of s-a-0 and s-a-1.

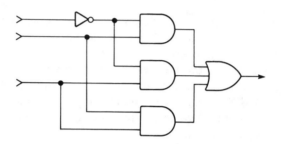

Fig. 7.39 Example circuit for Exercise 7.1.

7.4 Use the Boolean difference method to confirm the test cover found in Exercise 7.3.

7.5 Using the path-sensitization method, find a test for the output of the two-input NOR gate in the circuit of Fig. 7.40, s-a-0.

7.6 Derive the minimum form of the three-valued and four-valued functions defined in Fig. 7.41 using the connectives of Postian algebra.

7.7 Find the ternary Reed–Muller expansion of the operational domain map of Fig. 7.41a.

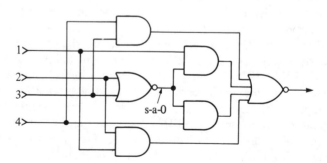

Fig. 7.40 Example circuit for Exercise 7.5.

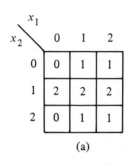

Fig. **7.41** Example functions for Exercise 7.6.

7.8 Find the quaternary Reed–Muller expansion of the operational domain map of Fig. 7.42b. Use the inverse transform to deduce the operational domain map of the function defined in Fig. 7.42b.

x_2 \\ x_1	0	1	A	B
0	0	A	B	1
1	A	0	1	B
A	B	1	0	A
B	1	B	A	0

(a)

	1	x_1	x_1^2	x_1^3
1	0	1	0	0
x_2	1	0	A	A
x_2^2	0	A	1	B
x_2^3	0	A	B	0

(b)

Fig. **7.42** Example functions for Exercise 7.8.

7.9 Derive the simplified T-gate representations of the following four-valued operations:
a) Postian min function,
b) Postian max function,
c) modulo-4 addition,
d) modulo-4 multiplication.

2.1

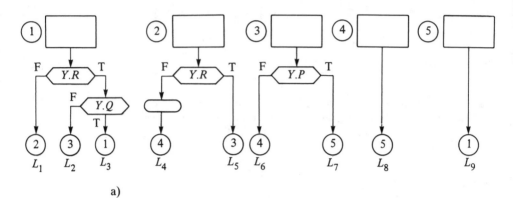

a)

Inputs			Present state	Next state	Inputs			Present state			Next state		
Y.R	Y.Q	Y.P			R	Q	P	A	B	C	NA	NB	NC
F	—	—	1	2	0	—	—	0	0	0	0	1	0
T	F	—	1	3	1	0	—	0	0	0	0	1	1
T	T	—	1	1	1	1	—	0	0	0	0	0	0
F	—	—	2	4	0	—	—	0	1	0	1	1	1
T	—	—	2	3	1	—	—	0	1	0	0	1	1
—	—	F	3	4	—	—	0	0	1	1	1	1	1
—	—	T	3	5	—	—	1	0	1	1	1	0	1
—	—	—	4	5	—	—	—	1	1	1	1	0	1
—	—	—	5	1	—	—	—	1	0	1	0	0	0

b)

Present state	Outputs			Present state			Outputs		
	H.SET	H.RND	L.CNT	A	B	C	H.SET	H.RND	L.CNT
1				0	0	0	0	0	1
2	A	A		0	1	0	1	1	1
3		A		0	1	1	0	1	1
4				1	1	1	0	0	1
5			A	1	0	1	0	0	0

c)

Inputs Y.R	Y.Q	Y.P	Present state	Outputs L.LOD		Inputs R	Q	P	Present state A	B	C	Outputs L.LOD
F	—	—	1			0	—	—	0	0	0	1
T	F	—	1			1	0	—	0	0	0	1
T	T	—	1			1	1	—	0	0	0	1
F	—	—	2	A		0	—	—	0	1	0	0
T	—	—	2			1	—	—	0	1	0	1
—	—	F	3	A		—	—	0	0	1	1	0
—	—	T	3	A		—	—	1	0	1	1	0
—	—	—	4	A		—	—	—	1	1	1	0
—	—	—	5			—	—	—	1	0	1	1

2.2

Link path	Inputs R	Q	P	Present state Sym.	A	B	C	Next state Sym.	NA	NB	NC	Outputs H.SET	H.RND	L.CNT	L.LOD
1	0	—	—	1	0	0	0	2	0	1	0	0	0	1	1
2	1	0	—	1	0	0	0	3	0	1	1	0	0	1	1
3	1	1	—	1	0	0	0	1	0	0	0	0	0	1	1
4	0	—	—	2	0	1	0	4	1	1	1	1	1	1	0
5	1	—	—	2	0	1	0	3	0	1	1	1	1	1	1
6	—	—	0	3	0	1	1	4	1	1	1	0	1	1	0
7	—	—	1	3	0	1	1	5	1	0	1	0	1	1	0
8	—	—	—	4	1	1	1	5	1	0	1	0	0	1	0
9	—	—	—	5	1	0	1	1	0	0	0	0	0	0	1

$$NA = BC + \bar{R}B \qquad NB = B\bar{C} + \bar{P}\bar{A}B + \bar{R}C + \bar{Q}C \qquad NC = B + R\bar{Q}\bar{C}$$

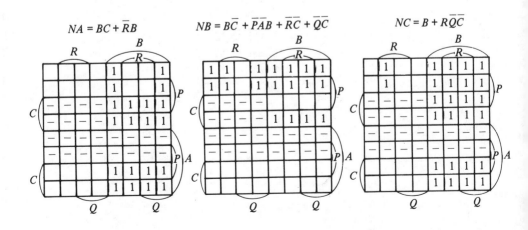

2.3

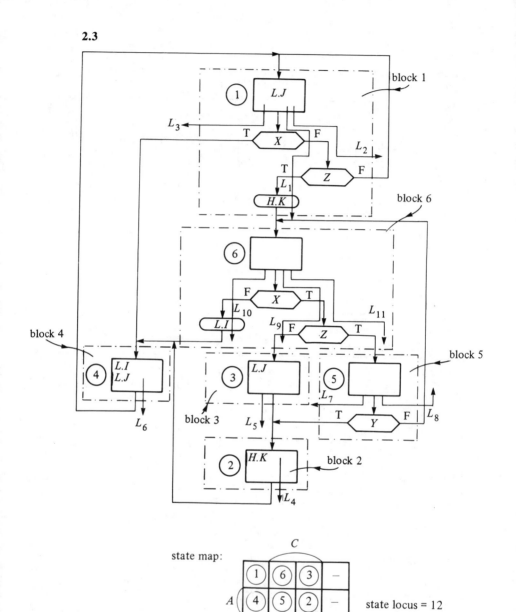

state map:

state locus = 12

| Inputs | | | Present state | | | | Next state | | | | Outputs | | |
X	Y	Z	Sym.	A	B	C	Sym.	NA	NB	NC	L.I	L.J	H.K
0	—	1	1	0	0	0	6	0	0	1	1	0	1
0	—	0	1	0	0	0	1	0	0	0	1	0	0
1	—	—	1	0	0	0	4	1	0	0	1	0	0
—	—	—	2	1	1	1	4	1	0	0	1	1	1
—	—	—	3	0	1	1	2	1	1	1	1	0	0
—	—	—	4	1	0	0	1	0	0	0	0	0	0
—	1	—	5	1	0	1	2	1	1	1	1	1	0
—	0	—	5	1	0	1	6	0	0	1	1	1	0
1	—	0	6	0	0	1	3	0	1	1	1	1	0
0	—	—	6	0	0	1	4	1	0	0	0	1	0
1	—	1	6	0	0	1	5	1	0	1	1	1	0

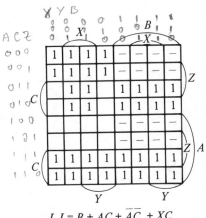

$$L.I = B + AC + \overline{AC} + XC$$

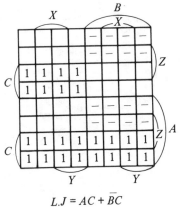

$$L.J = AC + \overline{B}C$$

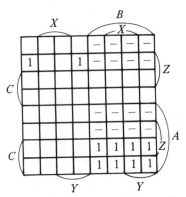

$$H.K = AB + \overline{X}Z\overline{A}\overline{C}$$

2.4

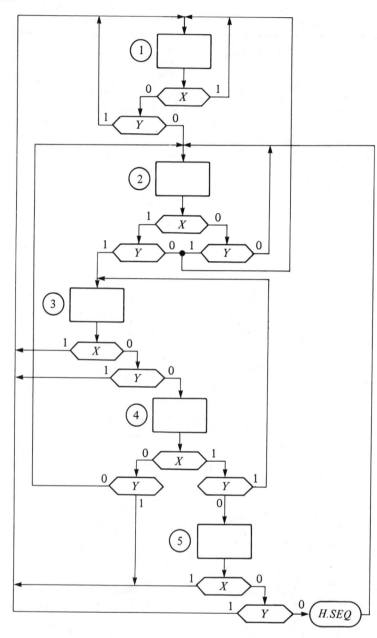

Inputs X Y	Present state	Next state	Output H.SEQ
1 —	1	1	
0 1	1	1	
0 0	1	2	
0 0	2	2	
0 1	2	1	
1 0	2	1	
1 1	2	3	
1 —	3	1	
0 1	3	1	
0 0	3	4	
0 0	4	2	
0 1	4	1	
1 0	4	5	
1 1	4	3	
1 —	5	1	
0 1	5	1	
0 0	5	2	A

2.5

state map:

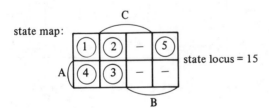

state locus = 15

| Inputs | | Present state | | | | Next state | | | | Output |
X	Y	Sym.	A	B	C	Sym.	NA	NB	NC	H.SEQ
1	—	1	0	0	0	1	0	0	0	0
0	1	1	0	0	0	1	0	0	0	0
0	0	1	0	0	0	2	0	0	1	0
0	0	2	0	0	1	2	0	0	1	0
0	1	2	0	0	1	1	0	0	0	0
1	0	2	0	0	1	1	0	0	0	0
1	1	2	0	0	1	3	1	0	1	0
1	—	3	1	0	1	1	0	0	0	0
0	1	3	1	0	1	1	0	0	0	0
0	0	3	1	0	1	4	1	0	0	0
0	0	4	1	0	0	2	0	0	1	0
0	1	4	1	0	0	1	0	0	0	0
1	0	4	1	0	0	5	0	1	0	0
1	1	4	1	0	0	3	1	0	1	0
1	—	5	0	1	0	1	0	0	0	0
0	1	5	0	1	0	1	0	0	0	0
0	0	5	0	1	0	2	0	0	1	1

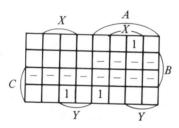

$$NA = XY\bar{A}\bar{C} + \bar{X}\bar{Y}AC + XYA\bar{C}$$

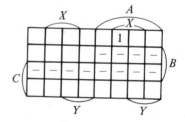

$$NB = X\bar{Y}A\bar{C}$$

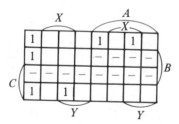

$$NC = \bar{X}\bar{Y}\bar{A} + \bar{X}\bar{Y}C + XYC\bar{A} + XY\bar{C}A$$

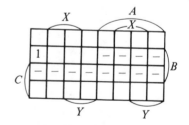

$$H.SEQ = \bar{X}\bar{Y}B$$

3.1

Inputs			Present state			(a) Next state						(b) Next state					
R	Q	P	A	B	C	JA	KA	JB	KB	JC	KC	SA	RA	SB	RB	SC	RC
0	—	—	0	0	0	0	—	1	—	0	—	1	—	0	1	1	—
1	0	—	0	0	0	0	—	1	—	1	—	1	—	0	1	0	1
1	1	—	0	0	0	0	—	0	—	0	—	1	—	1	—	1	—
0	—	—	0	1	0	1	—	—	0	1	—	0	1	—	1	0	1
1	—	—	0	1	0	0	—	—	0	1	—	1	—	—	1	0	1
—	—	0	0	1	1	1	—	—	0	—	0	0	1	—	1	—	1
—	—	1	0	1	1	1	—	—	1	—	0	0	1	1	0	—	1
—	—	—	1	1	1	—	0	—	1	—	0	—	1	1	0	—	1
—	—	—	1	0	1	—	1	0	—	—	1	1	0	1	—	1	0

3.2

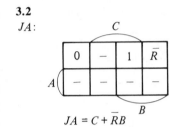

JA: $JA = C + \bar{R}B$

KA: $KA = \bar{B}$

SA: $SA = \bar{B} + R\bar{C}$

RA: $RA = B$

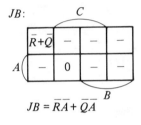

JB: $JB = \bar{R}\bar{A} + \bar{Q}\bar{A}$

KB: $KB = A + PC$

SB: $SB = C + RQ$

RB: $RB = \bar{C} + \bar{P}\bar{A}$

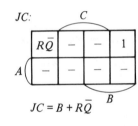

JC: $JC = B + R\bar{Q}$

KC: $KC = \bar{B}$

SC: $SC = A + \bar{R}\bar{B} + Q\bar{B}$

RC: $RC = \bar{A} + B$

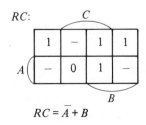

3.3

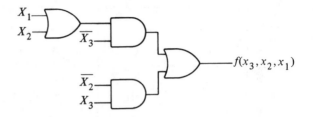

3.4

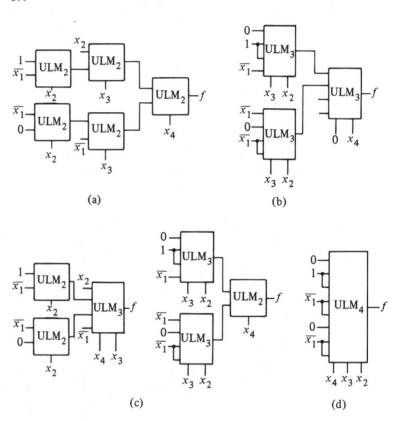

3.5

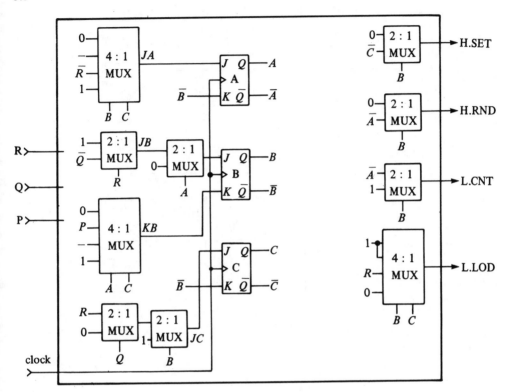

4.1

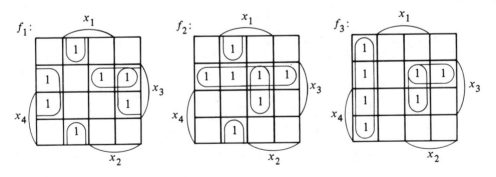

$$f_1 = X_3\overline{X}_1 + \overline{X}_3\overline{X}_2X_1 + \overline{X}_4X_3X_2 = t_1 + t_2 + t_3$$
$$f_2 = \overline{X}_3\overline{X}_2X_1 + X_3X_2X_1 + \overline{X}_4X_3 = t_2 + t_4 + t_5$$
$$f_3 = \overline{X}_2\overline{X}_1 + X_3X_2X_1 + \overline{X}_4X_3X_2 = t_6 + t_4 + t_3$$

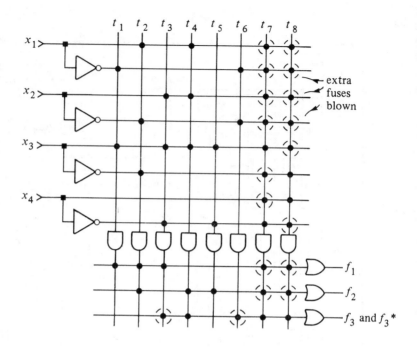

4.2

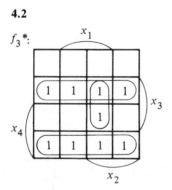

$f_3^* = \overline{X}_4 X_3 + X_3 X_2 X_1 + X_4 \overline{X}_3 = t_5 + t_4 + t_8$

$$= t_7 + t_4 + t_8$$

We need to duplicate t_5 in t_7 because it is no longer available for f_3. t_4 is still required.

4.3

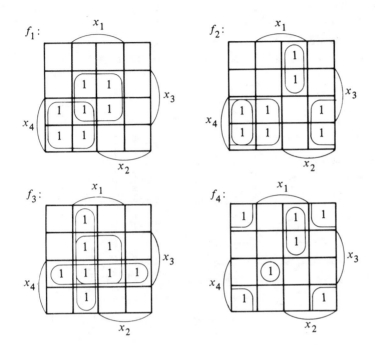

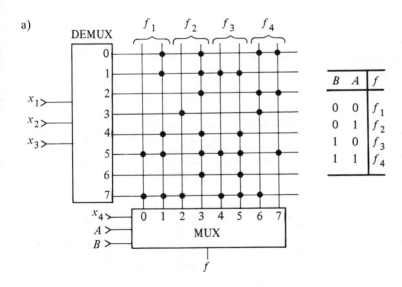

a)

b) $f_1 = X_3X_1 + X_4\overline{X}_2 = t_1 + t_2$

$f_2 = \overline{X}_4X_2X_1 + X_4\overline{X}_2 + X_4\overline{X}_1 = t_3 + t_2 + t_4$

$f_3 = \overline{X}_2X_1 + X_3X_1 + X_4X_3 = t_5 + t_1 + t_6$

$f_4 = \overline{X}_3\overline{X}_1 + \overline{X}_4X_2X_1 + X_4X_3\overline{X}_2X_1 = t_7 + t_3 + t_8$

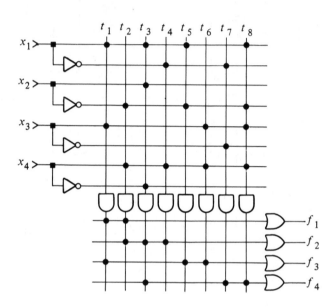

4.4

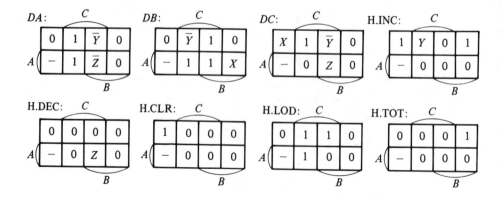

$$DA = \overline{B}C + \overline{Y}\overline{A}C + \overline{Z}AC = t_1 + t_2 + t_3$$
$$DB = AC + BC + \overline{Y}\overline{A}C + XA = t_4 + t_5 + t_2 + t_6$$
$$DC = \overline{A}\overline{B}C + X\overline{B}\overline{C} + \overline{Y}\overline{A}C + ZABC = t_7 + t_8 + t_2 + t_9$$
$$H.INC = \overline{B}\overline{C} + \overline{A}\overline{C} + YA\overline{B} = t_{10} + t_{11} + t_{12}$$
$$H.DEC = ZABC = t_9$$
$$H.CLR = \overline{B}\overline{C} = t_{10}$$
$$H.LOD = \overline{A}C + \overline{B}C = t_{13} + t_1$$
$$H.TOT = \overline{A}B\overline{C} = t_{14}$$

a)

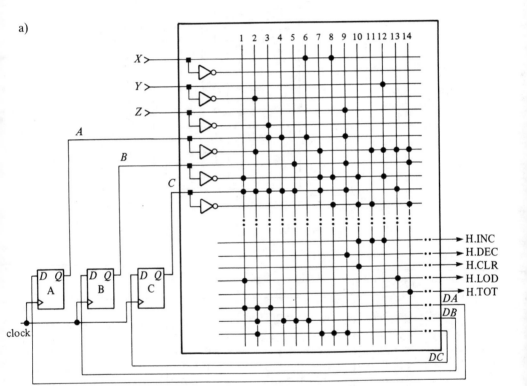

b)

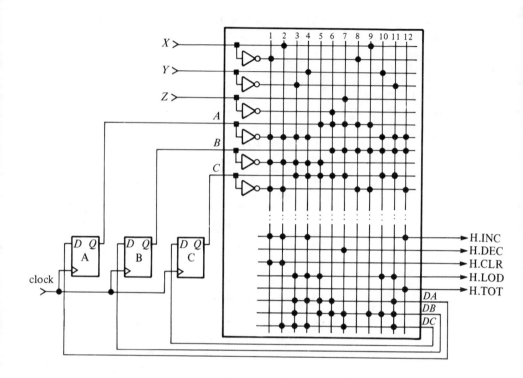

4.5
ASM table interpreted for SR-bistables for state register and output latches.

Inputs			Present state				Next state							Outputs									
														H.INC		H.DEC		H.CLR		H.LOD		H.TOT	
X	Y	Z	Sym.	A	B	C	Sym.	SA	RA	SB	RB	SC	RC	S	R	S	R	S	R	S	R	S	R
0	—	—	1	0	0	0	1	0	—	0	—	0	—	1	0	0	1	1	0	0	1	0	1
1	—	—	1	0	0	0	2	0	—	0	—	1	0	1	0	0	1	1	0	0	1	0	1
—	0	—	2	0	0	1	4	1	0	1	0	—	0	0	1	0	1	0	1	1	0	0	1
—	1	—	2	0	0	1	3	1	0	0	—	—	0	1	0	0	1	0	1	1	0	0	1
—	—	—	3	1	0	1	5	—	0	1	0	0	1	0	1	0	1	0	1	1	0	0	1
—	—	0	4	1	1	1	5	—	0	—	0	0	1	0	1	0	1	0	1	0	1	0	1
—	—	1	4	1	1	1	6	0	1	1	0	—	0	0	1	1	0	0	1	0	1	0	1
0	—	—	5	1	1	0	1	0	1	—	0	0	—	0	1	0	1	0	1	0	1	0	1
1	—	—	5	1	1	0	7	0	1	—	0	0	—	0	1	0	1	0	1	0	1	0	1
—	1	—	6	0	1	1	7	0	—	—	0	0	1	0	1	0	1	0	1	1	0	0	1
—	0	—	6	0	1	1	4	1	0	—	0	—	0	0	1	0	1	0	1	1	0	0	1
—	—	—	7	0	1	0	1	0	—	0	1	0	—	1	0	0	1	0	1	0	1	1	0

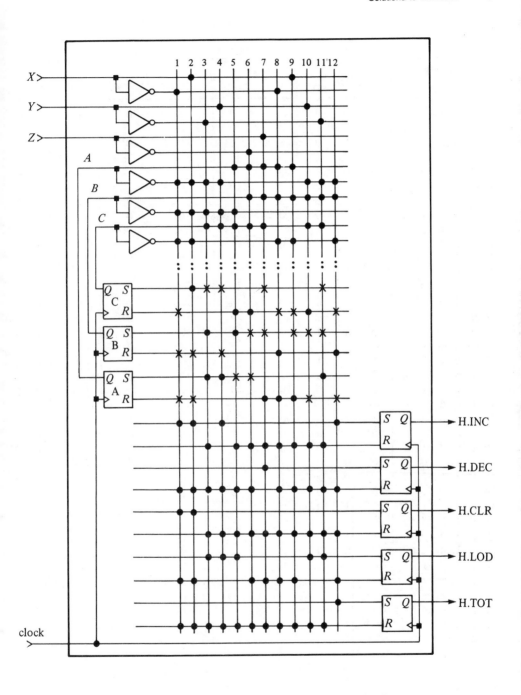

4.6

Address						DA	DB	DC	H.INC	H.DEC	H.CLR	H.LOD	H.TOT	Hex code	
X	Y	Z	A	B	C										
0	0	0	0	0	0	0	0	0	1	0	1	0	0	1	4
0	0	0	0	0	1	1	1	1	0	0	0	1	0	E	2
0	0	0	0	1	0	0	0	0	1	0	0	0	1	1	1
0	0	0	0	1	1	1	1	1	0	0	0	1	0	E	2
0	0	0	1	0	0	—	—	—	—	—	—	—	—	—	—
0	0	0	1	0	1	1	1	0	0	0	0	1	0	C	2
0	0	0	1	1	0	0	0	0	0	0	0	0	0	0	0
0	0	0	1	1	1	1	1	0	0	0	0	0	0	C	0
0	0	1	0	0	0	0	0	0	1	0	1	0	0	1	4
0	0	1	0	0	1	1	1	1	0	0	0	1	0	E	2
0	0	1	0	1	0	0	0	0	1	0	0	0	1	1	1
0	0	1	0	1	1	1	1	1	0	0	0	1	0	E	2
0	0	1	1	0	0	—	—	—	—	—	—	—	—	—	—
0	0	1	1	0	1	1	1	0	0	0	0	1	0	C	2
0	0	1	1	1	0	0	0	0	0	0	0	0	0	0	0
0	0	1	1	1	1	0	1	1	0	1	0	0	0	6	8
0	1	0	0	0	0	0	0	0	1	0	1	0	0	1	4
0	1	0	0	0	1	1	0	1	1	0	0	1	0	B	2
0	1	0	0	1	0	0	0	0	1	0	0	0	1	1	1
0	1	0	0	1	1	0	1	0	0	0	0	1	0	4	2
0	1	0	1	0	0	—	—	—	—	—	—	—	—	—	—
0	1	0	1	0	1	1	1	0	0	0	0	1	0	C	2
0	1	0	1	1	0	0	0	0	0	0	0	0	0	0	0
0	1	0	1	1	1	1	1	0	0	0	0	0	0	C	0
0	1	1	0	0	0	0	0	0	1	0	1	0	0	1	4
0	1	1	0	0	1	1	0	1	1	0	0	1	0	B	2
0	1	1	0	1	0	0	0	0	1	0	0	0	1	1	1
0	1	1	0	1	1	0	1	0	0	0	0	1	0	4	2
0	1	1	1	0	0	—	—	—	—	—	—	—	—	—	—
0	1	1	1	0	1	1	1	0	0	0	0	1	0	C	2
0	1	1	1	1	0	0	0	0	0	0	0	0	0	0	0
0	1	1	1	1	1	0	1	1	0	1	0	0	0	6	8

Address						DA	DB	DC	H.INC	H.DEC	H.CLR	H.LOD	H.TOT	Hex code	
X	Y	Z	A	B	C										
1	0	0	0	0	0	0	0	1	1	0	1	0	0	3	4
1	0	0	0	0	1	1	1	1	0	0	0	1	0	E	2
1	0	0	0	1	0	0	0	0	1	0	0	0	1	1	1
1	0	0	0	1	1	1	1	1	0	0	0	1	0	E	2
1	0	0	1	0	0	—	—	—	—	—	—	—	—	—	—
1	0	0	1	0	1	1	1	0	0	0	0	1	0	C	2
1	0	0	1	1	0	0	1	0	0	0	0	0	0	4	0
1	0	0	1	1	1	1	1	0	0	0	0	0	0	C	0
1	0	1	0	0	0	0	0	1	1	0	1	0	0	3	4
1	0	1	0	0	1	1	1	1	0	0	0	1	0	E	2
1	0	1	0	1	0	0	0	0	1	0	0	0	1	1	1
1	0	1	0	1	1	1	1	1	0	0	0	1	0	E	2
1	0	1	1	0	0	—	—	—	—	—	—	—	—	—	—
1	0	1	1	0	1	1	1	0	0	0	0	1	0	C	2
1	0	1	1	1	0	0	1	0	0	0	0	0	0	4	0
1	0	1	1	1	1	0	1	1	0	1	0	0	0	6	8
1	1	0	0	0	0	0	0	1	1	0	1	0	0	3	4
1	1	0	0	0	1	1	0	1	1	0	0	1	0	B	2
1	1	0	0	1	0	0	0	0	1	0	0	0	1	1	1
1	1	0	0	1	1	0	1	0	0	0	0	1	0	4	2
1	1	0	1	0	0	—	—	—	—	—	—	—	—	—	—
1	1	0	1	0	1	1	1	0	0	0	0	1	0	C	2
1	1	0	1	1	0	0	1	0	0	0	0	0	0	4	0
1	1	0	1	1	1	1	1	0	0	0	0	0	0	C	0
1	1	1	0	0	0	0	0	1	1	0	1	0	0	3	4
1	1	1	0	0	1	1	0	1	1	0	0	1	0	B	2
1	1	1	0	1	0	0	0	0	1	0	0	0	1	1	1
1	1	1	0	1	1	0	1	0	0	0	0	1	0	4	2
1	1	1	1	0	0	—	—	—	—	—	—	—	—	—	—
1	1	1	1	0	1	1	1	0	0	0	0	1	0	C	2
1	1	1	1	1	0	0	1	0	0	0	0	0	0	4	0
1	1	1	1	1	1	0	1	1	0	1	0	0	0	6	8

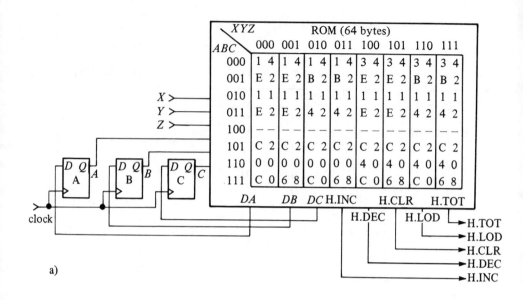

a)

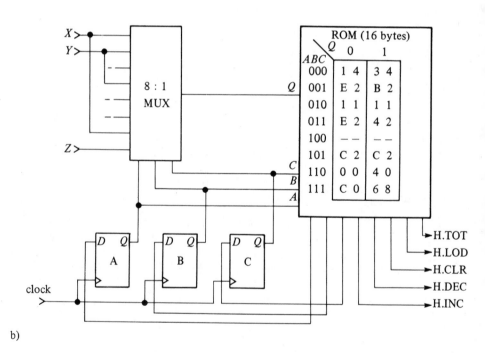

b)

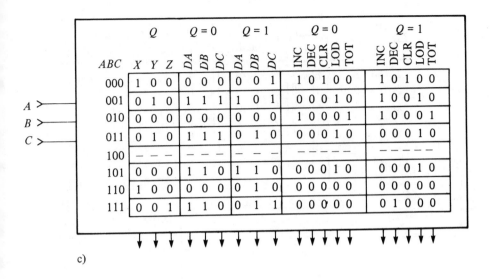

		Q			Q = 0			Q = 1		Q = 0					Q = 1				
ABC	X	Y	Z	DA	DB	DC	DA	DB	DC	INC	DEC	CLR	LOD	TOT	INC	DEC	CLR	LOD	TOT
000	1	0	0	0	0	0	0	0	1	1	0	1	0	0	1	0	1	0	0
001	0	1	0	1	1	1	1	0	1	0	0	0	1	0	1	0	0	1	0
010	0	0	0	0	0	0	0	0	0	1	0	0	0	1	1	0	0	0	1
011	0	1	0	1	1	1	0	1	0	0	0	0	1	0	0	0	0	1	0
100	–	–	–	–	–	–	–	–	–	–	–	–	–	–	–	–	–	–	–
101	0	0	0	1	1	0	1	1	0	0	0	0	1	0	0	0	0	1	0
110	1	0	0	0	0	0	0	1	0	0	0	0	0	0	0	0	0	0	0
111	0	0	1	1	1	0	0	1	1	0	0	0	0	0	0	1	0	0	0

c)

4.7

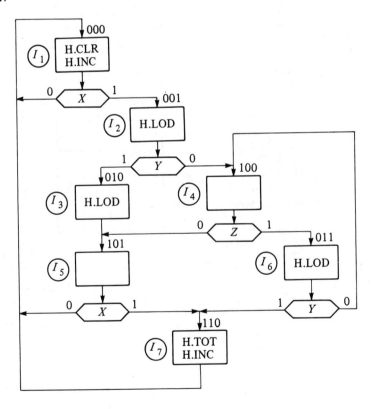

Inst.	Address			Qual. index		TF	Jump address			Commands			
										H.INC	H.CLR	H.LOD	H.TOT
I_1	0	0	0	0	1	0	0	0	0	1	1	0	0
I_2	0	0	1	1	0	0	1	0	0	0	0	1	0
I_3	0	1	0	0	0	0	1	0	1	0	0	1	0
I_6	0	1	1	1	0	1	1	1	0	0	0	1	0
I_4	1	0	0	1	1	1	0	1	1	0	0	0	0
I_5	1	0	1	0	1	0	0	0	0	0	0	0	0
I_7	1	1	0	0	0	0	0	0	0	1	0	0	1

5.1

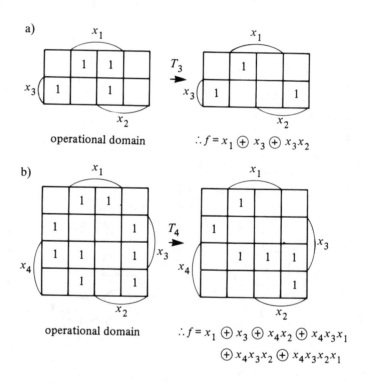

a)

operational domain

$\therefore f = x_1 \oplus x_3 \oplus x_3 x_2$

b)

operational domain

$\therefore f = x_1 \oplus x_3 \oplus x_4 x_2 \oplus x_4 x_3 x_1$
$\oplus x_4 x_3 x_2 \oplus x_4 x_3 x_2 x_1$

5.2

$$Z_{\langle 9\rangle} = Z_{1001} = \begin{bmatrix} 1 & 1 \\ 0 & 1 \end{bmatrix} * \begin{bmatrix} 1 & 0 \\ 0 & 1 \end{bmatrix} * \begin{bmatrix} 1 & 0 \\ 0 & 1 \end{bmatrix} * \begin{bmatrix} 1 & 1 \\ 0 & 1 \end{bmatrix}$$

$$Z_{\langle 9\rangle} = \begin{pmatrix}
1 & 1 & 0 & 0 & 0 & 0 & 0 & 0 & 1 & 1 & 0 & 0 & 0 & 0 & 0 & 0 \\
0 & 1 & 0 & 0 & 0 & 0 & 0 & 0 & 0 & 1 & 0 & 0 & 0 & 0 & 0 & 0 \\
0 & 0 & 1 & 1 & 0 & 0 & 0 & 0 & 0 & 0 & 1 & 1 & 0 & 0 & 0 & 0 \\
0 & 0 & 0 & 1 & 0 & 0 & 0 & 0 & 0 & 0 & 0 & 1 & 0 & 0 & 0 & 0 \\
0 & 0 & 0 & 0 & 1 & 1 & 0 & 0 & 0 & 0 & 0 & 0 & 1 & 1 & 0 & 0 \\
0 & 0 & 0 & 0 & 0 & 1 & 0 & 0 & 0 & 0 & 0 & 0 & 0 & 1 & 0 & 0 \\
0 & 0 & 0 & 0 & 0 & 0 & 1 & 1 & 0 & 0 & 0 & 0 & 0 & 0 & 1 & 1 \\
0 & 0 & 0 & 0 & 0 & 0 & 0 & 1 & 0 & 0 & 0 & 0 & 0 & 0 & 0 & 1 \\
0 & 0 & 0 & 0 & 0 & 0 & 0 & 0 & 1 & 1 & 0 & 0 & 0 & 0 & 0 & 0 \\
0 & 0 & 0 & 0 & 0 & 0 & 0 & 0 & 0 & 1 & 0 & 0 & 0 & 0 & 0 & 0 \\
0 & 0 & 0 & 0 & 0 & 0 & 0 & 0 & 0 & 0 & 1 & 1 & 0 & 0 & 0 & 0 \\
0 & 0 & 0 & 0 & 0 & 0 & 0 & 0 & 0 & 0 & 0 & 1 & 0 & 0 & 0 & 0 \\
0 & 0 & 0 & 0 & 0 & 0 & 0 & 0 & 0 & 0 & 0 & 0 & 1 & 1 & 0 & 0 \\
0 & 0 & 0 & 0 & 0 & 0 & 0 & 0 & 0 & 0 & 0 & 0 & 0 & 1 & 0 & 0 \\
0 & 0 & 0 & 0 & 0 & 0 & 0 & 0 & 0 & 0 & 0 & 0 & 0 & 0 & 1 & 1 \\
0 & 0 & 0 & 0 & 0 & 0 & 0 & 0 & 0 & 0 & 0 & 0 & 0 & 0 & 0 & 1
\end{pmatrix}$$

$$F = 1 \oplus \overline{X}_1 \oplus X_2 \oplus X_3\overline{X}_1 \oplus X_3 X_2 \overline{X}_1 \oplus \overline{X}_4 X_2 \oplus \overline{X}_4 X_3 \oplus \overline{X}_4 X_3 \overline{X}_1 \oplus \overline{X}_4 X_3 X_2 \overline{X}_1$$

5.3

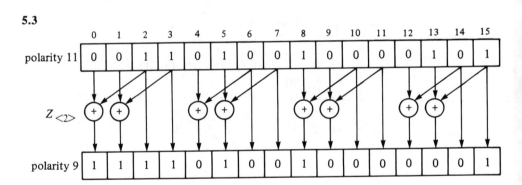

$$\therefore F = 1 \oplus \overline{X}_1 \oplus X_2 \oplus X_2\overline{X}_1 \oplus X_3\overline{X}_1 \oplus \overline{X}_4 \oplus \overline{X}_4 X_3 X_2 \overline{X}_1$$

5.4

$F_9 = Z_{(9)}F_0$ but $F_0 = T_4.D_0$

where D_0 is the operational domain coefficient. Therefore

$F_9 = Z_{(9)}.T_4.D_0 = W_{(9)}D_0$

$$
W_{(9)} =
\begin{bmatrix}
0 & 0 & 0 & 0 & 0 & 0 & 0 & 0 & 0 & 1 & 0 & 0 & 0 & 0 & 0 & 0 \\
0 & 0 & 0 & 0 & 0 & 0 & 0 & 0 & 1 & 1 & 0 & 0 & 0 & 0 & 0 & 0 \\
0 & 0 & 0 & 0 & 0 & 0 & 0 & 0 & 0 & 1 & 0 & 1 & 0 & 0 & 0 & 0 \\
0 & 0 & 0 & 0 & 0 & 0 & 0 & 0 & 1 & 1 & 1 & 1 & 0 & 0 & 0 & 0 \\
0 & 0 & 0 & 0 & 0 & 0 & 0 & 0 & 0 & 1 & 0 & 0 & 0 & 1 & 0 & 0 \\
0 & 0 & 0 & 0 & 0 & 0 & 0 & 0 & 1 & 1 & 0 & 0 & 1 & 1 & 0 & 0 \\
0 & 0 & 0 & 0 & 0 & 0 & 0 & 0 & 0 & 1 & 0 & 1 & 0 & 1 & 0 & 1 \\
0 & 0 & 0 & 0 & 0 & 0 & 0 & 0 & 1 & 1 & 1 & 1 & 1 & 1 & 1 & 1 \\
0 & 1 & 0 & 0 & 0 & 0 & 0 & 0 & 0 & 1 & 0 & 0 & 0 & 0 & 0 & 0 \\
1 & 1 & 0 & 0 & 0 & 0 & 0 & 0 & 1 & 1 & 0 & 0 & 0 & 0 & 0 & 0 \\
0 & 1 & 0 & 1 & 0 & 0 & 0 & 0 & 0 & 1 & 0 & 1 & 0 & 0 & 0 & 0 \\
1 & 1 & 1 & 1 & 0 & 0 & 0 & 0 & 1 & 1 & 1 & 1 & 0 & 0 & 0 & 0 \\
0 & 1 & 0 & 0 & 0 & 1 & 0 & 0 & 0 & 1 & 0 & 0 & 0 & 1 & 0 & 0 \\
1 & 1 & 0 & 0 & 1 & 1 & 0 & 0 & 1 & 1 & 0 & 0 & 1 & 1 & 0 & 0 \\
0 & 1 & 0 & 1 & 0 & 1 & 0 & 1 & 0 & 1 & 0 & 1 & 0 & 1 & 0 & 1 \\
1 & 1 & 1 & 1 & 1 & 1 & 1 & 1 & 1 & 1 & 1 & 1 & 1 & 1 & 1 & 1 \\
\end{bmatrix}
$$

and

$$
\begin{aligned}
W_{(9)} &= \begin{bmatrix} 0 & 1 \\ 1 & 1 \end{bmatrix} * \begin{bmatrix} 1 & 0 \\ 1 & 1 \end{bmatrix} * \begin{bmatrix} 1 & 0 \\ 1 & 1 \end{bmatrix} * \begin{bmatrix} 0 & 1 \\ 1 & 1 \end{bmatrix} \\
&= \left(\begin{bmatrix} 1 & 1 \\ 0 & 1 \end{bmatrix} \cdot \begin{bmatrix} 1 & 0 \\ 1 & 1 \end{bmatrix} \right) * \left(\begin{bmatrix} 1 & 0 \\ 0 & 1 \end{bmatrix} \cdot \begin{bmatrix} 1 & 0 \\ 1 & 1 \end{bmatrix} \right) * \left(\begin{bmatrix} 1 & 0 \\ 0 & 1 \end{bmatrix} \cdot \begin{bmatrix} 1 & 0 \\ 1 & 1 \end{bmatrix} \right) * \\
&\quad \left(\begin{bmatrix} 1 & 1 \\ 0 & 1 \end{bmatrix} \cdot \begin{bmatrix} 1 & 0 \\ 1 & 1 \end{bmatrix} \right) \\
&= \left(\begin{bmatrix} 1 & 1 \\ 0 & 1 \end{bmatrix} * \begin{bmatrix} 1 & 0 \\ 0 & 1 \end{bmatrix} * \begin{bmatrix} 1 & 0 \\ 0 & 1 \end{bmatrix} * \begin{bmatrix} 1 & 1 \\ 0 & 1 \end{bmatrix} \right) \cdot \begin{bmatrix} 1 & 0 \\ 1 & 1 \end{bmatrix} \\
&= Z_{(9)}.T
\end{aligned}
$$

5.5

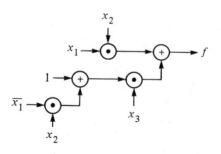

5.6

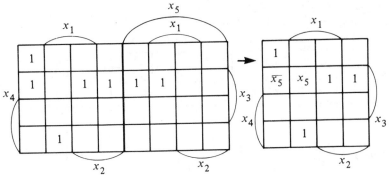

or

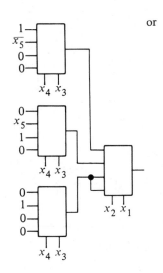

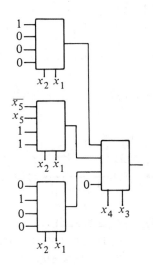

6.1

$X_i = \ldots 0001000 \ldots$

$Z_i = \ldots 0001100111000 \ldots$

$X_s = \ldots 0001111 \ldots$

$Z_s = \ldots 000100010111 \ldots$

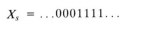

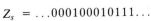

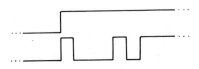

Null sequence

$X_0 \quad = \ldots 000001111001001010100110100001 -$
$\quad\quad\quad -000101101111110101110000110 -$
$\quad\quad\quad -011101100000111100 \ldots$
$\quad\quad\quad\quad\quad\quad \underbrace{\quad\quad\quad} \text{repeats}$

$Z_0 \quad = \ldots 000001000 \ldots$

6.2

$$H_1(D) = \frac{Z_1(D)}{X(D)} = \frac{1 \oplus D \oplus D^2 \oplus D^5 \oplus D^6 \oplus D^8}{I \oplus D^2 \oplus D^3} = I \oplus D \oplus D^4 \oplus D^5$$

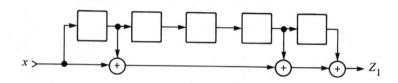

$$H_2(D) = \frac{Z_2(D)}{X(D)} = \frac{I \oplus D^2 \oplus D^3 \oplus D^6 \oplus D^7 \oplus D^8 \oplus D^{10}}{I \oplus D^2 \oplus D^3} = I \oplus D^6 \oplus D^7$$

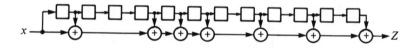

$$H_{\text{eff}} = H_1(D) . H_2(D) = (I \oplus D \oplus D^4 \oplus D^5)(I \oplus D^6 \oplus D^7)$$
$$= I \oplus D \oplus D^4 \oplus D^5 \oplus D^6 \oplus D^8 \oplus D^{10} \oplus D^{12}$$

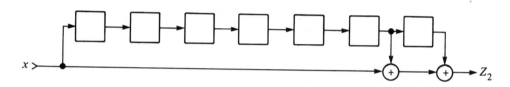

$$Z(D) = H_{\text{eff}}(D) . X(D)$$
$$= (I \oplus D \oplus D^4 \oplus D^5 \oplus D^6 \oplus D^8 \oplus D^{10} \oplus D^{12})(I \oplus D \oplus D^2)$$
$$= I \oplus D^3 \oplus D^4 \oplus D^6 \oplus D^9 \oplus D^{11} \oplus D^{13} \oplus D^{14}$$

when $X = \ldots 000111000 \ldots$
then $Z = \ldots 000100110100101011000 \ldots$
or

6.3

$$H_1(D) = \frac{Z_1(D)}{X(D)} = \frac{I \oplus D^2 \oplus D^3 \oplus D^4 \oplus D^6}{I \oplus D \oplus D^2} = I \oplus D \oplus D^2 \oplus D^3 \oplus D^4$$

$$H_2(D) = \frac{Z_2(D)}{X(D)} = \frac{I \oplus D \oplus D^2 \oplus D^3 \oplus D^4 \oplus D^5 \oplus D^6 \oplus D^7 \oplus D^8}{I \oplus D \oplus D^2}$$

$$= I \oplus D^3 \oplus D^6$$

$$H_3(D) = \frac{Z_3(D)}{X(D)} = \frac{I \oplus D \oplus D^3 \oplus D^4 \oplus D^5 \oplus D^7 \oplus D^9}{I \oplus D \oplus D^2}$$

$$= I \oplus D^2 \oplus D^5 \oplus D^6 \oplus D^7$$

a) $H_{\text{eff}}(D) = H_1(D) \oplus H_2(D) \oplus H_3(D)$
   $= I \oplus D \oplus D^4 \oplus D^5 \oplus D^7$

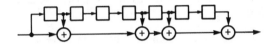

b) $H_{\text{eff}}(D) = H_1(D) . H_2(D) \oplus H_3(D)$
   $= D \oplus D^6 \oplus D^7 \oplus D^8 \oplus D^9 \oplus D^{10}$

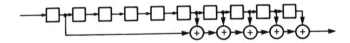

c) $H_{\text{eff}}(D) = H_1(D) . H_2(D) . H_3(D)$
   $= I \oplus D \oplus D^3 \oplus D^4 \oplus D^8 \oplus D^{10} \oplus D^{13} \oplus D^{15} \oplus D^{17}$

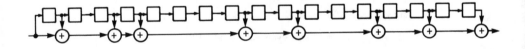

6.4
$H(D) = I / I \oplus D \oplus D^2 \oplus D^4 \oplus D^6$

Autonomous sequences:

i)	111111011000100011100	length 21 digits
ii)	111100001011101010110	length 21 digits
iii)	000001101001100100101	length 21 digits
iv)	000000...	length 1 digit

Therefore cycle set $= \{1, 3(21)\}$

$$Z(D) = \frac{H(D) \cdot f(D)}{I \oplus D^k} = \frac{I \oplus D^2 \oplus D^5 \oplus D^7 \oplus D^8}{(I \oplus D \oplus D^2 \oplus D^4 \oplus D^6)(I \oplus D^9)}$$

$$= \frac{I \oplus D \oplus D^2}{I \oplus D^9}$$

$$= I \oplus D \oplus D^2 \oplus D^9(I \oplus D \oplus D^2) \oplus D^{18}(I \oplus D \oplus D^2) \oplus \dots$$

Therefore, when

$X = \,.\,.00, \; 101001011, \; 101001011, \; 101001011, \; \text{etc.}$
$Z = \,.\,.00, \; 111000000, \; 111000000, \; 111000000, \; \text{etc.}$

6.5

$$\phi(s) = s^{11} \oplus s^{10} \oplus s^7 \oplus s \oplus 1 = (s^2 \oplus s \oplus 1)(s^3 \oplus s^2 \oplus 1)(s^6 \oplus s^5 \oplus 1)$$

$$= \phi_1(s) \cdot \phi_2(s) \cdot \phi_3(s)$$

All factors are primitive polynomials. Therefore cycle-set of

$\phi_1(s) = \{1, 1(3)\} \quad n_1 = 2, \; e_1 = 3, \; m_1 = 1$
$\phi_2(s) = \{1, 1(7)\} \quad n_2 = 3, \; e_2 = 7, \; m_2 = 1$
$\phi_3(s) = \{1, 1(63)\} \quad n_3 = 6, \; e_3 = 63, \; m_3 = 1$

Cycle set of $\phi_1(s) \cdot \phi_2(s) = \{1, 3, 7, 21\}$
Therefore cycle set of $\phi(s) \equiv \{1, 1(3), 1(7), 1(21)\} * \{1, 1(63)\}$

$$= \{1, 1(3), 1(7), 1(21), 1(63), 3(63), 7(63), 21(63)\}$$

$$= \{1, 3, 7, 21, 32(63)\}$$

6.6

$$\phi(s) = \phi_1(s) \cdot \phi_2(s) \phi_3(s)$$

$\phi_1(s) \rightarrow n_1 = 6, \; e_1 = 9$

Therefore $m_1 = 7$ and cycle set $= \{1, 7(9)\}$.

$\phi_2(s) \rightarrow n_2 = 6, \; e_2 = 21$

Therefore $m_2 = 3$ and cycle set $= \{1, 3(21)\}$.

$\phi_3(s) \rightarrow n_3 = 4, \; e_3 = 5$

Therefore $m_3 = 3$ and cycle set $= \{1, 3(5)\}$.

$\phi_1(s) \cdot \phi_2(s) \rightarrow \{1, 7(9)\} * \{1, 3(21)\} = \{1, 7(9), 3(21), 63(63)\}$
$\phi(s) \rightarrow \{1, 3(5)\} * \{1, 7(9), 3(21), 63(63)\}$

$$= \{1, 3(5), 7(9), 3(21), 21(45), 63(63), 9(105), 189(315)\}$$

6.7

a)

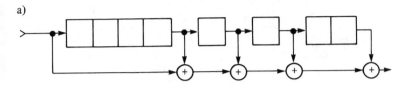

b)

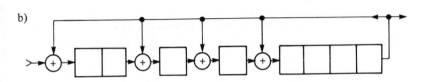

$$(x^{12}\oplus x^{11}\oplus x^5\oplus x^3\oplus 1)(x^8\oplus x^4\oplus x^3\oplus x^2\oplus 1) = x^{20}\oplus x^{19}\oplus x^{16}\oplus x^{12}\oplus x^6\oplus x^5$$
$$\oplus x^3\oplus x^2\oplus x\oplus 1$$

$$\frac{x^{12}\oplus x^{11}\oplus x^5\oplus x^3\oplus 1}{x^8\oplus x^4\oplus x^3\oplus x^2\oplus 1} = x^4\oplus x^3\oplus 1$$

remainder $x^3\oplus x^2\oplus x$

7.1

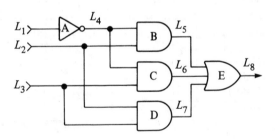

Gate	Inputs	Type	Output
A	L_1	NOT	L_4
B	L_2, L_4	AND	L_5
C	L_3, L_4	AND	L_6
D	L_2, L_3	AND	L_7
E	L_5, L_6, L_7	OR	L_8

7.2

Pass	Step	L_1	L_2	L_3	L_4	L_5	L_6	L_7	L_8
1	New inputs	0	0	0	?	?	?	?	?
	Gate A	0	0	0	1	?	?	?	?
	Gate B	0	0	0	1	0	?	?	?
	Gate C	0	0	0	1	0	0	?	?
	Gate D	0	0	0	1	0	0	0	?
	Gate E	0	0	0	1	0	0	0	0
2	New inputs	0	0	1	(1)	(0)	(0)	(0)	(0)
	Gate A	0	0	1	1	(0)	(0)	(0)	(0)
	Gate B	0	0	1	1	0	(0)	(0)	(0)
	Gate C	0	0	1	1	0	1	(0)	(0)
	Gate D	0	0	1	1	0	1	0	(0)
	Gate E	0	0	1	1	0	1	0	1
3	New inputs	0	1	1	(1)	(0)	(1)	(0)	(1)
	Gate A	0	1	1	1	(0)	(1)	(0)	(1)
	Gate B	0	1	1	1	1	(1)	(0)	(1)
	Gate C	0	1	1	1	1	1	(0)	(1)
	Gate D	0	1	1	1	1	1	1	(1)
	Gate E	0	1	1	1	1	1	1	1
4	New inputs	1	1	1	(1)	(1)	(1)	(1)	(1)
	Gate A	1	1	1	0	(1)	(1)	(1)	(1)
	Gate B	1	1	1	0	0	(1)	(1)	(1)
	Gate C	1	1	1	0	0	0	(1)	(1)
	Gate D	1	1	1	0	0	0	1	(1)
	Gate E	1	1	1	0	0	0	1	1
	etc.								

7.3

Test			No fault	L_1 s-a-0	L_1 s-a-1	L_2 s-a-0	L_2 s-a-1	L_3 s-a-0	L_3 s-a-1	L_4 s-a-0	L_4 s-a-1	L_5 s-a-0	L_5 s-a-1	L_6 s-a-0	L_6 s-a-1	L_7 s-a-0	L_7 s-a-1	L_8 s-a-0	L_8 s-a-1
X	Y	Z	f_0	f_1	f_2	f_3	f_4	f_5	f_6	f_7	f_8	f_9	f_{10}	f_{11}	f_{12}	f_{13}	f_{14}	f_{15}	f_{16}
0 0 0			0	0	0	0	1	0	1	0	0	0	1	0	1	0	1	0	1
1 0 0 1			1	1	0	1	1	0	1	0	1	1	1	0	1	1	1	0	1
2 0 1 0			1	1	0	0	1	1	1	0	1	0	1	1	1	1	1	0	1
3 0 1 1			1	1	1	1	1	1	1	1	1	1	1	1	1	1	1	0	1
4 1 0 0			0	0	0	0	0	0	0	0	0	0	1	0	1	0	1	0	1
5 1 0 1			0	1	0	0	1	0	0	0	1	0	1	0	1	0	1	0	1
6 1 1 0			0	1	0	0	0	0	1	0	1	0	1	0	1	0	1	0	1
7 1 1 1			1	1	1	0	1	0	1	1	1	1	1	1	1	0	1	0	1

Test	f_1, f_8	f_2, f_7	f_3	f_4	f_5	f_6	f_9	$f_{10}, f_{12}, f_{14}, f_{16}$	f_{11}	f_{13}	f_{15}	
T_0			1		1			1				←
T_1		1		1					1		1	←
T_2		1	1				1				1	←
T_3											1	
T_4								1				
T_5	1			1				1				←
T_6	1					1		1				
T_7				1		1				1		←

minimum test set $\{T_0, T_1, T_2, T_5, T_7\}$

7.4

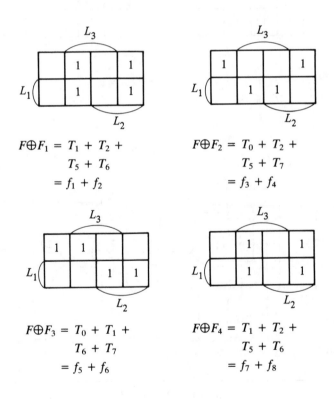

$$F \oplus F_1 = T_1 + T_2 + T_5 + T_6 = f_1 + f_2$$

$$F \oplus F_2 = T_0 + T_2 + T_5 + T_7 = f_3 + f_4$$

$$F \oplus F_3 = T_0 + T_1 + T_6 + T_7 = f_5 + f_6$$

$$F \oplus F_4 = T_1 + T_2 + T_5 + T_6 = f_7 + f_8$$

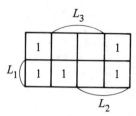

$$F \oplus F_5 = T_0 + T_2 + T_4 +$$
$$T_5 + T_6$$
$$= f_9 + f_{10}$$

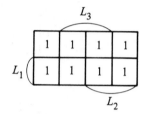

$$F \oplus F_6 = T_0 + T_1 + T_4 +$$
$$T_5 + T_6$$
$$= f_{11} + f_{12}$$

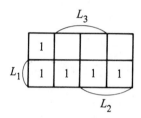

$$F \oplus F_7 = T_0 + T_4 + T_5 +$$
$$T_6 + T_7$$
$$= f_{13} + f_{14}$$

$$F \oplus F_8 = 1$$
$$= f_{15} + f_{16}$$

7.5

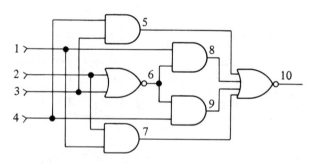

Line Nos. →	1	2	3	4	5	6	7	8	9	10
Test	1	0	0	1	0	$\bar{D}$	0	$\bar{D}$	$\bar{D}$	D

7.6

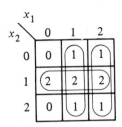

	x_1		
x_2	0	1	2
0	0	1	1
1	2	2	2
2	0	1	1

$$F(X_2, X_1) = j_1(X_2) + 1 \cdot j_1(X_1) + 1 \cdot j_2(X_1)$$

	x_1			
x_2	0	1	2	3
0	0	2	0	3
1	0	2	0	3
2	1	2	1	3
3	1	2	0	3

$$F(X_2, X_1) = j_3(X_1) + 2 \cdot j_1(X_1) + 1 \cdot j_2(X_2) + 1 \cdot j_3(X_2)j_0(X_1)$$

7.7

	x_1		
x_2	0	1	2
0	0	1	1
1	2	2	2
2	0	1	1

$\xrightarrow{\;T_2\;}$

	1	x_1	x_1^2
1	0	0	1
x_2	1	0	1
x_2^2	1	0	1

$$F(x_2, x_1) = x_1^2 \oplus x_2 \oplus x_2 x_1^2 \oplus x_2^2 \oplus x_2^2 x_1^2$$

7.8

	x_1			
x_2	0	1	A	B
0	0	A	B	1
1	A	0	1	B
A	B	1	0	A
B	1	B	A	0

$\xrightarrow{\;T_2\;}$

	1	x_1	x_1^2	x_1^3
1	0	A	0	0
x_2	A	0	0	0
x_2^2	0	0	0	0
x_2^3	0	0	0	0

$$F(x_2, x_1) = Ax_2 \oplus Ax_1$$

	1	x_1	x_1^2	x_1^3
1	0	1	0	0
x_2	1	0	A	A
x_2^2	0	A	1	B
x_2^3	0	A	B	0

$S_2 \longrightarrow$

$x_2 \diagdown x_1$	0	1	A	B
0	0	1	A	B
1	1	1	A	B
A	A	A	A	B
B	B	B	B	B

7.9

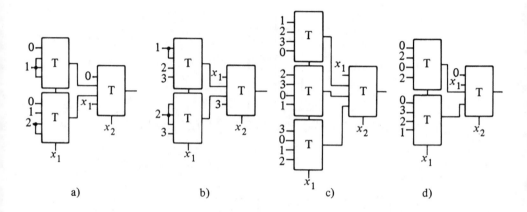

a)   b)   c)   d)

Bibliography

Almaini, A.E.A. and M.E. Woodward, (1977) "An approach to the control variable selection problem for universal logic modules", *Digital Processes*, No. 3, 190–206.

Bannister, B.R. and D.G. Whitehead, (1983) *Fundamentals of Modern Digital Systems*, Macmillan, London.

Bennett, L.A.M., (1978) "The application of map-entered variables to the use of multiplexers in the synthesis of logic functions", *Int. J. Electron.* **45** (4) 373–379.

Bennetts, R.G., (1978) *Introduction to Digital Board Testing*, Arnold, London.

Bennetts, R.G., (1984) *Design of Testable Logic Circuits*, Addison-Wesley, Wokingham.

Berlekamp, E.R., (1968) *Algebraic Coding Theory*, McGraw-Hill, Maidenhead.

Bernstein, B.A., (1928) "Modular representation of finite algebras", *Congress of Math.* Vol. **1**, University of Toronto Press, pp. 207–216.

Besslich, Ph.W., (1983) "Efficient computer method for ExOR logic design", *Proc. IEE,* **130**, Part E CDT, No. 6, 203–206.

Blakeslee, T.R., (1975) *Digital System Design with Standard MSI and LSI*, Wiley, Chichester.

Blunden, D.F., A.H. Boyce and G. Taylor, (1977) "Logic simulation Part 1", *Marconi Rev.* **XL**, 157–171; and "Part 2" *ibid.* **XL**, 236–253.

Breuer, M.A. and A.D. Friedman, (1976) *Diagnosis and Reliable Design of Digital Systems*, Pitman, London.

Breuer, M.A. and A.D. Friedman, (1980) "Functional level primitives in test generation", *IEEE Trans. Comp.* **C-29**, 223–235.

Chappell, S.G., P.R. Menon, J.F. Pellegrin and A.M. Schowe, (1976) "Functional simulation in the Lamp system", *Proc. 13th Design Automation Conference*.

Clare, C., (1972) *Designing Logic Systems using State Machines*, McGraw-Hill, Maidenhead.

Comer, D.J., (1984) *Digital Logic and State Machine Design*, Holt, Rinehart & Winston, Eastbourne.

Dagless, E.L., (1983a) "Logic design with emphasis on the ASM method", in Hicks, P.J. (Ed.), *Semi-custom IC Design and VLSI*, Peter Peregrinus, Stevenage.

Dagless, E.L., (1983b) "PLA and ROM based design", in Hicks, P.J. (Ed.), *Semi-custom IC Design and VLSI*, Peter Peregrinus, Stevenage.

Davio, M., J.-P. Deschamps and A. Thayse, (1978) *Discrete and Switching Functions*, McGraw-Hill, Maidenhead.

Davio, M., J.-P. Deschamps and A. Thayse, (1983) *Digital Systems with Algorithmic Implementation*, Wiley, Chichester.

Dimond, K.R., (1983) "A review of simulation techniques", in Hicks, P.J. (Ed.), *Semi-custom IC Design and VLSI*, Peter Peregrinus, Stevenage.

Edwards, C.R. and S.L. Hurst, (1976) "An analysis of Universal Logic Modules", *Int. J. Electronics* **41** (6) 625-628.

Edwards, M.D. and D. Aspinall, (1983) "The synthesis of digital systems using ASM design techniques", *IFIP 6th Int. Symp. on Computer Hardware Description Languages,* North-Holland, Amsterdam.

Elspas, B., (1959) "Theory of autonomous linear sequential networks", *Trans. IRE* **CT-6**, 45-60.

Floyd, T.L., (1982) *Digital Fundamentals*, 2nd Edn., Merrill.

Forrest, J. and M.D. Edwards, (1983) *The Automatic Generation of Programmable Logic Arrays from Algorithmic State Machine Descriptions.*

Gill, A., (1966) *Linear Sequential Switching Circuits*, Holden-Day.

Golomb, S.W., (1964) *Digital Communications*, Prentice-Hall, Englewood Cliffs, N.J.

Golomb, S.W., (1967) *Shift Register Sequences*, Holden-Day.

Green, D.H. and I.S. Taylor, (1974) "Modular representation of multiple-valued logic systems", *Proc. IEE* **121** 409-418.

Green, D.H. and I.S. Taylor, (1976) "Multiple-valued switching circuit design by means of generalised Reed-Muller expansions", *Digital Processes* **2**, 63-81.

Green, D.H. and K.R. Dimond, (1970) "Polynomial representation of nonlinear feedback shift-registers", *Proc. IEE* **117** (1) 56-60.

Green, D.H. and M. Edkins, (1978) "Synthesis procedures for switching circuits represented in generalised Reed-Muller form over a finite field", *Computer and Digital Techniques* **1** (1) 22-35.

Hill, F.J. and G.R. Peterson, (1974) *Introduction to Switching Theory and Logical Design*, 2nd Edn, Wiley, Chichester.

Holdsworth, B., (1982) *Digital Logic Design*, Butterworths, London.

Huffman, D.A., (1956) "The synthesis of linear sequential coding networks", in Cherry, C. (Ed.), *Information Theory, London Symposium on Inf. Th.,* Butterworth, London.

Hurst, S.L., (1978) *The Logical Processing of Digital Signals*, Arnold, London.

Jablon, A., R. Wakefield and R.G. Bennetts, (1977) "Sequential logic design based on ASM charts", *Digital Processes* **3**, 273-287.

Jack, M.A., (1983) "Design for testability", in Hicks, P.J. (Ed.), *Semi-*

custom IC Design and VLSI, Peter Peregrinus, Stevenage.

Kautz, W.H., (1965) *Linear Sequential Switching Circuits*, Holden-Day. (NB. Includes both Elspas and Huffman's papers quoted above.)

Kinnemint, D.J., (1983) "The programmable logic array: implementation and methodology", in Hicks, P.J. (Ed.), *Semi-custom IC Design and VLSI*, Peter Peregrinus, Stevenage.

Lala, P.K., (1985) *Fault Tolerant and Fault Testable Hardware Design*, Prentice-Hall, Englewood Cliffs, NJ.

Lee, C.Y. and W.H. Chen, (1956) "Several-valued combinational switching circuits", *Trans. AIEE* **75** (1) 278-283.

Lee, S.C., (1978) *Modern Switching Theory and Digital Design*, Prentice-Hall, Englewood Cliffs, NJ.

Lewin, D., (1972) *Theory and Design of Digital Computers*, Van Nostrand Reinhold, Wokingham.

Lewin, D., (1974) *Logical Design of Switching Circuits, 2nd Edn.*, Van Nostrand Reinhold, Wokingham.

Lewin, D., (1977) *Computer-Aided Design of Digital Systems*, Arnold, London.

MacWilliams, F.J. and N.J.A. Sloane, (1977) *The Theory of Error-Correcting Codes*, North-Holland, Amsterdam.

Mano, M.M., (1984) *Digital Design*, Prentice-Hall, Englewood Cliffs, NJ.

Memory Devices Ltd., (1981) *Programmable array logic family, Monolithic Memories*.

Morris, N.M., (1976) *Logic circuits*, 2nd Edn, McGraw-Hill, Maidenhead.

Mowle, F.J., (1976) *A Systematic Approach to Digital Logic Design*, Addison-Wesley, Wokingham.

Mukhopadhyay, A. and G. Schmitz, (1970) "Minimisation of exclusive-OR and logical equivalence switching circuits", *IEE Trans. Comp.* **C-19** (2) 132-140.

Mullard Technical Publications M81-1064, (1981) *Signetics Integrated Fuse Logic*.

Muller, D.E., (1966) "Application of Boolean algebra to switching circuit design and to error detection", *IRE Trans. Electron. Comp.* **EL-15** (4) 578-585.

Peterson, W.W. and E.J. Weldon, (1972) *Error-Correcting Codes*, 2nd Edn., MIT Press.

Post, E.L., (1921) "Introduction to a general theory of elementary propositions", *Am. J. Math.* **43**, 163-185.

Reddy, S.M., (1972) "Easily testable realisations for logic functions", *IEE Trans. Comp.* **C-21** (11) 1183-1188.

Reed, I.S., (1954) "A class of multiple-error-correcting codes and their decoding scheme", *IRE Trans. Inf. Th.* **PGIT-4**, 38-49.

Rine, D.C. (Ed.), (1977) *Computer Science and Multiple-Valued Logic*, North-Holland, Amsterdam.

Roth, P., (1980) *Computer Logic, Testing and Verification*, Pitman, London.

Tabloski, T.F. and F.J. Mowle, (1976) "A numerical expansion technique and its application to minimal multiplexer logic circuits", *IEE Trans. Comp.* **C-25** (7) 684-702.

Wilcox, P., (1979) "Digital logic simulation at the gate and functional level", *Proc. 16th Design Automation Conference*, pp. 242-248.

Winkel, D. and F. Prosser, (1980) *The Art of Digital Design*, Prentice-Hall, Englewood Cliffs, NJ.

Wu, X., X. Chen and S.L. Hurst, (1982) "Mapping of Reed-Muller coefficients and the minimisation of exclusive-OR switching functions", *Proc. IEE* **129** (E CDT) 15-20.

Yau, S.S. and C.K. Tang, (1970a) "Universal logic circuits and their modular realisations", *Proc. AFIPS, Spring Joint Comp. Conf.*, pp. 297-305.

Yau, S.S. and C.K. Tang, (1970b) "Universal logic modules and their applications", *IEE Trans. Comp.* **C-19** (2) 141-149.

Index

algorithm 21
algorithmic state machine 21, 23
ASM block 28
ASM chart 27, 29
ASM state assignments 39
ASM tables 43, 47
asynchronous circuits 1, 15
asynchronous inputs 77
asynchronous outputs 77
autonomous sequential circuits 177
auxiliary ULMs 89

backward trace 205
binary-to-Gray code conversion 160
Boolean differential calculus 198, 200

canonical form 3, 142, 215
cascade connection 172
characteristic equation 178
combinational circuit 1
combined ASM table 47
compatible pairs 12
compiled-code simulation 192
completely specified functions 2
composite polynomials 181
conditional output box 27
conditional output list 28
conditional output table 46
conjuction operation 212
control path 20, 23
critical race 15, 77
cycle set 180
cyclic redundancy check 184
cycling operation 212

D-algorithm 205
D-cubes 205
D-drive 206, 207
D-frontier 207
data path 20, 23

decision box 27
discrete gate implementation 72
disjunction operation 212
disjunctive canonical form 3, 215
direct implementation 109, 112
documentation 21
don't care terms 2, 12

error-detecting codes 162
error-correcting codes 162
essential prime implicant 7
event scheduling 194
exit path 28
exponent 180
extension field 221

factorization 73, 147
fault cover 207
fault detection 191, 198
fault location 200, 210
fault matrix 198
feedback filters 174
feedback shift registers 176, 177
feedforward filters 165
field programmable gate arrays 92
field programmable logic arrays 92
field programmable logic sequencers 92
finite field 133, 217
finite state machine 9, 177
forward trace 205
full decode 115
function domain 136
function domain map 137

Galois field 133, 217
general state machine 23
generalized RM expansions 142
generator polynomial 183
GF(2) 133, 177
GF(3) 217

GF(5) 217, 221
GF(8) 222
GF(p) 133, 221
GF(p^k) 221
GF(q) 133, 221
Gray code 30, 151, 160
Gray code-to-binary conversion 160

Hamming code 163
hazard 16

immediate outputs 26, 78
implicant 5
impulse response 167
impulse sequence 166
instructions 24, 122
interdomain transforms 134, 160,
    187, 219, 221, 225
interface 24

j-operators 214

Karnaugh map 4, 7, 59, 136
Krönecker product 144, 202, 220

linear combinational circuit 159
linear function 159
linear sequential circuit 165
link path 29, 34, 109
linked state machines 50
logic simulation 191, 192

m-sequences 179, 182
map-entered variables 56, 59, 81,
    157
mapping variables 63
max function 212
maximal compatibles 12
Mealy model 10, 30
memory module 23
microinstruction formats 124
microprogram 122
microprogram store 122
microprogramming 121
min function 212
minimum test set 198, 200
minterms 3, 136, 139, 214
modulo-2 algebra 132
modulo-p algebra 212
Moore model 10, 17, 30

multilevel circuit 73, 147, 154
multiple-path sensitization 205
multiple-valued GRM expansion
    225
multiple-valued logic 191
multiple-valued switching circuits
    211
multiple-valued RM expansion 217
multiplexers 56, 79, 156, 225

next-state excitation 55, 56
next-state functions 10, 12, 25, 34
next-state variables 25
non-linear FSRs 182
null sequence 171

operational domain 136
operational domain map 137
optimum polarity 149
order of an element 222
output function 23, 33

parallel connection 173
parallel linking 52
parity checks 162
path sensitization 198, 205
pdcf 206
piterms 136
polarity 142
polynomial 178, 182, 222
polynomial division 185, 222
polynomial roots 222
polynomial multiplication 184, 221
Postian algebras 212
pseudo-inputs 193
pseudo-outputs 193
pseudo-random binary sequences
    182
pre-selection of qualifiers 118
prime implicant 5, 217
primitive D-cube of failure 206
primitive elements 222
primitive flow-table 18
primitive polynomial 180, 222
products of cycle sets 181
programmable array logic 56, 92,
    111
programmable gate arrays 92, 95
programmable logic arrays 56, 92,
    93, 97

programmable logic sequencers 56,
    92, 103, 107
propagation delay 15

qualifier 23
qualifier pre-selection 118
qualifier selection 119
Quine−McCluskey method 7

races 15
read-only memories 24, 56, 113
read−write memories 24
reduced dependency assignment 43,
    77
Reed−Muller circuit tree 154, 225
Reed−Muller codes 163
Reed−Muller expansion 136, 207
Reed−Muller fault-testing 208
Reed−Muller transform matrix 134
Reed−Muller ULM 156
residues 60, 76, 80, 157
ROM-based designs 112
roots of polynomials 222
row-merging 18

s-a-0 fault 198
s-a-1 fault 198
scalar multiplier 159, 186
sequential circuit 1, 9, 15
serial linking 50
series connection 172
series/parallel connection 174
shared decision box 38
simulation 191, 192
square-wave input sequence 169
square-wave response 170
stable state 15
state 5, 23, 179
state assignment 10, 28, 40
state box 27
state code 28
state diagram 9, 17

state locus 40
state map 40
state name 28
state output list 28
state output table 46
state register 39
state time 25
state-transition table 10, 43
state variables 12, 25
step-input sequence 166
step-response 167
stuck-at faults 198
sum-of-products 3
synchronous circuits 1

T-gates 225
table-driven simulation 193
terminal mnemonics 21, 26
ternary logic 211
ternary Reed−Muller expansion
    218
ternary switching circuits 211
testing 191, 197
time wheel 196
top-down design 8, 20
transfer function 166
transform matrix 134, 143, 150,
    160, 162, 187, 202, 219
transform module 23
transition matrix 178
triangular transform method 141
truth table 2
two-level circuit 6, 147

unary operators 213, 214
uncommitted gate array 77, 93
universal logic modules 56, 79, 156,
    225
universal tree circuit 74, 154, 225
unstable states 15

zero polarity expansion 142, 149